Kenneth E. F. Watt

LICENSE TO STEAL

LICENSE TO STEAL

The Secret World of Wall Street
and the Systematic Plundering
of the American Investor

Anonymous AND **Timothy Harper**

HarperBusiness
A Division of HarperCollins*Publishers*

HarperCollins books may be purchased for educational, business, or sales promotional use. For information please write: Special Markets Department, HarperCollins Publishers, Inc., 10 East 53rd Street, New York, NY 10022.

FIRST EDITION

Designed by Eric Coates

Library of Congress Cataloging-in-Publication Data
Anonymous.
    License to steal : the secret world of Wall Street brokers and the systematic plundering of the American investor / Anonymous and Timothy Harper.
—1st ed.
        p.   cm.
    ISBN 0-88730-992-5
    1. Stockbrokers—United States.   2. Stockbrokers—Corrupt practices—United States.   3. Investments—United States.
I. Harper, Timothy, 1950–   .   II. Title.
HG4928.5.G55   1999
332.6'2'0973—dc21   99-16917

00 01 02 03 ❖/RRD 10 9 8 7 6 5 4 3 2

CONTENTS

PREFACE

This is a cautionary tale of Wall Street. In a sense, it's the book your stockbroker doesn't want you to read. It's a walk down the dark side of Wall Street, the true story of brokers who broke the law and violated their professional ethics. Beyond the outright crooks, however, it is also a lesson in how brokers routinely mislead their clients and abuse their trust.

One of the most remarkable changes in late-twentieth-century American society has been the way the general public has come to regard the stock market over the past two decades. The number of Americans owning stock has increased dramatically, corresponding to the extraordinary bull market that began in the early 1980s. People talk about the market today the way they talk about the weather or sports: what's up, what's down, what we invested in, what we'd like to invest in, and what we wish we had invested in.

Yet most Americans, including investors with their life savings tied up in the market, know surprisingly little about Wall Street and how it works. This book lifts the green veil that has long shrouded the inner workings of brokerage firms and the motivations of brokers themselves.

"My broker." We love to say it. Despite the growth of discount investment houses and new technology that allows us to buy and sell shares with a mouse click from our spare bedrooms, the majority of investors with significant shareholdings still use stockbrokers. We ask them to make us rich, and then do whatever they advise.

This is the era of personal service: the cleaning lady, the lawn guy, the personal trainer, the administrative assistant—and the broker. We love the idea of professional service. We love the idea of having an expert on our side, especially one who is smarter than our neighbor's expert. We love the idea of someone who knows more than we do, out there in the financial jungle representing us, always on the lookout for ways to make more money for us. It's a reassuring image. It is also an illusion. Let's put it simply. For a vast number of stockbrokers, the top priority is not to make money for their clients. The top priority is to make money for the brokers themselves.

There's a basic conflict of interest, an inherent contradiction, in the brokerage business. Virtually every broker advises prospective clients that the best way to make money in the market is to go for solid long-term investments. "I'm a long-term kind of guy," brokers say. "My attitude is buy and hold."

Brokers don't make money, however, if you buy and hold. Brokers make money by buying and selling stocks on your behalf. Yes, they try to get you to invest more and more with them, as much as you can. But what about when you're tapped? When your portfolio is maxed out, and there's no new money to invest? The only way for brokers to make money is to sell some of the stocks you own, and buy different stocks. If the client makes money, too, that's wonderful. But brokerage houses, big and small, exist primarily to make money for themselves, not for clients. Brokers like to present themselves as investment counselors. Some are. But first and foremost, they are salesmen.

•　•　•

Preface

This is a true story of Wall Street in the 1990s, but the details of each incident and anecdote have been obscured because the brokers involved preferred not to be identified by name for professional or legal reasons. To put it bluntly, this book could not have been written without the cloak of anonymity. Naming names, telling exactly who did what, when, and where—and to whom—is less important than telling what these stockbrokers did and saw, and how they and other stockbrokers routinely abused their relationships with clients. Some of the incidents related by our young broker in the book involve brokers who paid fines, served suspensions, and in several cases went to prison because of their wrongdoing. Many others involve brokers who did little or no wrong themselves, but would not agree to be identified by name because they did not want to be tainted by association with wrongdoers or wrongdoing. Nevertheless, their stories should be told.

The Authors
June 1999

1

Thursday Night and Friday Morning

Lazlo was feeling good, and so was I. It was a warm spring evening in Manhattan, and we were young and healthy and making more money than we knew what to do with. Princes of the City. Masters of the Universe. We were determined to spend some of that money and have some fun. Lazlo was tall and thin, in good shape, his curly hair well trimmed and blown. Perhaps the best word describing him, back then anyway, was sleek. He was wearing an Armani suit, a charcoal-gray, double-breasted wool crêpe. His powder-blue shirt, with a navy-blue monogram on the French cuff, had been handmade personally for Lazlo by a tailor who came into our office to measure him. His Hermès tie had subtle navy and charcoal overlapping stripes. His shoes and his belt were crocodile. He was wearing a Rolex, the President model, eighteen carats.

I was dressed similarly, except I didn't have a Rolex. I had a Cartier. Lazlo was one of the most productive (highest-earning, in other words) stockbrokers at the brokerage firm where I had started working after I got my own broker's license the year before. I was beginning to make serious money, but still had a way to go before I would catch up to Lazlo. He was pulling down half a million a year, maybe more.

I wanted that. And I was on my way. Two and a half years earlier, I had started in the financial services industry at $3.50 an hour. Now I was bringing home more than $100,000 in my first full year as a broker. In five or six years, when I was Lazlo's age—early thirties—I'd be making more than he was, a millionaire many times over.

It must have been obvious to Lazlo that I admired him. He often joked around with the younger guys. He encouraged them in his own way, which could be characterized as Leading by Outrageous Example. He seemed to have taken a particular liking to me. So when he asked me to go out that September evening, I quickly said yes. It was a Thursday, almost the end of the week, a good night for going out. I called my girlfriend and told her I was having dinner with Lazlo. I told her not to wait up.

We went to Lazlo's apartment on one of the upper floors of one of those new residential skyscrapers on the East Side. He poured us some drinks and showed me around: bedroom, dining room, kitchen, living room. It was a big place for an apartment in that neighborhood, about 1,700 square feet, Lazlo told me. With its marble entryway and polished parquet floors, the apartment was furnished as if straight out of *Architectural Digest*. There was an unbelievable view of Central Park from almost every room. My tongue must have been hanging out, imagining myself living in a place like that in a year or two. It was obvious that he enjoyed impressing me. Over three or four drinks— vodka tonics made with Absolut—we talked, as we always did, about business, about our jobs, our colleagues, our clients. Especially the clients. Lazlo made fun of his clients, laughed at them, and bragged about how they did whatever he told them to do. "Putty in my hands," he crowed.

From downstairs, the doorman buzzed. A cold caller, one of the young guys who dialed numbers of prospective clients all day, was in the lobby. Once somebody came on the line and expressed the mildest interest, the cold caller quickly passed the call to a more experienced broker like Lazlo. Lazlo had invited the cold caller, too. He told the doorman to send the guy up. He was a nice kid, maybe twenty-five, a couple of years younger than me. He was where I had been eighteen months earlier, but I didn't think he could move up as rapidly as I had. I was confident I was going to be the best. Or at least, in a couple of years of watching Lazlo and other big-commission brokers, I would be right up there with them. We had another drink with the cold caller, and Lazlo suggested, "Hey, men, let's go get some dinner."

We went to a little Italian place around the corner. It was one of those evenings when all of Manhattan seemed soft and warm. We sat at an outside table, talking, laughing, Lazlo and I joking around about how much money we were making, how much we were saving, and, especially, how much he was spending. Lazlo showed us his new sunglasses ($350) and told us about his new Porsche 911 Turbo with the black leather seats that had been specially treated to smell like Breath of Heaven. After another round of drinks, the menus came. "Don't worry," Lazlo assured us. "It's all on me." After a long discussion about what to eat, we decided to keep it light. "So we'll have plenty of room for plenty of booze later," Lazlo said.

We shared steamed calamari, grilled Chilean sea bass, and salad. We washed it all down with a bottle of Antinori Chianti Classico Reserve, and then another. Lazlo ordered cognac all around and pulled out three Cohiba Robusto cigars. We fired them up. Life was good. We started talking to two nicely dressed couples having dinner at an adjacent table. The women were great-looking. The guys asked about our cigars. They told us they were investment bankers, and joshed with Lazlo about deal rumors and talked about people until they found a couple of mutual acquaintances. He bought them drinks. The women never said anything, but laughed when we laughed. After a while, the couples left and our cigars were burned down to the bands.

"Hey," Lazlo said, "you guys want to go to a club with me? The babes are unbelievable." Sure, we said. Lazlo pulled out a cell phone, the smallest one I had ever seen, and called the limo company where he had an account. Within minutes a gleaming black stretch limo was parked in front of us. Lazlo remarked approvingly that it appeared to be brand-new. "They know I only want the best," he said. He started talking to the two new couples who had come in and taken over the table next to us, and ended up ordering drinks for them, too. We talked to them for maybe half an hour while the limo waited. We were about to go when Lazlo said, "Oh shit, I forgot. I'm supposed to go see my aunt. She's in the hospital up in Westchester. She's just had surgery. I gotta go see her." He sat back in his chair with his cognac and thought hard for maybe ten seconds. "I got it," he said. He said he'd call for a second limo (at $125 an hour) and take that one out to see his aunt. The cold caller and I could take the first limo to the club, and Lazlo would catch up with us later.

The club turned out to be an exclusive, expensive strippers' bar. The cold caller and I didn't know what to do with the limo, so we told the driver to wait. We walked into the club, told the doorman we were guests of Lazlo's, and were shown to a good table. The cover, our drinks, everything was on Lazlo's tab. Lazlo himself joined us about an hour later, assuring us that his aunt was recovering nicely. He ordered more drinks, and some big cigars for all three of us. We sat there for a while, sucking on the stogies and trying to blow smoke rings at the beautiful naked woman dancing on the stage above us.

Lazlo nudged me and nodded toward the bathroom downstairs. "Have a hit," he urged, handing me a "bullet" of cocaine, a little device that you turn over to "load" with coke inside. You put it up your nose, push the plunger on the bottom of the bullet, and get a nice measured hit. We made a couple of trips to the restroom, then ran out of coke. "Let's get a breath of fresh air," Lazlo said. We walked out, leaving the cold caller at the table. Outside, I saw that Lazlo had kept his limo waiting, too. Two limos. I tried to figure out, at $250 an hour, what it was costing, and how much we could save by just taking taxis, but my brain was too bleary. "C'mon," Lazlo said, opening the door of one of the limos. "I want to go home and get something." I climbed in.

Back at Lazlo's apartment, we sat down at his dining room table, a big tinfoil package of cocaine between us. I had never seen this much dope. We sat there for what seemed like a long time, doing lines off his marble tabletop and talking business. He told me how much he loved being a stockbroker, the feeling of power, of control, of knowing what's going to happen before it happens. He told me about his clients. How much they trusted him. And how stupid they were. How he could get them to buy or sell anything. Lazlo told me he thought I had a great future in the business. I was a young, good-looking guy, a smooth talker, a natural salesman. That's the most important part of being a broker, he said. You gotta be able to sell. I lapped up what he was saying even more enthusiastically than I snorted up his cocaine.

After a while—I had no idea of how long we had been gone, or what time it was, but it seemed like Thursday must certainly have turned to Friday by then—Lazlo decided we should go find the cold caller. Down to the limo, back to the club, we saw the second limo was still there. Lazlo let one limo go, but told the other one to keep waiting. Inside, the cold caller was still there, amid empty glasses and cigar stubs and dozens of implant-perfect bare breasts. "Where you guys been?" he demanded, slurring his words a bit. Lazlo flashed him a glimpse of a cocaine bullet, and the cold caller said, "Hey, I'm jealous." Lazlo handed him the bullet and he disappeared downstairs to the bathroom.

While he was gone, Lazlo and I laughed at how the cold caller was reveling in all this, sitting there in an exclusive strip club, drinking expensive booze and smoking Havana cigars, ogling high-priced women, all on his salary of less than $1,000 a month. When the cold caller returned, his eyes bright, Lazlo suggested we move up to the next level of the club. The VIP level, he called it, the Champagne Room. The cold caller and I followed him upstairs to a plushly furnished room where we sat back in easy chairs around a small marble-topped table.

Lazlo ordered a bottle of Absolut ($150) and three bottles of Cristal champagne ($350 each), plus assorted mixers and buckets of ice. "Hey, we're making our own party," he said. Within minutes there were half a dozen strippers around us—dressed now, but provocatively. They all seemed to know Lazlo, and they fawned over him, saying his name over and over. They made sexually suggestive remarks to all three of us, and held out crystal flutes for tastes of our champagne. Every now and then Lazlo would toss one of them a $100 bill. "Just to keep them interested," he muttered. Women came and went, sometimes to dance. Some left and returned, occasionally wearing different clothes. It felt late. A man approached our table. I hadn't seen him in the club at any time earlier in the evening. He was swarthy, short, and stocky. "Hey, Lazlo," he said, ignoring everyone else at the table. "You wanna play tonight?" Lazlo didn't think twice.

"Yeah," he said. "Sure. I'll play."

"Okay," the man said. "We're open now."

"Yeah," Lazlo said. "In a little while."

"Okay," the man said. "You know where we are."

Lazlo didn't say anything to the rest of us. He just kept laughing and drinking and teasing the women. After what seemed like another hour, he turned to me. "Hey, you want to play some cards?" I don't know, I said. I'm drunk, I'm high, I'm tired, I've never been much of a card player. "C'mon," Lazlo prodded. "It's just blackjack. What's the big deal? You got balls." I said okay, and we began making a move.

"Hey, let's grab a couple of girls to take with us," Lazlo said. Grab a couple of girls? "Yeah, pick any one you want. I've already got mine picked out," he said, winking at a voluptuous redhead who was all but bursting out of her Wonderbra. I reminded him that I was in a serious relationship, and declined. The cold caller, with a hopeful note in his voice, volunteered that he was not involved with anyone. Lazlo sneered at me, handed the cold caller eight crisp new hundred-dollar bills, and pointed to a small group of women chatting in a corner of the Champagne Room.

The cold caller walked over, said excuse me to one of the women, a beautiful blonde, handed her the $800, and asked her if she'd like to go play cards with us. She took the money and turned back to her friends, ignoring him. Lazlo saw what had happened. "Let me straighten this out, you rookie," he told the cold caller. He went and talked to the blonde who had taken the money, and in a few minutes came back with another woman, also blonde and just as pretty. "Okay, rook, I know you like blondes, so I got you a better one. Say hello to Pam," he told the cold caller with a laugh. She just smiled at the cold caller. The five of us—Lazlo, me, the cold caller, and two strippers—burst noisily out of the club, onto the street, and into the still-waiting limousine. The driver had been sleeping, but he woke up instantly. His expression never changed when we all clambered into the car, laughing and hollering.

We drove to a rough part of Hell's Kitchen, on the far west side of Midtown, and pulled up in front of what appeared to be an abandoned warehouse. Lazlo found the button for an intercom next to the bare door, and announced himself. The door buzzed open, and Lazlo led us onto a small, dirty elevator. Upstairs, the elevator opened into a full-blown casino: craps and blackjack tables in green felt, clicking roulette wheels, dealers and croupiers in white jackets, managers in black tuxedos, leggy cigarette girls, a curved bar with three bartenders working in front of mirrored shelves of bottles. It was like a scene out of a movie.

Lazlo, the cold caller, and I sat down at a blackjack table. The two strippers stood alongside, watching. I started to pull some money out of my wallet, but the dealer stopped me. "No, sir, please, no cash," the dealer said, looking at Lazlo for help. Lazlo explained that everything was on credit. The cold caller and I could get a line of credit because we knew Lazlo, but we'd have to settle up at the end of the evening. Lazlo asked for $2,000 worth of chips. The cold caller said he wanted $1,000, and so did I. The bets were $40 minimum, $200 maximum. We ordered drinks. Lazlo got out his coke and started sharing it with us and the strippers. "Is it okay, right out in front of everybody?" I whispered, motioning toward the nearest manager, who was watching us. Lazlo laughed at me and took a hit from a bullet.

Meanwhile, we were losing steadily. But it wasn't enough action for Lazlo. He got a line of credit for the redhead, and started playing her hand, too. Lazlo said the problem was that we were playing too conservatively. We needed to be more aggressive to get our money back. "Besides," he said, "it's only money. It's meaningless. I'll get it back tomorrow at work, from clients." The strippers seemed turned on by all this. He asked if he could bet $500 a hand instead of $200, and the dealer said yes. The cold caller went from $100 to $200 a hand, and I went from $40 to $100. After twenty minutes of playing more aggressively, I was down $1,500, which seemed like a ton of money to me, but the other two guys had it a lot worse. The cold caller was down $9,000—more than he would earn in his job in the remaining seven months of the year. Lazlo was down $21,000. Tossing his last hand in, cursing, he said, "Forget it. This is no good. We're getting ripped off. Let's get out of here."

For the first time in hours, I looked at my watch. It was four-thirty. Lazlo spoke to the swarthy, stocky guy from the club, who had reappeared as we were getting up to leave. The stocky guy took him off into a corner to talk to someone else for a few minutes. Lazlo came back to us, grim-faced, and said he had made arrangements for us to pay off our debts within seven days. He led the other four of us downstairs, back to the limo. We woke up the driver again, but this time Lazlo didn't have any immediate instructions. He didn't want to take us all back to his place. We sat silently for what seemed like a full minute, waiting for Lazlo to speak. "I know," he said finally, smiling again, as if nothing had happened. "Take us to the Meridien Hotel. We'll get a suite."

At the hotel, he and the cold caller and the two women climbed out of the limo. I stayed put, and told the driver to take me home.

The cold caller was already at his cubicle and on the phone when I walked into the office a few hours later that Friday morning. I was late. It was almost ten o'clock, and I could tell that people were noticing I was late. One guy raised his eyebrows at me, and a secretary gave me a sympathetic little smile, as if she could tell how bad my hangover was. I ignored them. The cold caller and I exchanged shamefaced grimaces as I walked past, but we didn't speak. I went straight to Lazlo's office. He was already there, but he didn't appear to be doing any work. He was sitting at the big desk, his head in both hands, staring blankly. He looked terrible. "Good morning," I said, my voice hoarse.

He tried to smile. His face was ashen. "Morning. God, I think I feel as bad as you look." I told him he didn't look that great, either. After a couple of minutes of unconvincing talk about what a great time we had the night before, Lazlo told me to go to my desk and he would call me in a few minutes to discuss "our problem." I sat at my desk, mouth scratchy and dry, head pounding, wishing I was home in bed, wishing I would wake up and the whole night, especially the gambling, would just be a bad dream. The phone rang. It was Lazlo and the cold caller, on an intra-office conference call. Lazlo wanted to talk about the gambling debts. What were we going to do? These were tough guys, he said. He had dealt with them before. He didn't have enough ready cash to cover the money lost by the cold caller and me. He didn't have enough to cover his own debts. We needed to get our share of the money to Lazlo so he could get it to the casino. It was a Friday. He needed the money by the following Friday.

"My grandfather was a big publisher, and he set up a trust fund for me," the cold caller said. "I'll get the nine grand from that. It's not what the money is for, but I don't know what else to do. I'll have it for you by the middle of next week." He hung up.

I told Lazlo that I would have a $1,500 check for him on Monday. I asked him not to tell anyone I had lost so much money. He just kind of snorted, which I took for a promise. I asked him what he was going to do. He said he had a plan for raising the money.

Our brokerage firm was running a "special" that day on a bloc of a particular stock that we had in inventory. The bloc of TechnoStock (not its real name) probably had been owned by a large investor: maybe one of the company's insiders, maybe an institutional investor, or perhaps a fund, or another brokerage house. The previous owner wanted to unload the bloc of stock but knew that dumping it all at once on the open market would send the share price into a free fall. So the institutional investor transferred the shares, at a deep discount, directly to our brokerage firm. As a result, the firm had accumulated a big bloc of TechnoStock at a dirt-cheap price—$5.75 per share, when it was listed as trading at $7.

The $1.25 "spread" between what the firm had paid for the stock and its listed selling price was pure profit, a hidden commission that the firm would split with the brokers who sold it to their clients. Clients who bought the stock for the listed $7 price would never know that the firm had bought it for only $5.75. And no broker was about to tell them, least of all Lazlo. We brokers officially received commissions of 5 percent per trade. That's what was listed on the trade confirmation forms sent to clients. A client who bought 1,000 shares of TechnoStock would pay $7,000, plus $350 for the 5 percent commission: $7,350. Actually, however, the commission was $350 plus $1.25 per share—an additional $1,250. The true commission was $1,600, more than 20 percent, which was split fifty-fifty between the brokerage house and the individual broker.

Lazlo needed to generate more than $80,000 in gross commissions to pay off his $21,000 debt. Half of the gross commission would go to the brokerage house. Of the $40,000 that was Lazlo's share, about half would be withheld in income taxes. Figuring $1.25 in hidden commissions and 35 cents for his 5 percent straight commission—for a total of $1.60 per share in commissions—he needed to sell 50,000 shares of TechnoStock to generate $80,000 in gross commissions. He got on the phone to our firm's trading department. "How much TechnoStock is still available on that special?" he demanded. "You've got 50,000 shares? Great. I'll take it all." The trading department was pleased because it had locked in the $1.25 per share hidden commission on TechnoStock—$62,500. Lazlo was pleased because all he had to do was sell 50,000 shares and he would cover his gambling debts.

It didn't matter to Lazlo whether TechnoStock was any good, what it was really worth, what would happen to it after he unloaded it, or to whom he might try to sell it. He didn't care about anything except booking all the TechnoStock that day. He figured that if he sold the 50,000 shares by the time the market closed, he could take his trade receipts to the casino that evening and convince the stocky guy that he would pay his debts, no doubt with some interest, as soon as he got his commissions from our firm in about three weeks. Lazlo told me that if he didn't make some arrangements, there was a decent chance someone would knock on his door in the next few days and offer to break his legs. Lazlo said that once he had paid off all the debts, he and I could do the whole evening all over again, except next time we'd win. I gave a noncommittal answer, but I thought he was crazy. No way was I going out with him again.

I went back to my desk and tried to do what business I could through my hangover and Lazlo's frequent interruptions to give me progress reports. He was having problems, he told me. His clients didn't want to buy this cheap little stock they'd never heard of. They wanted to hold on to their past investments, the stocks he'd told them to buy and hold.

It didn't help that Lazlo hadn't done much research on Techno-Stock. Actually, he hadn't done any. Nonetheless, when I walked by his office to get some water for an aspirin I overheard him giving a client some made-up statistics over the phone. I paused outside his door to listen. He fibbed about our research department giving a recommendation, and some analyst rating it as a "buy," and some nonexistent newsletter tipping TechnoStock as an undiscovered bargain. Oh yes, he assured the dubious client, this stock is really a hot tip. There's a real inside buzz about it. No, Lazlo couldn't tell the client where he had received his information. He was an extraordinarily good liar. One convincing touch was telling the client that he, Lazlo, personally had purchased 14,000 shares that same morning. That was a nice number for a lie, I thought: 14,000. It sounded believable.

I don't know if that client bought any shares in TechnoStock, but it seemed as though most of the people Lazlo called were not interested. It was supposed to be a nice weekend coming up, so it was hard to get a lot of clients on the phone that Friday afternoon. Many of them had already taken off for the weekend. By late afternoon, Lazlo had sold barely 10,000 of the 50,000 TechnoStock shares. "I gotta get this shit booked, quick," he said, looking even more haggard than he had that morning. "If I don't move these goddam shares, I'm gonna choke on 'em." He couldn't take the stock back to the trading department. Not at our firm. The traders would laugh at him. If Lazlo kept the shares in his own account, he'd have to pay for them on Monday. Even if he'd had the money, he didn't want to pay $7 for shares that were worth $5.75, and would probably be worth even less the following week.

Lazlo told me there was only one thing to do: buy the shares on behalf of clients without telling them first. This would have been easy if Lazlo had any clients who were "discretionary" accounts—clients who had given him the discretion to make trades on their behalf without their prior approval. He would have been able to unload the shares on those clients, and the problem would have simply gone away. Oh, sure, the clients might have been unhappy for a while. Maybe they would have dumped him as their broker for abusing the discretionary authority they had given him to trade their accounts. But it was a moot point. Lazlo didn't have that option. He didn't have any discretionary accounts. No client would trust him with a discretionary account, with the authority to make trades without explicit, prior approval. And with good reason. What Lazlo did next showed that all those clients were right not to trust him with their money.

He decided to unload the leftover TechnoStock on his clients without telling them first. Sure, he'd get caught, but he wouldn't get caught that day. He'd buy himself a few days. He picked the easiest clients, the ones who never argued or complained. Some of them followed every recommendation Lazlo made to them. Some of them, incredibly, really thought he was always looking out for their best interests. Others knew that brokers could be ethically fast and loose, but regarded brokers like Lazlo as "street smart," the kind of guys who got an edge any way they could, and sometimes passed it along to their clients. They thought Lazlo was slick and smart—the same way he thought of himself.

Lazlo didn't hold those clients, the "easy" ones, in the same regard. He called them pikers and suckers and fish and worse. And he ditched his TechnoStock on them that Friday afternoon. What he did was an illegal practice called "parking." He bought the stock in his clients' names for their accounts, but without their knowledge. He wrote "tickets" ordering the trades so that the shares would be moved out of the trading department by the end of the day—and he would not be liable for them. Instead, his clients were liable for the stock he had parked in their accounts: a few thousand here, a few thousand there, over a dozen accounts.

But Lazlo knew this wasn't the end of his headaches with Techno-Stock. Within a few days, the clients whose accounts had bought TechnoStock would receive confirmation notices in the mail. Those who had not authorized the trades would begin calling the following week and demanding to know what was going on:

"What's this stock doing in my account?"

"Did we talk about this? Why didn't we talk about this?"

"What do you mean, you want me to sell one of my other positions to pay for this?"

Lazlo fully anticipated that most of the clients saddled with TechnoStock would say no, they didn't want it, they wouldn't pay for it, they couldn't pay for it. If they canceled the purchases, he'd be right back in hot water again. Not only could Lazlo forget about his commissions, but he would also lose net dollars. The fact that our firm was running a special on TechnoStock meant that the stock was probably overvalued, and was likely to fall in price in the near future. By the middle of the following week the share price probably would be down to $6, maybe $5. Lazlo would not only owe money to the hoodlums who ran the underground casino, but he'd also owe money to our firm—tens of thousands of dollars, depending on what happened to the share price—for all that TechnoStock he was committed to sell.

"All right, what do you do now? This only buys you the weekend. You're out of your mind. This is idiotic. What happens when your clients start calling in all pissed off?" I asked Lazlo after he told me he had parked the unsold TechnoStock in the accounts of unsuspecting clients. Lazlo had no answers. But he did have another idea, and a request. "Come with me to talk to Rex," he said.

We went down the hall to the office, even bigger than Lazlo's, inhabited by the broker known as Rex. It was after four o'clock by then, and Lazlo was afraid that Rex had already charged off to launch the weekend with his first martini. But he was still there, barely. "Hey, guys, c'mon in," he said as he snapped his briefcase shut. "Jesus, you guys look like hell." I didn't know Rex well. We said hi in the hall or the elevator or the men's room, but that was about it. He was a big guy, but smooth in appearance and demeanor. Somebody told me he got a haircut every day.

Rex was also a big producer, in a different league from me. He earned more than Lazlo, significantly more, and had been doing it for years. All of us younger guys at the firm talked about him, wondered about him, marveled at him, and lusted after his work style and lifestyle. But we also heard that he had lots of problems with clients. Or that he had problem clients, depending on how you looked at it. Any way you looked at it, Rex sailed pretty close to the wind, ethically. Everybody seemed to think that someday he was going to end up in big trouble. But for now, Lazlo was there to seek his help. I was there because I was curious.

Lazlo started to tell Rex his problem, beginning with the gambling debt. Rex stopped him with an upraised hand, walked over and closed his office door, and then motioned for us to sit down and continue. When Lazlo finished, despairing at what was going to happen next week when outraged clients began calling, Rex just smiled at us. "This is an easy problem, boys," he said. He pointed at me. "I'm not surprised that you don't know the answer."

Then he aimed his finger at Lazlo. "But I'm amazed that you don't know what to do by now." Lazlo, looking defensive, started to say something but nothing came out. It was the only time I ever saw him speechless.

"Boy, you gotta call Travis," Rex went on. "Travis is the answer to your problems. Well, not all your problems. Even when this is over you're still gonna be an ugly bastard with a goofy Hungarian name. But Travis is the answer to your immediate problems." I was dumbfounded. Travis? Was that an acronym? My mind raced. Travelers International Securities? Nah. The only person I had ever known named Travis was the stooped, middle-aged guy in the firm's mailroom, a guy who dressed like an old Detroit hepcat, in shiny trousers, those knit short-sleeved shirts that button all the way down the front, pointed half-boots, and sometimes even a straw fedora. Once in a while you could hear him humming old Motown songs, Marvin Gaye or the Temptations and all that.

As it turned out, that Travis was the very one Rex was talking about. Rex laid it out quickly for Lazlo. Get downstairs before the mailroom closed and Travis went home. Slip him a couple of bills, and he'd pull the confirmations on every one of those trades made on behalf of unsuspecting accounts. Travis would give them to Lazlo, or destroy them himself. They would never go out. It would be weeks until the clients got their quarterly statements and noticed the TechnoStock purchases.

Clients who had sufficient cash in their accounts to cover the TechnoStock purchases wouldn't know they had bought it until they got their statements. Clients who didn't have the cash in their accounts would soon be getting notices from our firm demanding cash for the purchases. Maybe Lazlo could go back into their accounts and sell enough of their existing portfolio to cover the TechnoStock purchase. That might keep the clients in the dark for a while longer, but eventually they would find out what he had done. They would still lose their money in buying and selling TechnoStock. But it gave Lazlo a few weeks—until the next client account summary statements went out—to figure out something else.

Lazlo said thanks over his shoulder and bolted out of Rex's office, all but running down the hall back to his own office. He got on the phone, talked to Travis urgently, and then hung up. "Travis says no problem," Lazlo told me when I came in, trailing along. It was the first time I had seen him smile since he had picked up the red-haired stripper at the club the night before. A few minutes later, Lazlo's phone rang. It was Travis, asking to meet him out on the street. Lazlo motioned me to follow. I didn't. I went back to my desk. Later, Lazlo told me that after a quick stop at the cash machine down the block, he gave Travis $500, and Travis gave him a paper bag containing all the confirmation notices that would have gone out to the not-so-proud new owners of TechnoStock. He told Travis he would need him to pull some more notification mailings on Monday, when he sold shares from some of the portfolios to cover the TechnoStock purchases. "No problem," Travis said again.

Over that next week, Lazlo called all the clients who had bought TechnoStock without knowing it. He sounded them out, cautiously, talking about how great TechnoStock was, and how this latest dip in the price—back down under $7—was just a glitch in what was sure to be a stairway to heaven for the stock. At the same time, he talked down some other perfectly good—indeed, much preferable—stock in their portfolios, and urged them to sell it so they could buy TechnoStock. Some said okay, and agreed to buy what they already unknowingly owned.

A couple of clients flatly refused, and a few days later Lazlo called them and apologized for the godawful mistake that had been made: somehow, somebody in the back office had confused the day's trades, and they had ended up with TechnoStock after all. He was sorry, but there wasn't much he could do. He took the stock out of their accounts, at a loss to the clients, and parked it in other clients' accounts. Once again, he bought time by asking Travis to give him the trade confirmations instead of sending them to the clients.

It wasn't until a few weeks later, when they got their statements, that some of the clients realized they had owned TechnoStock. Some of them chewed Lazlo out and told him not to do it again. A couple of them were angry enough to close their accounts. I never heard of any clients filing formal complaints against Lazlo—not for this, anyway. He had explained that it was just a mistake, and the clients couldn't prove otherwise without taking a lot of time and trouble. It wasn't worth it to them.

So Lazlo lost a couple of clients, but that was a small price to pay for what he regarded at the time as a completely satisfactory outcome—for him, anyway. Lazlo collected his commissions and paid his gambling debts without any hoodlums coming to take him for a ride in the Meadowlands. A few clients lost some money, but so what? I didn't go to the underground casino anymore, but I know Lazlo went back many times—too many. Meanwhile, word spread through our firm about what he had done. He had committed a number of ethical violations. He had broken securities laws, both state and federal. But none of our co-workers criticized him. None of our bosses did, either.

2

Conflict of Interest

What Lazlo did was wrong. However, as I came to learn, it was not all that unusual. During my years as a stockbroker, I have seen many more examples of fellow brokers misleading, tricking, cheating, and defrauding the clients who trusted them. I don't think that all stockbrokers are crooks. But there is a basic conflict of interest in the securities industry, and most clients don't seem to recognize it. It doesn't take a rogue broker such as Lazlo to mislead a client, or not tell the client the whole truth about why a certain stock has a "buy" recommendation. I know of no broker who tells his clients the whole truth about every transaction—and particularly about the hidden commissions that many brokers collect without their clients' knowledge.

Like most brokers, I always wanted to make money for my clients. But, like any other broker, I was more likely to make recommendations from the handful of stocks that I followed—all stocks that gave me higher commissions. That was not and is not against any of the rules and regulations of the securities industry. It is an accepted, everyday part of the business. It is also an ingrained conflict of interest. Most brokers try to make money for their clients, and truly believe in the companies that they recommend. But unlike their clients, brokers *know* that they will make money off every transaction.

One of the striking things about my introduction to the securities industry was learning how much most clients don't know about the way the business works. Even people who consider themselves sophisticated investors usually don't know that their brokers' annual commissions can amount to 10 percent, 20 percent, sometimes more of their total portfolios. At the same time, I saw that the typical broker's attitude was "What the client doesn't know won't hurt him." I have known many brokers who earned more off their clients' money than their clients did. If clients knew the extent of the hidden commissions they pay, would they care? Many probably wouldn't. A raging bull market for most of two decades covers a multitude of brokers' sins. Most investors were happy if they were anywhere near the 20-plus percent average rise in the market in years such as 1995, 1996, 1997, and 1998. Even if their portfolios were outperformed by the market, most didn't care as long as they were seeing at least double-digit returns.

Relatively few of the hundreds of brokers I have worked with have been outright crooks, of course. But a surprising number were. Beyond those who intentionally cheated clients, many brokers I have worked with almost seemed brainwashed by their brokerage houses and by the securities industry in general. They were taught, and seemed to believe, that what they were doing—focusing on making money for themselves and the brokerage house first and their clients second—was actually in the clients' best interest.

Greed, of course, is at the heart of the stock market. Greed on the part of brokers. And, it must be said, greed on the part of investors. Before I began working in the securities industry, what little I knew about it was largely from the film *Wall Street*, which supposedly outlined the excesses of the financial services industry in the 1980s. At first, I thought the cynical viewpoint of Oliver Stone, the director, was an exaggeration for dramatic purposes, a form of literary license.

I came to learn that Stone and his film had barely scratched the surface. I knew brokers who used to rent the movie just to laugh at how naïve it was.

Gordon Gekko, the Michael Douglas character in the movie, exulted, "Greed is good." That's still a mantra on Wall Street, especially among young brokers. Gordon Gekko is not a villain to them. He was and is a hero to many of today's brokers. That's because the 1990s echoed the 1980s. The 1990s roared just as much as the Roaring Eighties, maybe more. The difference was that most of us brokers learned the lessons of the 1980s. Don't brag. Don't be too showy. Don't call too much attention to yourself. Sure, there were throwbacks, brokers like Lazlo who flaunted their wealth, who rubbed their clients' noses in it. But many other brokers today, like me, keep relatively low profiles—and their huge commissions.

I learned that a major real-life difference between the 1990s and the 1980s was that the money, and the greed, was spread more broadly throughout society. It wasn't just the big wheeler-dealers who were making more money than they ever imagined. The middle class got positively rich by investing in the stock market in the 1990s. And as clients got richer, they got greedier. Brokers and others in the securities industry quickly learned how to capitalize on the desire of so many investors to make a quick score. Consider the IPO (Initial Public Offering), when companies float their stock to the public for the first time. Through the 1990s, investment banking exploded, primarily through taking companies public. From 1996 to 1998, more than 1,800 U.S. companies offered Initial Public Offerings, raising more than $120 billion. IPOs have come to be seen by many investors, large and small, as manna from above. If you can get in on the ground floor of an IPO, goes the considered wisdom, the stock will run up the first day. If you don't think the company is fundamentally a good one, you sell the first day, or "flip" the stock, and pocket a nice chunk of change. If you believe in the company, you hold on to the stock and count on it continuing to appreciate, though more gradually, for months or years.

As a cold caller, I used that line of thinking to persuade investors to give their money to brokers they never heard of, to invest in companies they never heard of. Today, investors who scorn brokers and embrace online trading find themselves being sucked in the same way by stock promoters on the Internet. But many investors by now have realized that not every IPO is that mirage of investing, The Sure Thing. Indeed, it is becoming increasingly clear that many companies doing IPOs should not be going public at all—and many of them that went public in the 1990s should have remained private, for their own sake and especially for the sake of their investors. I've been involved in IPOs that were at best ridiculous, such as the one for a company that raised millions based on cookies a couple of guys made in their kitchen at home. No matter how ridiculous, however, there always seemed to be rapacious investment bankers and vulturous corporate managers preying upon clients blinded by their own greed.

I saw firsthand how corporate managers and investment bankers sell brokers on their companies, convincing us that the companies will grow and that investors will make money. Brokers, believing what they hear and looking for reasons to help their clients (and themselves), convince their clients to invest. Calling up strangers and advising them how to spend their money is a difficult, daunting job. I wouldn't have been able to do it if I didn't believe in the companies I was supporting. Yet the investors were the least likely to profit. The managers and the bankers were sure to make money, and so were the brokers.

Clients should not believe that they can trust their brokers just because they are with investment houses that have network TV commercials. Some of the biggest names on Wall Street, among them Merrill Lynch, Goldman Sachs, Salomon Smith Barney, Paine Webber, and J. P. Morgan, were among the firms paying tens of millions in fines in 1999 for alleged share price-fixing and stock manipulation that cheated clients out of several billion dollars. Dozens of brokers were suspended, but only temporarily. Some were back at work within three weeks.

Here's another aspect of the conflict of interest inherent in the securities industry: Analysts supposedly make recommendations that predict what specific stocks will do–"buy" recommendations for stocks that will go up, "sell" recommendations for stocks that go down. How often do brokerage firms put sell recommendations on stocks? A recent study of 26,000 reports by Wall Street analysts showed that only 1 percent were sell recommendations. The brokerage business is aimed at encouraging people to buy stocks, not sell them. That's the way brokers make their money.

I'm going to tell you about things I saw and heard that were not necessarily in the best interests of clients. From starting as a cold caller (maybe I was one of those guys who interrupted you at home or work on more than one occasion) to becoming a trainee to emerging as a full-fledged, licensed broker and ultimately being anointed a senior vice president, I saw many examples of how clients' interests took a back seat to their brokers' interests. Churning. Parking. Taking kickbacks and payments under the table. Manipulating a stock's price to create a bigger spread—and bigger hidden commissions—between the buy and sell prices. Cornering the sales of a stock to make sure shares don't end up with "outsiders" who might sell the stock at the real market price rather than at their own artificial price. Crossing transactions—matching buy and sell orders to leave clients in exactly the same position, except for the commissions they've paid to their brokers. Skimming favorably priced shares, particularly in IPOs, for their own and their friends' accounts before making them available to clients.

This is a book that stockbrokers do not want their clients to read. Stockbrokers will admit that the stories in this book are true, but will assure clients that their firms don't operate that way, and that they personally don't do business that way. Maybe. But the basic conflict of interest remains: Brokers routinely persuade their clients to buy or sell shares when it is in the best interest of the brokers rather than the clients.

3

A Born Broker

Looking back, I see how I fit a common profile for a stockbroker. We are personality guys, people who like to make money and spend it. We are natural salesmen who enjoy contact with people, who respond to pressure and stress, who see selling as a gratifying pursuit, and who like to revel in and share our successes.

My dad, now retired, was a successful entrepreneur and business manager. He never went to college. He started working at a trucking company in the dispatcher's office as a teenager, and ended up running several rental-car franchises and auto dealerships. We had a nice home in a well-to-do area in the New York suburbs, and we took nice vacations. We were a happy family. We didn't hurt for anything. My mother stayed home and took care of my brother and sisters and me and the house. Growing up was for the most part unremarkable. It was fun. The only thing that bothered me, on the rare occasions when I thought about it, was that my dad wasn't around more. He was a good-looking man who was always well groomed and well dressed, just right for whatever occasion. He always drove a big Lincoln, never more than two years old. I thought of him as a big shot. I wanted to emulate him.

School wasn't hard for me, but I was a marginal student. I could do the work, but I didn't like it. I was more interested in sports, my friends, and having fun. In high school I played soccer and hockey and tennis, and got seriously into chasing girls. My folks wanted me to do well, but there wasn't a lot of pressure to get good grades. My dad got where he was not because of good grades, but because of hard work, toughness, and the ability to get along with people. He could sell, and he could close a deal. To me, those were the keys to success.

After graduating from high school in the late 1980s, I worked, sort of, at one of my dad's car rental agencies for the summer, and then went off in the autumn to Bucknell University in Pennsylvania, where I majored in having a good time. I graduated with a lot of casual friends and a few very good ones.

I took a job out on Long Island as a sales rep, selling office-building security and lighting systems. The starting salary was only $18,000, but I cared more about the position and the job than about the salary. I just needed an apartment, a car, and enough money to have fun. The guy who hired me told me it was possible to earn up to two-thirds of my base salary in bonuses and commissions, and said some guys were able to do that within three or four years. I did it the first year, and could have made more if not for that two-thirds limit. I found out that not only could I sell, but that I was good at it.

That $30,000 was decent money, especially for a twenty-two-year-old, in the early 1990s. I went out almost every night, and partied a lot. I had a company car, and got an apartment with another young guy in a singles-dominated complex. Its real name was Pheasant Hills, but everybody called it Pleasant Thrills. It had a pool, a hot tub, tennis courts, and a clubhouse, and there was usually a party either going on or waiting to be started.

My regional managers at the security company loved me, and I thought they were great bosses. Their motto was "Work hard, play hard, sleep fast." They sent me on training courses, and taught me a lot about the way to treat customers and run a sales business. I started winning incentive sales contests, and on one of them I flew down to the Bahamas and played golf with the president of the company. I was on my way. I loved working. I was proud of myself, and it seemed like my dad was proud of me, too. I thought maybe after a few years I could join him in his business, and perhaps take over his companies myself someday.

After a year or so, I became restless. I was doing well in my job, but in some ways it was too easy. It offered me a nice life, but it wasn't a way to get really rich, plus the security and lighting business wasn't exactly sexy. It sounded almost blue-collar. I felt like I needed a change, but I had no idea what. Every now and then I'd go into Manhattan with some friends for the evening, and we'd get together with other friends from high school or college who were living and working in the city. One Saturday night at a sports bar, mutual friends introduced me to Larry, a guy about five years older than me. We started talking about the hockey game on the big TV, and he seemed like a good guy. Larry told me he was a stockbroker, and that it was a great business. I was intrigued. I had never met a stockbroker before. I didn't even know if my folks owned any stocks or bonds.

I became part of a regular group of guys, including Larry, who hung out in the city on weekends. We met in bars and went to a lot of sporting events and parties together. Sometimes we double- or tripled-dated. Through Larry, I met several other stockbrokers from his firm, and I liked them, too. They always seemed to have a great time. They were confident but not arrogant, and got along great with people. They made friends everywhere we went. They had plenty of money, and didn't mind spending it on good times. They were generous, including with me. Over time, they explained their work to me. It was sales, basically. They worked for a firm that specialized in raising money for little startup companies that had great promise. They helped the people who invested in those companies make money for themselves on new issues. I had no idea what a new issue was, but it all sounded good. In comparison, my job out on Long Island seemed dull.

By the time I had been at the security and lighting job for almost two years, I was making $4,000, $5,000, sometimes $6,000 a month. Not bad for a twenty-three-year-old. But I was bored stiff and looking for any excuse to quit. Larry and his buddies gave me one. Half a dozen brokers had planned a ski vacation in Vail, but at the last minute one of them couldn't go. He had a big deal coming down, and he couldn't get away. He offered me a half-price deal on his plane ticket (it was the first time I had ever flown first-class) and his room in the luxury chalet they had rented in Vail. We skied all day every day, and partied hard every night. It wasn't just the plane flight; everything about that week, and about those guys, was first-class. Their ski equipment and clothing. Their meals. Their whiskey. Their cigars. The women they chatted up and sometimes took back to the chalet with them. That week in Colorado changed my life. Staying with those guys, I realized that they weren't happy-go-lucky high rollers only when I hung out with them in Manhattan on weekends. It was all the time. This was their life. And I wanted it to be my life, too.

On the plane on the way back to New York, I told Larry and the other brokers that I was thinking of quitting my job and trying to become a broker. They told me that I should do it, that I had the right kind of personality to be a successful broker. For the entire flight, we talked about the securities business and how to break in. They described cold calling and getting leads and opening accounts. They told me hundreds of calls would produce a handful of leads, and those would lead to one new account. They told me a lot of guys would be stockbrokers if they could, but it took a special kind of person. Most trainees never made it. But they thought I could beat the odds. They warned me that it would be lousy work at first, for a few weeks anyway, but once I passed the broker's test and got my license—the Series 7, they called it—I could start making big bucks, just like them. A couple of them, including Larry, said maybe they could get me on at their firms. I was intrigued with the idea, and I loved talking about it, but I was leery of starting out at their firms. I didn't want to be under anybody's wing. They had made it on their own, why couldn't I?

Back home, I called my dad and told him I was thinking of becoming a broker. He suggested we get together for dinner in the city, which was something we tried to do once a month or so. We usually went to a good steak house, and this time we went to Peter Luger's in Brooklyn. I was surprised when he told me that he and my mom had owned some stocks for years—nothing huge, but some tidy holdings in a few blue chips. "They might help you kids pay for college for your own kids one of these days," he said. My dad didn't seem to know a lot about the stock market, but said he liked and trusted his broker. He told me the man's name, but I had never heard of him. My dad was always happy to talk about running a company with us kids, but he had never been much for discussing money with any of us. He told me he thought being a broker was an honorable profession, and he said he liked the idea of my helping people manage their money and make investments that would provide security for themselves and their families. He didn't say anything that would discourage me.

With my dad's blessing, the next morning I looked in the help-wanted section of the newspapers and found classified ads for trainee stockbrokers at several brokerage houses, including one that I had heard Larry and the other brokers describe as the cream of the cream, the Harvard of financial institutions. Why not aim high?

I called the number and was invited in for an interview at the firm's main office, just off Wall Street.

I had never been to Wall Street, and I had to look it up on a map to figure out how to find the brokerage house. Inside, the place looked like Harvard, or at least the way I thought Harvard should look. Everything was big, heavy, dark wood, thick carpeting, and plush upholstery. The waiting room had big club chairs. It seemed sophisticated to me, like a rich man's library without the books. I was twenty-three years old, I was applying for a job to become a stockbroker trainee, and I knew absolutely nothing about stocks, bonds, or other investments. I was nervous, but I was confident. I knew I could sell.

The Harvard interviewer was not what I expected. She was a tall blond woman, very friendly. When she came and got me from the lobby, I thought she was taking me to meet someone else, probably a distinguished man with gray hair. But she took me straight into a conference room and interviewed me herself, one on one. We talked about my sales experience for a few minutes, and that was about it. I was surprised that she never asked me why I wanted the job. I was even more surprised that she didn't tell me anything about the job. "So, would you like me to show you around?" she asked. I said sure.

We left the conference room and walked down a hallway. I could hear voices raised, and a raspy loudspeaker. The hallway opened up into a huge room that she called the board room. Big mahogany desks, dozens of them, stood in rows, with a big green office armchair behind each one. Each big desk had one or more smaller desks grouped around it, with armless orange chairs behind the smaller desks. Almost every chair, orange or green, had a person in it. The vast majority were men, and nearly all were talking on the phone. Those that weren't on the phone seemed to be shouting at each other. The woman turned to me and smiled. "See that gentleman over there," she said, pointing. "He made eighty thousand dollars last month. Take-home. That's right, last month." She smiled, knowing I was incredulous even though I tried hard not to show it. "That gentleman over there,'" she said, pointing again. "He made one hundred and fifty thousand dollars last month." One of my goals had been to make $100,000 a year by the time I was thirty. I could feel myself setting new goals. Inside, I felt a yearning, an actual kind of hunger. I wanted to be one of these guys.

We strolled through the room. I took in as much as I could, trying to remember it all. Everyone ignored us. One guy, sitting in one of the big green chairs, was getting his shoes shined while he talked on the phone. I had never seen that, but suddenly I wanted it to be me getting my shoes shined. I had no understanding of what was going on, but I liked it and I wanted to be part of it. The place felt like money. Ten minutes later, we were back in the conference room. "Any questions?" the woman asked.

"Yeah," I said, joking. "When do I start?" I thought that surely I'd have to take some tests or be interviewed some more.

She considered, as if she was thinking about it. "How's Monday?" she suggested.

I was surprised, but not so surprised that I couldn't blurt out, "Great!" I walked out on a cloud. On the way back home I realized I hadn't asked about the pay, the working hours, benefits, vacation, or even what I would be doing. But it didn't matter. I didn't care. I would do whatever it took to be a success—for a year. I vowed that if I wasn't making money in a year, I would quit and go back to the security and lighting firm.

Over the weekend before I started my new job, my parents could tell how excited I was. They wanted to know more. About all I could tell them was that Harvard was known for the highest commissions per broker on Wall Street, year after year. Harvard brokers knew they were expected to generate higher commissions than brokers at other firms, and they usually did. It made them feel superior, but it wasn't just about the money they earned from those commissions, the houses and cars and vacations and expensive clothes. They were the best, the winners. That was the way it was at all of Harvard's branches around the country, I told my mom and dad, but especially at the headquarters on Wall Street, the crown jewel in the Harvard operation, the branch with the highest commissions per broker in the entire country.

I told my folks that the Harvard brokers' overall attitude was comparable to that of college fraternity boys who were sure they had pledged the best frat house, the one everyone else wanted to join. There was an aura about the Harvard board room, an aura of success, confidence, and rampant egos. I admitted that I was more than a little intimidated. I was nervous, excited, eager to do well. But more than anything, I yearned to be one of them, to be part of their sleek, smug fraternity. Some of them made $100,000 a month. Even if I was average at it, I figured I could make at least $10,000 a month. I could see my future. I was going to be a stockbroker.

4

"Hello, I Can Make You Rich . . ."

If I had known what cold calling was like, I might never have shown up for my first day of work. Being a cold caller was like being an invisible man.

I walked into Harvard at a little before nine o'clock on a Monday morning. I told the receptionist I was there to start work, and she just pointed wordlessly, without even looking me in the eye, down the hall toward the board room. In the board room, the brokers were just coming out of a meeting in a conference room at the far end. They were all talking, gesturing, laughing. No one even glanced at me. They were part of the fraternity, and I wasn't. I saw the guy who had made $150,000 the previous month. I tried to pick out other guys who looked like they were big earners. It wasn't so much the clothes. It was the attitude, the bearing. They seemed like gods to me, and I was a long way from even the foothills of Mount Olympus.

Finally, after standing around for fifteen minutes—it seemed like three hours—a woman came over to me, asked my name, and introduced herself. She rounded up five other guys standing around like me, reporting for their first day of work. She told us she was in charge of the cold callers. That was the first time anyone had told me what

I would be doing. Cold calling. I had suspected that's where I would start, based on what my broker buddies had told me. But up until that point I still had a faint notion that some manager would size me up as a future superstar and order me into a special training program. I had never heard of such a program, but in my fantasy one would be created just for me. No. The queen of the cold callers—that's what we called her, the Queen—showed us the time clock. We actually had to punch in every morning, and punch out at night. I hadn't done that even when I swept floors at my dad's office during summers in high school. I tried to act like it was no big deal. I took my time card and successfully punched in for the first time in my life. The Queen never told us anything about the job. She took me over to a desk right in the middle of the board room and introduced me to Tom. "You'll work with Tom today, and maybe tomorrow," she said. "He'll show you the job." And she walked away.

Tom didn't seem especially interested in me, or in talking about the job. "Watch and listen for a while," he said. "You can try it when you're ready." He had a big sheet of perforated three-by-five cards, and was bending and tearing off the individual cards. He put them in a stack.

Tom tore up sheet after sheet. His stack of single three-by-five cards got higher and higher. Lead cards, he called them. Tom showed me a card. It had a name, address, and phone number. That was it. I noted that these cards were from Dun & Bradstreet, but he told me that other companies sold them, too. Brokerage houses bought the cards by the tens of thousands. They were supposed to be lists of people who invested in the stock market, or fit the profile of people who might invest in the market. Tom said the cards were culled from databases and mailing lists: people who subscribed to a financial magazine, or who had bought a luxury car or an expensive stereo, or who had taken a cruise, or maybe who simply lived in a zip code with a high population of well-off residents.

When the stack of cards was almost a foot high, Tom handed me a sheet of paper with a script typed on it. It had both sides of the conversation, the caller and the respondent:

Hello. This is Mr. Jones's office.
HELLO, IS MR. JONES IN, PLEASE?
Who's calling, please?
IT'S MR. SMITH'S OFFICE.
Mr. Smith? From where?
FROM NEW YORK.
What is this regarding?
IT'S A PERSONAL BUSINESS MATTER.

Most calls were taken by secretaries. The secretary usually either put the call through to the guy whose name was on the card, or else she hung up. Tom was a cold caller for a young broker named Samms, so he would say the call was from Mr. Samms's office. Every once in a while he got a secretary who actually may have believed her boss knew Mr. Samms and they had some personal business history. Most secretaries, though, knew it was a cold call from a securities house boiler room. (I myself never heard the term "boiler room" until several weeks later. I preferred to continue thinking of it as the board room.) Either way, if a secretary put the call through, it was a good sign that her boss was the kind of guy who would listen to a cold call.

When Tom did get the boss on the line, he quickly transferred the call to Samms, who sat at the big desk in the green chair next to us. Cold callers weren't allowed to talk to clients or potential clients, Tom told me. Federal regulations. "You gotta have your license," he said. Gradually, talking to Tom and to other cold callers, I figured things out. Cold callers typically served an apprenticeship of at least 120 days before they could take the Series 7 test to get a broker's license. If you were doing well after six or eight weeks, the Queen would give you a set of the study books to help you prepare for the test.

If you passed the test and got your Series 7 license, you didn't automatically start working as a broker. You might keep cold calling for a while until you moved up to become a qualifier, one step above a cold caller. If a cold caller got a potential investor on the line, the call would quickly be transferred to a qualifier. The qualifier spoke to the potential client and tried to find out if he had more than $100,000 invested in stocks and at least $10,000 in any single stock, and if he was interested in talking to a Harvard broker about investment ideas. If the investor met those criteria, he qualified.

At that point, the investor officially became a lead. The qualifier told him that some information about Harvard would be mailed to him, and that a broker would be calling him in a week or so. The qualifier filled out a form confirming the lead's contact information, along with any information the qualifier might have picked up, especially if it concerned the lead's investments. That form was stapled to the original perforated lead card and put into a stack on the broker's desk. The broker—or, more likely, the broker's secretary—mailed each lead a standard packet of information about investing in general and Harvard in particular, with the broker's business card. The lead card went into a tickler system, and ten days later the broker plucked out the card, called the lead, pitched him on some possible investments, and tried to get him to open an account.

The most productive brokers at Harvard, the biggest earners, each had two cold callers and a qualifier. At the next level, the brokers who were big producers but not the superstars had one qualifier and one cold caller. The rest of the brokers had a single cold caller and acted as their own qualifiers. When Tom got a potential investor to come on the line, he quickly passed the call to Samms. Samms, who did not yet merit a qualifier, would find out if the guy qualified—$100,000 in the market and at least $10,000 in one position—and fill out the lead forms himself.

• • •

I watched that whole first day, and the first half of the second day. The second day, I went out for a quick slice of pizza for lunch with Tom and a couple of other cold callers, and then started making calls myself in the afternoon. The phone on my desk, and on every cold caller's desk, was one of those old black rotary jobs that you had to dial. No push buttons. Brokers had sleek new push-button phone consoles, with multiple lines, number memory, speed-dial, and headphones. The headphones looked expensive, like the kind that come with a good stereo system. Brokers put their headphones on in the morning and didn't take them off until they left the building. If they went to the restroom, they unplugged the wire from the jack on the phone and pulled the headphones down off their ears to rest around their necks. They'd swagger around the office with the headphones dangling from their necks, like they were doctors with stethoscopes. I thought it was stupid and arrogant, but I wished more than anything that I had my own set of headphones to wear when I went to the restroom.

Within a couple of hours I got a blister on my index finger, and had to switch to another finger. Then I tried dialing with a pencil. I was nervous and awkward with my first few calls, but I quickly got over it. Once I got the rap down, I tried to raise the energy level in my voice so I would sound more confident, and I sensed a hesitation in the secretary's voice before she hung up on me. I concentrated on sounding more positive, more important. On about the twentieth call, a secretary put me through to her boss. I transferred the call to Samms, and then I grinned at Tom. He just stared back at me.

Over the course of the afternoon, I got through to five more potential investors for Samms. Before we quit for the day, I asked Tom what he thought about cold calling. "It's shit," he said. "But you gotta do it if you're going to get over there." He nodded toward a wall near the windows, where the big producers' desks lined the outside of the board room. I agreed with him. The work was shit. I hated it already. The worst part was when I got a potential investor on the line and Samms was on another call. I'd hold the phone toward him, gesturing. If he couldn't break away from the call he was on, he would raise one finger and wave it in a circle, like a baseball umpire's signal for a home run. He was telling me to offer the call to the rest of the board room. I had to stand up and shout out, "Call!" Other brokers or qualifiers who wanted to take the call would shout out their extension numbers, and I would transfer the call to one of them. I found it humiliating, but no one cared how I felt. Harvard did not waste potential leads.

As I punched out that second day, the Queen of the Cold Callers buzzed past. "How'd it go?" she asked, a big fake smile on her face.

"Great," I said. "I love it. I can't wait 'til tomorrow."

She actually stopped and studied me for a moment. She didn't say anything, but the fake smile gave way to a kind of half-quizzical, half-amused expression. I don't think she believed me for a second. Looking back, however, I think she recognized that I might have what it took to survive cold calling, to pass the Series 7 test, and to actually become a broker at Harvard. "You'll work with Tom again tomorrow" was all she said. I said okay, but I really didn't want to work with Tom any-more. He was depressing. He had no energy, no interest in the job. He sounded bored on the phone. He might not have admitted it to him-self yet, but he thought this was a dead-end job, and he was never going to be a broker.

When I closed my eyes that night, all I could see was a closeup of an old telephone dial, with the black numbers against white circles showing through the finger holes. I didn't sleep well. When I woke up the next morning, I had a stiff neck from the way I had been holding the phone. Getting up, getting dressed, and going back to Harvard that third morning was one of the hardest things I have ever done in my life. But I did it. I got in a few minutes before nine, punched in, and stood in the line of cold callers with Tom as the Queen handed out stacks of perforated cards. I noticed that the cold callers who worked for the big producers got more lead cards than Tom or any of the cold callers working for the less productive brokers.

The lead cards were the basic fuel of the boiler room, I came to learn. They were the raw material for building a business. Brokers for the most part treated cold callers miserably or ignored them as much as they could. But they fought and scrapped and argued with the Queen and her boss, the Branch Manager, for their cold callers to get more cards each morning. "The Branch Manager says you get more cards when you do more with the ones you got," I overheard her tell one broker who was whining that his cold caller should get more lead cards.

A cold caller ordinarily wouldn't call the number on a card only once. He'd recycle the cards, calling again and again. If a secretary hung up on him in the morning, he'd try in the afternoon. If the secretary hung up on him in the afternoon, he'd try lunchtime, then early in the morning, then late in the day, hoping the boss would pick up the phone himself. A cold caller had to be convinced that he was never going to get the boss on the phone before he would throw away a lead card. Sometimes he would put the card away and then call back in a couple of weeks, hoping that the secretary had forgotten his voice or, better yet, that she had been fired and replaced. The only other way that cold callers threw away cards was if the lead, the person named on the card, came on and said he wasn't interested.

The third day, I made about 200 phone calls and got 22 potential investors to come on the line. About half of those I passed to Samms, and the other half I passed to other brokers who shouted out their extensions when I stood up and yelled, "Call!" When five or six guys were all shouting out extension numbers, it sounded like some kind of crazy bingo game. Over the coming weeks, I came to recognize some of the extension numbers, and the faces that went with them. Once in a while, usually on the way out in the evening, one or two qualifiers would stroll by and say something like, "Hey, man, thanks for the call today. It was a good one." I made it a point to throw more calls toward those guys.

In contrast, on my third day of work Tom got only a dozen people on the line. To me, it was as if there was a giant scoreboard all lit up right there in the board room: Rob 22, Tom 12. I was competing with everybody at Harvard, and Tom was the first one who happened to be in my sights. By the end of my third day, he was dead meat as far as I was concerned, and he knew it. The fourth day, he didn't show up for work. Nobody knew what happened to him. He didn't resign. He just never showed up again.

Talking to other cold callers over the next few days, I learned that his departure was no big deal. There was an incredible turnover among cold callers. Of the other five cold callers who started the same day I did, one didn't come back the second day, four were gone within two weeks, and all five were gone within a month. Harvard would bring in five to ten new cold callers every week, thirty or forty in a month. Of every hundred cold callers, maybe eight would get their books and take the Series 7 exam. Five or six would pass the exam, get their broker's licenses, and become qualifiers. The goal was to work for a few months, maybe a year or two, as a qualifier. Gradually, working with a broker, a qualifier would learn how to open accounts, how to build and run a business. Then, in theory, the qualifier could become a broker with his own big desk, green chair, and cold caller.

Even with a license, however, it was rare for a qualifier at Harvard to move up to become a Harvard broker. Quite a few qualifiers, after they were allowed to talk to clients, found out they weren't that good at selling. Some would quit the business altogether. A few would stay at Harvard for years as permanent qualifiers, or become sales-clerks who kept track of the bookkeeping and administrative side of a broker's business. Some were good at selling but not quite good enough to work at Harvard. After a year or two, they would get jobs as brokers at other firms. Harvard qualifiers were always in demand as brokers at smaller firms. Only the very best qualifiers became brokers at Harvard. When I was there, of the eighty brokers in the board room, I could find exactly three who had started like me, as cold callers in that same room. Most of them had come from other firms where they had graduated from training programs and gone on to be superstars before they were recruited away by Harvard. All in all, I figured the odds were at least 100–1 against me getting one of those big desks and green chairs. But I still thought I would do it.

My fourth morning, the morning that Tom didn't show, I picked up Samms's allotment of perforated cards and ripped them up myself. That came to be my favorite part of the day as a cold caller, ripping up the cards and stacking them. It was the only physically satisfying part of the job. That fourth day on the job, I started doing something else that helped me get through the day. The thought of spending eight hours cold calling, from nine to five, was so depressing that I couldn't bear it. I told myself I just had to make it until ten o'clock. That's all I had to do. One hour. At ten I told myself one more hour. I just had to make it to eleven o'clock. I did that all day, until five. And I did it every day for the next four months.

With Tom gone, I assumed his spot as Samms's cold caller. Nobody said I should or could. I just did it. Samms didn't seem at all surprised. I had quickly dismissed Samms as an also-ran because he had only one cold caller. But we talked occasionally during the four weeks I was his cold caller—which was unusual, because Harvard brokers rarely spoke to cold callers, even their own. I didn't think he was going to be a heavy hitter at Harvard, but he still seemed like a nice guy. I was stunned when he told me that he was part of a special training program.

Samms had never been a cold caller or a qualifier. He was an accountant who was changing careers. Harvard had brought him in as a trainee, put him through some classes, and started him off at the big desk in the green chair. He and the other trainees got a draw of $4,000 a month for six months while they were training, and then it was sink or swim. No punching the time clock for him. How come I hadn't heard about this program? How come Harvard hadn't looked at me, and put me into the program? I was jealous, and it must have showed. "With your experience, you should be starting as a trainee, not a cold caller," Samms told me after I'd been there a few days.

I agreed. Most of the other cold callers were straight out of college, and looked it. They wore khakis and cheap sports jackets, or suits that looked like they were off the rack from one of those discount houses. I had just turned twenty-four. I already had started wearing designer suits. I had proved I could sell. I had made more than $40,000 the previous year. Some of the other cold callers didn't believe me when I told them that, or if they did, they thought I was nuts. They certainly thought I was nuts when I asked them what we got paid. I hadn't asked, and no one had told me. I started to think I was nuts, too, when I got my first paycheck. I was making $3.50 an hour.

I did pretty well as Samms's cold caller. The Queen kept a chart near the time clock, a running day-by-day list of rankings: total contacts, contacts per hour, dials per day. The most important daily figure was total contacts, the number of calls that were passed along to qualifiers. I decided it was my goal to be in the top three every day, and within a couple of weeks I was. On a good day I would make 500 calls, and pass along 60 or 70 contacts. Most days I was on top of the Queen's rankings, or at least in the top three.

There was little glory in this, or satisfaction. I was just a body to Harvard at that point, a finger and a voice to get people on the phone. I realized that the managers at Harvard didn't even call us cold callers. They called us dialers. They had no interest in grooming us, or training us. They called where we worked the board room, but we called it the pit. I shouldn't use the term "we," I suppose, because I never really thought of myself as being part of a group with the other cold callers. I talked to them and went out for a quick lunch with a few of them once in a while, but I pretty much kept to myself. I didn't want to be friends with them. I wasn't like them. Ninety-nine percent of them were going to be losers at Harvard. I wasn't.

Whenever I talked to another cold caller, I had two standard questions. First, "How long have you been here?" Second, "How much longer do you think it will take for you to get your books?" I was gathering information, continually recalibrating my own timetable. I was also checking out the competition. If a guy had been there more than six months, he was probably a loser. But I still might pick his brain a little. Who are the best brokers to work for? Do you know any cold callers who took their tests after 120 days? When did they get their books? If I had gotten whatever information I could from a loser, I probably didn't talk to him after that. And there were a lot of losers among the cold callers. There was a guy who had been there two years. That was incredible to me.

"So when are you going to take your test?" I asked the guy.

"Whenever they're ready to give it to me," he said.

"Not me," I said. "If they won't let me take it on the hundred and twenty-first day, I'm gone." I couldn't imagine two years of this degradation for $3.50 an hour. How could that cold caller possibly think he was ever going to become a broker? How could he possibly think any of the managers at Harvard were interested in him?

Of course, the managers at Harvard weren't interested in me, either. Not as a cold caller, anyway. But I knew that if I lasted long enough and was tenacious enough to pass the Series 7 test and become a qualifier, they might show a tiny amount of interest. I set a goal. If I didn't get the study books within 120 days, I was leaving. But I was determined to work as hard as I could, and to keep my mouth shut, until then. The Queen didn't check to make sure that the cold callers were telling the truth when they told her how many contacts they had passed along to qualifiers at the end of each day. Nobody checked. We could

have lied about our totals to make it onto the top of the daily rankings. I thought about it, but I never inflated my contacts. I don't think
any other cold callers did, either. We were all too scared that we might
somehow get caught, and blow our chance of grabbing the brass ring.

Like every other cold caller, I had become an invisible man. All
around me were people doing business. I could see them and hear
them. They couldn't see or hear me unless I stood up and shouted,
"Call!" I could have been a machine, except I probably worked cheaper
than a machine. Less maintenance, and easier to throw away. But an
invisible man can absorb a lot. I looked and listened and learned. The
workings of the stock market had been a complete mystery to me.
Gradually, as a cold caller, I figured out the basics of how the market
worked, and what made individual stocks and the Dow Jones go up
and down. The market had crashed in 1987, and brokers still murmured darkly sometimes about Black Friday and Black Monday. But
that was ancient history to me. Watching brokers work, I saw that it
was easier to sell stock in a company that was doing well, and when
the market was getting better. But it wasn't necessary. To brokers, any
time was a good time to buy stocks. If a stock had been going up, it
was time to jump on the bandwagon. If it was going down, it was a
buying opportunity because it was undervalued and would surely go
up again.

Time and again I heard brokers tell new clients that their investment philosophy was to buy and hold. That's the way they made
money for their clients, they said. They were conservative, they said.
After the new clients opened an account, sent in their money, and
bought something, the brokers were on the phone again peddling an
even better opportunity. They wanted clients to send in more money
for this next purchase. But when clients wouldn't or couldn't send in
more money for the new purchase, the broker usually shifted gears.
Well, he said, let's sell out the first position and use that money to
buy this other stock. It was an opportunity just too good to pass up,

the broker said. Either way—sending in new money or using old money already in the portfolio—it was a commission for the broker. A typical commission for a modest-sized trade was $200, $300, $400, somewhere in that range. A good-sized trade would yield a commission in the thousands. Not bad for a five-minute phone call. I began to see how the money could add up for stockbrokers.

5

If a Woman Answers, Hang Up

Cold calling was invented by Harvard, or so I was told. As I came to learn more about the business, I heard many more claims, both from brokerage houses and individual brokers, that they had been the ones to invent cold calling. Who knows? Certainly it was the lifeblood of the Harvard operation—calling strangers and asking them for money. Brokers at old-line, traditional brokerage firms such as Merrill Lynch, Paine Webber, Dean Witter, Lehman, Shearson—"wire houses," we called them—tried to build up their business by networking. They gave talks to local organizations, or joined clubs, or served on committees. They became known in their communities as solid citizens, and tried to present themselves to friends, neighbors, and acquaintances as careful, conservative, reliable financial advisors. They also did cold calling, but were nowhere near as aggressive or as organized about it as Harvard.

When I got my sheets of fresh lead cards each morning, I would tear them along the perforations and stack them by time zones. I'd start calling the East Coast first, because of the time difference, and work my way west. The cards were supposed to have office numbers only, but sometimes I'd get a home phone. I would act like I was a business associate who had been given the wrong number, and ask for the correct number for the office. Whoever answered the phone, usually a wife or kid but surprisingly often a maid or babysitter, usually gave it to me.

Some states were especially fertile ground for cold calling. Ohio, for some reason, became my favorite state. There were lots of rich people in Ohio, and most of their secretaries seemed too polite to hang up on me. Texas was good. A stack of cards in the morning from Texas and Ohio would make my day. Connecticut was good, and so was New Jersey. I hated New York cards. The secretaries were sophisticated; they had taken hundreds of cold calls, and knew the drill better than I did. They had no qualms about hanging up on me. California was trouble. Lots of suspicious people in California. Florida was pretty good because even though the cards had an inordinately high percentage of home numbers, they were often retired guys who didn't have anything better to do than hold on for a minute while I transferred them to a qualifier.

Every day as a cold caller seemed like a month to me. The Queen encouraged us cold callers to work overtime, to stay past five o'clock. There was no extra pay for staying late, but some cold callers did it anyway, trying to show how earnest they were, trying to get on top of the list of most contacts. I never did. I punched out at five o'clock. As much as I hated the job, however, I worked hard on my technique as a cold caller. I began to take pride in how quickly I could transfer a call to a qualifier. I wasn't determined to be the best cold caller in the world. That wasn't my goal. But I knew that being on top of those daily rankings would help me get the Series 7 study books sooner. I also realized, reluctantly, that cold calling could help me become a better salesman.

Cold calling taught me the salesman's greatest weapon: patience. Later, as a broker, I opened many accounts and made many big sales simply because I refused to give up. It didn't matter what a client said to me, I wasn't going to end the call. If you wanted to end a conversation with me, you either had to say yes or hang up on me. I learned that from cold calling. When I got a secretary on the line, she—out of the tens of thousands of calls I made, I encountered only a handful of male secretaries—was going to have to either put her boss on the phone or hang up on me. I wasn't going to say, "Okay, sorry, I'll try again later."

The only exception was when the prospective client turned out to be a woman. Most of the time, a lead card had a man's name on it, or only a first initial. If it had an obvious woman's name—Mary, say, or Jane or Susan—I wouldn't call the number. I'd throw the card away. All the cold callers did that. It was one of the first things I learned as a cold caller. Brokers didn't want to talk to women. They didn't want women for clients. "They're a pain in the ass," one broker said. "It's really hard to get them to open an account, and if they do then they're more trouble than they're worth. It's too hard to sell them on an idea, and they keep asking all these questions about their accounts."

Sometimes I couldn't tell by the first name on a client card if it was a man or a woman. Dale. Marty. Terry. Initials only. Richie fooled me once. I'd always call and ask for Mr. So-and-So, but sometimes a secretary would put me through to a woman, or the woman would answer herself and say, "I'm Dale So-and-So." I'd hang up. Every cold caller hung up on women—except maybe women cold callers, but I don't know. So few women were cold callers that I don't recall ever talking to one. One or two would show up at Harvard every now and then, but they never seemed to last more than a few days.

Only a handful of Harvard brokers were women, but none of them seemed like former cold callers. It seemed like they had gotten their jobs through connections. One woman broker was a tall, gorgeous blonde who was married to another broker, one of the big producers, a guy about ten years older than she was. She did some business, not a lot, but no one seemed to mind. "Don't matter how much business she does," one broker growled. "She's decorative." We cold callers figured the bosses kept her on just to keep her husband there, happily pumping out those big commissions he shared with Harvard. I thought that she should get her own slick little brochure printed up, complete with her picture, and send it out with the packet of Harvard materials that went to leads. I figured that would help her open accounts, especially if she wore something with a plunging neckline. The more alluring the picture, the more accounts she would open. But I never had the nerve to suggest it to her.

Another woman broker worked with her brother, also a broker, as a team. It seemed to me like there should have been some nepotism rules, but apparently there weren't. She and her brother, working together, did a lot of business, and that was all that mattered at Harvard. Once, when she was in the office but her brother wasn't, she had an epileptic seizure. She started flailing around, fell out of her chair, and kept seizing on the floor. Out of the dozens of other brokers in the board room, not one moved to help her. A couple of cold callers got down on the floor with her and tried to keep her from thrashing her limbs into a desk or chair and hurting herself. A couple of secretaries screamed, and one of them ran to get the Branch Manager, who told her to call 911. The Branch Manager hovered around the scene, but he seemed more intent on making sure there was minimal disruption to normal business. The other brokers all turned to look now and then during their phone calls, but no one came over. The paramedics came and took the woman broker away on a stretcher. She was back at work a few days later, and I saw her grin with embarrassment when some of the brokers teased her about doing anything to get some time off.

Even though I saw myself as a broker of the future, a potential big producer, it repeatedly was made clear to me that no one else thought I was anything special. One day, as I returned to my desk from the restroom, I walked by the Queen's desk while she was on the phone. As I passed, she caught my eye and with one hand held up the big glass she sipped water from all day. It was empty. She held it out toward me and raised her eyebrows expectantly. She snapped her fingers. She wanted—no, she expected—me to go fill up her water glass. I wanted to ignore her, I wanted to curse at her, I wanted to dump the glass of water on her head and walk out the door and never come back. Instead, I took the water glass, went over to the cooler, filled it up, and brought it back to her with a tight smile. She took it and kept talking on the phone. She didn't give any sign of thanks. She didn't even look at me.

One morning, after I'd been at Harvard about a month, the Queen said, "You'll work with Maynard today," as she handed out the lead cards. She said it offhandedly, but I was electrified. It was a promotion for me. I walked past Samms's desk on my way to my new desk and told him, "I've got to sit by Maynard today." Samms grimaced and shrugged. "Okay, it was nice working with you," he said. "Good luck." I didn't even stop walking, and he didn't get up. We didn't shake hands. As a trainee, it was sink-or-swim time for Samms, and it looked like he was treading water with iron underwear. He hung around for a couple more weeks. I would see him on the phone, following up on his diminishing stack of leads, trying to qualify some of the contacts I had left behind, and maybe even dabbling in cold calling himself. Then one day there was some other trainee at his desk. I never found out, but I hoped Samms went back to being an accountant and that he was happy with it.

Maynard's desk was away from the center of the pit—excuse me, the board room—where Samms had been. It was near a window. The nameplate on his desk said Senior Vice President. Maynard was enormous. He must have weighed 400 pounds. He had expensive clothing, but it looked like an unmade bed on him. He wore French cuffs, but all I would notice were those incredibly chubby wrists poking out of them. He wore imported silk ties, but they were always loose under his chins, as if they wouldn't actually fit around his bulging neck. My first day, Maynard just grunted at me, but I heard him complaining over the phone to his ex-wife when she called. She was trying to get money out of him, and he didn't like it. "I made hundreds of thousands when I was with you, and I lost hundreds of thousands," he said. "If you can find it, you can have it." I couldn't believe my ears. Hanging around these brokers, I was beginning to see how someone could earn hundreds of thousands of dollars. But I still couldn't imagine losing hundreds of thousands. Like I said, I didn't know much about the stock market. I wanted to learn as much as I could from Maynard. He was "my" broker now, and I knew that the more he liked me, the sooner he would tell the Queen that I was ready to get the books to begin studying for the exam.

The second day, Maynard bought me lunch. Well, actually, he gave me some money and sent me down to the deli to bring back sandwiches for both of us. I didn't mind. I was making $3.50 an hour, so somebody spending $4 on me for lunch was meaningful. Cold callers at Harvard were kind of like bicycle messengers. We did a necessary job, but nobody would describe it as important. Nobody paid any attention to us. We didn't speak unless we were spoken to. Brokers rarely initiated conversations with cold callers. On the day Maynard bought me a tuna salad on a hard roll, however, I started talking to him. I presented myself as curious, interested, ambitious, but not aggressive. I sucked up to him. Most brokers are emotional egotists who love to talk, who love to get a response from people, who love to hear people talk about them. Brokers in social settings might discuss a lot of different topics, but what they're really saying one way or another is "So, hey, whaddya think of me now?" Over the first week with Maynard, we got to the point where we would talk easily but not often, maybe for a minute or two, maybe three or four times a day. I never asked him specifics, like "What are you buying today?" I came to recognize one of the ironies of the business: brokers like to talk about what they are buying *for* their clients, when in truth what they are doing is selling *to* their clients.

• • •

Maynard and most other brokers, not just at Harvard but at every firm, treated cold callers like their personal serfs. Sometimes they asked us to run personal errands for them–not just fetching their lunches, but also picking up their dry cleaning, or taking their bank cards to the local ATM machine and getting cash out for them. Maynard routinely had me do all those things for him, but he didn't trust me with certain jobs, and I'm glad he didn't. He had a special arrangement with another cold caller, and I wanted no part of it. The other cold caller would come to Maynard at the end of the day, and Maynard would hand him a package. The next morning the cold caller would hand Maynard back the package, along with a stack of lead cards. I got a glimpse of them once, and they were handwritten, not typed out like the usual lead cards we got from the Queen.

I went out for a beer after work one day with the cold caller, and he explained that Maynard was giving him microfiche transcripts of account statements from another brokerage firm. The transcripts were from the tops of the account statements, though, and had only the names and addresses of the clients, not the phone numbers. There were about 100 of them in each package. The cold caller took them home, and spent a couple of hours on the phone with directory assistance. He got numbers for as many of the names as he could, usually about half of them, wrote them up on lead cards, and brought them in the next day. Maynard paid him $20 a night, Monday through Friday, and the cold caller earned an extra $100 a week in cash.

A few weeks later the cold caller told me Maynard had refined the operation. Instead of giving him microfiche transcripts, Maynard was giving the cold caller actual microfiche. He also had given the cold caller a machine, a microfiche reader, that the cold caller kept at his apartment. Now the cold caller was reading the entire microfiche statements on the machine, and giving Maynard lists of clients who had at least $100,000 invested with the other firm. The cold caller guessed that the microfiche must have been stolen from the other investment house. Maynard probably bought it from some guy in the other firm's mail-room. The cards the cold caller filled out for him were more valuable than the usual run-of-the-mill Harvard lead cards because they were, in effect, already qualified. Those people were known investors. They were leads. Moreover, Maynard could look at the account information, call one of the investors, and say, "You've got $20,000 in IBM, and everybody knows IBM is going to be stagnant for the next six months. I've got a couple of other ideas for you to consider . . ." The client might think, "Hey, my regular broker didn't tell me IBM was going to be stagnant." Maybe the client hadn't heard from his broker in a while. Here was some guy who was showing an interest, who seemed to be eager to work for him. Usually the investors would tell Maynard they weren't interested, but sometimes they were.

I don't know why Maynard never asked me to do the microfiche job but, given that the whole thing was highly illegal, I'm glad he didn't.

By the time I was about halfway through the 120 days, I realized that I had a better chance of getting my books and taking the test if I was working for a broker who needed a qualifier. A broker who already had a qualifier wouldn't be pushing to promote one of his cold callers. He'd be happy with the way things were. A broker who needed a qualifier would want to promote a cold caller so that he wouldn't have to waste time talking to contacts himself to qualify them as leads. He could spend his time pitching ideas to leads. Maynard didn't have a qualifier. He had two cold callers: me, and a young guy who recently had begun going out to dinner with him. I decided to be blunt. "So, Maynard, what about me becoming your qualifier when I pass the Series 7?" I asked him one day. He didn't like the question. He tried to be evasive. "Oh, yeah, well, we'll see," he murmured, picking up the phone to end the conversation. He wanted to string me along because

I was a good cold caller. He didn't want to lose me. But he was sweet on the young guy. Maybe that's why he wasn't married anymore. Anyway, he wanted to keep the young guy happy, even if that meant promoting him to qualifier instead of me.

I started looking for a way to escape from Maynard, to get in position to get my books, take the test, and become a qualifier. Maynard wasn't in the very top tier of Harvard brokers. I guessed that he probably earned $300,000 a year, which was good but not great. I thought it was time for me to move up to the best. I wanted to work with the Bald Shadow. He got that nickname because he was a tall pale guy who apparently had been a good basketball player at one time, like on that old TV series *The White Shadow,* about a basketball coach. Except the Bald Shadow was hairless as a billiard ball.

The BS, as we called him, was a big producer, and his rank in the Harvard board room was obvious. Every morning at a quarter to nine, all the brokers would gather in the glassed-in conference room at one end of the board room. The Branch Manager, a small, buttoned-down man given to strutting like a bantam rooster, presided. These swaggering brokers, seemingly so confident and fearless, were afraid of the Branch Manager. In the immediate sense, they feared him for his scathing public criticism. Long-term, they feared him for the way he got rid of brokers who weren't producing. Brokers used to joke that if you were called into the Branch Manager's office, the first thing you did was hang your tongue on the hook right inside the door. At the morning meeting, he would occasionally chide brokers who were not producing as much as he thought they should. He would also laud brokers who were doing well. The Bald Shadow sat front and center in the conference room—nobody else dared sit in his chair—and was often praised by the Branch Manager. Cold callers were allowed to attend the morning meeting—before punching in, on their own time. I rarely missed one. I envisioned myself sitting where the Bald Shadow sat, looking so smug, acting like he didn't care about the praise and envy.

The Bald Shadow had a big book—literally, a looseleaf book that listed all his clients and all the transactions he did for them. But the number of clients was not as important as the amount of money they had. "How big is your book?" one broker would ask another. The other broker would never say, "I have two hundred clients." He would give the dollar amount that he had under management for all his clients put together. "My book is one million dollars," he might say. Or $5 million. Or, in the Bald Shadow's case, about $20 million. That was a good-sized book in the mid-1990s.

The BS, as we called him, made sure the money in his book kept moving. One of the measures of a Harvard broker's success was the percentage of commissions that he generated from his book. At the wire houses, a broker might have $40 million under management and generate commissions that amounted to only 1 percent or 2 percent of his book—$200,000 to $400,000 in gross commissions, of which the broker netted about 40 percent, on average. Those were old-fashioned, lazy brokers, we learned at Harvard. They were probably old men. The Bald Shadow's $20 million book generated more than $2 million in gross commissions for Harvard—more than 10 percent of the total under management. Like every other broker at Harvard, he got 45 percent of his gross commissions: $1 million or more a year, usually. That was the kind of broker I wanted to be.

I found the Queen of the Cold Callers back by the time clock and told her that I wanted to leave Maynard and work for the Bald Shadow. I didn't say anything about Maynard's crush on the other cold caller. I simply said I wanted to take my test after 120 days and become a qualifier, and this was the surest way to make that happen. She said she'd think about it, and let me know. I assume she talked to somebody—maybe the Branch Manager, maybe Maynard, maybe the Bald Shadow himself. I don't know. But the next morning she told me to go work with the Bald Shadow.

6

The Bald Shadow

The Bald Shadow was intimidating. He seemed so unapproachable, so aloof. He had the reputation of being hard on his people, his cold callers and qualifiers and other assistants. He was very demanding, I was warned. But when I sat down at one of the clutch of small desks near his, we hit it off immediately. He was a dour guy, and really focused on business. But the reason he didn't talk to people more was that nobody talked to him. His social skills were limited. He was pretty much incapable of small talk. I quickly realized that what he liked to talk about was money, and that was fine with me. He had a photo of a little girl on his desk, and I asked about her. The BS said he was in the process of a divorce (I can't say I was shocked), and had custody of his daughter on every other weekend. I pretended to be interested in the kid. The BS told me that a relative had given him a collection of thirty old first-edition Nancy Drew books, in mint condition, with the idea that he could read them to his daughter, and pass them along so she could read them to her daughter someday. The Bald Shadow didn't have much interest in that kind of sentimentality. He had the collection of books appraised, and when he found out how much they were worth, he sold them.

The Bald Shadow related this story to me matter-of-factly, without inflection. Then he stared at me, stone-faced, waiting for some reaction. I told him I would have done the same thing. He smiled at me, kind of a smirk, one money-crazed bastard recognizing another, and I could tell we were going to get along just fine.

Over the months we were together, I heard him make scathingly critical remarks to other people who worked for him, really vicious personal comments, when they made mistakes or didn't do something the way he thought it should have been done. Once a month or so his parents, who must have been elderly and apparently lived out in the Midwest somewhere, would call and try to talk to him. He never lasted more than a minute or two. He'd act angry at them for interrupting him at work. If they told him they needed something or had some problem, he raised his voice. "You let the doctor send you a bill for that? How could you be so goddamn stupid?" he would demand. I couldn't fathom ever talking to my mother or father that way. I decided that if the Bald Shadow ever started carving me up the way he did other people, I would return fire. Maybe he sensed that, because he never spoke harshly to me. Most people were afraid of him, but I think he was a little afraid of me.

The BS, as one of Harvard's biggest producers, had a lot of support: a qualifier, two cold callers, and a sales assistant who took care of most of the administrative and bookkeeping chores. When I joined the team, the qualifier was in the process of preparing to give a presentation, a mock stock pitch, to the Branch Manager. If he did well, he would become a Harvard broker. He would get his own big desk and green chair. I was pulling for him because I wanted to be the BS's next qualifier. I was hoping the spot would be kept open for a few weeks until I passed my Series 7. But I found out that the other cold caller was about to take his Series 7, a month ahead of me. He expected to be the BS's qualifier, too, and he would be eligible for the job at least four weeks before me. I was bummed out, but not for long. If I couldn't be the Bald Shadow's qualifier, I could still learn from him, and he could still help me get my books to study for the Series 7. The overall goal was what was really important.

I put my nose to the grindstone and tried to be the best cold caller I could for the Bald Shadow. And I kept talking to him whenever I could. One day, when he was getting his tax stuff together for his accountant, he showed me his last pay stub for the previous year. Under "Year-to-Date" was this number: $1,144,885.43. This was all but unbelievable to me. I had heard the numbers bandied about, but to see proof of it right there in black and white . . . I was speechless.

Despite the stratospheric income, however, the BS was a tightwad. Maynard used to buy my lunch. The BS sent me down to buy his, and when I brought it back he counted the change.

Around the time I started at Harvard, I met a girl. Mutual friends introduced me to Melanie one evening at one of those free outdoor jazz concerts at the South Street Seaport. We started talking, hit it off, and ended up leaving the group to go out to dinner. I hadn't had a serious girlfriend in years, since college, and I wasn't in the market. I dated a lot, but was really resistant to the idea of settling down even a little bit. But it was different with Melanie, maybe because she was so different. I had always been drawn to women with long dark hair who were very outgoing and vivacious, real party girls. Melanie had short blond hair and was more serious. She taught special education in the public schools. She read the *New York Times* cover to cover every day, and seemed to know a lot about current events. She asked me a lot of questions about myself that first evening, and I found myself talking to her in a more personal, intimate way than I ever had with any other woman. And I found myself being uncharacteristically honest with her.

"My goal is to make a lot of money on Wall Street," I said. "I want to be a big success, but it's important to me that I make it on my own. I'm afraid I might fail, but I'm more afraid of what will happen to me if I don't give it my best shot. I hate the idea of living a dull, dreary, ordinary life punching a clock nine to five." Unlike a lot of other women, Melanie seemed neither attracted nor repulsed by the notion that I wanted to make a lot of money. She seemed fascinated with everything about me, though, and always wanted to know more. She seemed to accept me.

Melanie was from Long Island, from a family of teachers who lived a middle-class life surrounded by books and liberal causes. She marched against breast cancer and volunteered at an animal shelter and organized contributions from her friends for Thanksgiving food drives. I found myself looking forward to seeing her every couple of days or so. She was a quiet person, not given to flash and glitz and being entertained. She said she liked my energy, but she never made me feel that I constantly had to be performing and making her laugh, like most other women did. But I did make her laugh. We quickly became very comfortable with each other, and a few weeks later, when her roommate moved out, I moved into her cramped little one-bedroom apartment on the Upper West Side.

Looking back, that was a crazy, fun time for Melanie and me. We scraped by on her teacher's salary and my measly $3.50 an hour. There were months when we could barely pay the $1,100 rent. We couldn't afford a car or a vacation. Going out meant a pizza in some greasy neighborhood joint, and once in a while a movie on Saturday night. If someone invited me for a beer after work, I had to think about whether I could afford to pick up my dry cleaning the next day. On Sunday nights we sat down and counted out how much money we had for the coming week. It was never very much. One Sunday night I remember we had $37.75, and it had to last us until we got paid on Friday. I gave Melanie the $20 bill and took the $17.75 for myself. Somehow we made it to Friday.

I took the bus to work once, but hated it. Too slow, and I didn't see anyone else on the bus with whom I could identify. Old people, kids, and blue-collar types. Once in a while I took the subway, which was a little better. There were plenty of old people, kids, and blue-collar types on the subway, too, and some people who were well dressed, reading the *New York Times* or *Wall Street Journal*. But the subway connections weren't very good from our neighborhood to the Harvard office. I had to walk several blocks at both ends of the subway. Melanie and I started taking cabs.

Yellow cabs were more expensive, so sometimes we tried to grab a gypsy cab, one of those unlicensed cars driven by a guy just trying to make a buck by ferrying people around in his old beater. It usually cost us around $10 for a gypsy cab to drop Melanie off at her school in TriBeCa, and then take me to Wall Street. One morning we got a guy in a rusty blue Buick Electra who charged us only $8. "Listen," I told the guy. "Pick us up at the same place, right in front of our building, at the same time tomorrow." To our amazement, he was waiting for us the next morning. He told us his name was Sami, and we told him we wanted to hire him permanently. I may not have had a pot to piss in, and I may have been a humble cold caller, but by God I had a limo and a private chauffeur. Once in a while when I was feeling generous I'd invite a friend to meet us in the morning, and the friend would ride along. We paid Sami $40 a week for about a month, and then one morning he didn't show up. We were both a little late for work that day after standing there waiting for him. He never came again. "Deported," Melanie suggested. She had a wry sense of humor.

Some of my broker friends invited Melanie and me to party with them on New Year's Eve that year, but they were all going to a SoHo restaurant for champagne, dancing, a big meal, and so on. I said no without asking how much it would cost because I knew we wouldn't be able to afford it. Instead, we went out for a quiet dinner in a neighborhood place and then walked around, just watching people and soaking up the festive atmosphere. It seemed momentous that we could do something simple together, just walking through Manhattan on New Year's Eve, and really be happy. Wall Street, which I now saw as my future, was starting to roar again, as it had in the 1980s. It seemed like there was lots of money out there just waiting for me to grab it. We decided to call our parents on a pay phone, and got in line at a phone behind a Puerto Rican guy. He was obviously drunk, and I thought he'd be finished with the phone in a minute. But he never got off the phone. He just kept shouting, "Happy Year!" both into the phone and, every thirty seconds or so, to us and anyone else who happened to be walking by. Melanie and I broke up laughing, and finally gave up and walked away with our arms around each other. That might have been the happiest New Year's Eve we ever had.

I was a senior cold caller, if there was such a thing. I was in the top three of the daily contacts tallies pretty much every day. But it was more than the scores. I didn't feel like or act like the typical cold caller. "You don't look like a cold caller, you look more like one of the top brokers," the Bald Shadow's qualifier told me a couple of days after I started working with him. He mentioned my suits and my watch, which he called a "Rolodex." I didn't correct him and tell him it was a Rolex, both because the watch wasn't a Rolex and because I didn't want to embarrass the guy. I appreciated his comment because it was exactly the sort of impression and image I wanted. A few days after I moved over to the Bald Shadow's desk, something extraordinary happened. The Branch Manager, making one of his usual twice-daily strolls through the board room, looked at me as he walked by and said, "Hiya, Burtelsohn." The guys working near me noticed. Their heads jerked up. "Hi," I said back, in a state of mild shock but trying to act like it was no big deal. It *was* a big deal. I was high as a kite that evening, and I kept talking about it. Melanie couldn't understand why it was so important. "This is huge," I kept telling her. "The Branch Manager not only knew my name, he spoke to me."

Once a week, on Wednesdays, the cold callers gathered in the conference room for a lunch meeting. Harvard brought in pizza, and the Queen presided. She usually asked a broker to come in and talk about the firm or some aspect of the business. One week in December, not long after I started with the Bald Shadow, she asked me to speak. It was a rare honor for a mere cold caller, and an important step toward getting my study books. I wondered what to talk about, and she just said, "Tell them about being a cold caller. Tell them what you do, and how you do it." I didn't disappoint her. I didn't tell the other cold callers how much I hated the job. I didn't tell them that they had a one-in-a-hundred chance of getting a big desk and a green chair. Instead, I told them how hard I worked, and how much I had learned, and what a great place Harvard was. The Queen watched from the back of the room with her usual stern expression. I thought at one point I saw a flicker of amusement on her face. I spoke for about ten minutes and answered a couple of stupid questions. After the meeting, she said thanks, and I felt like I had passed a test.

It was the moment I had been waiting for. A couple of days later I told her I wanted her to give me the books so I could start studying for the Series 7 exam. The test was given just once a month at that time, on the third Saturday, and Harvard gave out the books just once a month, about four weeks before the test. She went into her usual act about not knowing whether I was really ready, but I cut her off. "Look, your job here is to pick the best to take the test, and I'm the best," I said. "I want the books. I deserve them." She backed down right away, to my surprise, and said okay. "You'll get the books in a few days," she said, "and I'll make sure you get put on the list to take the test next month."

I was ecstatic. It was happening just as I had hoped, maybe even a little faster. I figured it out. The date of the test was 111 days after I had started at Harvard. I wasn't even going to have to wait the full 120 days. I told Melanie about that, but no one else. I didn't want anybody in the office pointing out that I was taking the test before putting in the minimum apprenticeship. They might make me wait another month.

The study books were actually looseleaf binders, each several inches thick. One was a textbook, the other was practice exams. I hadn't tried to study since college. I couldn't remember the last time I'd read a book all the way through to the end. Probably in college, but I couldn't say for sure. I'd purchased one right after college graduation, when it seemed like the thing to do; I think it was *The Art of Selling*. I moved it around back and forth between my bedside and living room, and I actually opened it a few times. But I don't think I ever got past the preface. Sitting down and reading had always been an almost physically painful experience for me. I was determined, however, to spend as much time as possible studying the Series 7 books in the four weeks before the test. I started with the textbook. It might as well have been in Chinese. I couldn't find anything in the book that related remotely to my experiences at Harvard, to what I had been learning and what I had been doing.

I started plowing my way through the books. It was difficult. I'd sit down and open the textbook with every intention of reading for a few hours. I'd last maybe twenty minutes. That wasn't working, so I started taking the practice tests. Maybe that would help. There were eighteen practice exams, and the booklet suggested taking each one at least twice. Each one took two hours. On the first practice exam, I scored a 27. The passing grade was 70. I didn't allow myself to be discouraged. I kept plowing through the textbook and kept taking the sample exams. Gradually my scores moved into the thirties and forties. I still didn't understand most of the material, but somehow I was absorbing it. I'd go to work, come home at six, eat with Melanie, study from seven o'clock until ten, take a half-hour break, and then study for another hour or so until eleven-thirty or midnight. When she finished grading papers or working on lesson plans, Melanie often helped me. She drilled me over and over, asking me sample test questions and then reading back the correct answers. Slowly, slowly, I started to understand a little more, and my test scores moved into the fifties.

One of the problems was that 40 percent of the exam was going to be on options and municipal bonds. Harvard's brokers worked very little with options and not at all with municipal bonds. None of Harvard's brokers, not the Bald Shadow or anyone else, could have passed that part of the test without studying for it all over again. I started asking guys in the office what they had scored when they had passed their Series 7 exams. Most of them either couldn't remember or didn't want to remember. It became clear that a high score didn't matter. In fact, I couldn't find anyone who had scored above the low 80s. Most were in the 70s. The brokers themselves regarded anything above 70 as overkill, as wasted effort. When they talked about people who had scored in the high 80s or even the 90s, it was with disdain. They were eggheads. "Guys who score real high on the Series 7 never make good brokers," one broker told me. "They've got the book smarts but not the street smarts. They can't sell. Too intellectual."

I studied even on weekends. I'd sleep late, hit the books around ten o'clock, go straight through till four, take off an hour, and then go back for two or three hours. In theory, someone who flunked the Series 7 the first time could take it again. It wasn't that unusual to run into a broker who had to take it two or even three times before passing. But none of them were brokers at Harvard.

7

Hidden Commissions

As the date of my Series 7 approached, my practice test scores got better and I got more nervous. I was consistently in the 70s, and once I cracked the 80s. I felt like I knew the material on the practice tests, but I remained far from confident. "There's still a lot I don't know," I told Melanie. "What if all the questions I don't know are the ones that are on my test?" Practice Exam No. 12 was supposed to be the hardest of the sample tests, and the one most like the real test. I took No. 12 over and over. I must have done it six or seven times. Each time, I'd go back and check the answers, and try to remember the right answers to the questions I had gotten wrong. I still didn't feel like I had any great knowledge about the securities industry, but if a certain question was worded a certain way and there were certain possible multiple-choice answers, I was getting to the point where I could remember which one was right.

There were cram courses, and I wanted to take one. One choice was to go to two evening classes a week, two and a half hours per class, for three weeks. The other was to take a week off work and go for eight hours a day for five days. I wanted to take the week off, but I didn't know if the Bald Shadow would let me. I was pleased when he said okay. I wasn't so pleased when I found out that Harvard wouldn't pay me for that week, but I decided it was worth the financial sacrifice to just concentrate on the test and nothing else in the five days leading up to the test.

The classes were run by the National Association of Securities Dealers in a building on Wall Street. There were about thirty of us in the class. Most of the guys—they were all men—were from brokerage firms with recognized, good names: Merrill Lynch. Dean Witter. Lehman Brothers. Shearson. Since I was from Harvard, I was one of them. We'd go out to lunch and talk about different firms. Like me, most of them had no assurances that they would end up working as brokers for the firms where they had worked as cold callers or clerks.

The classes ran from nine to five. A woman instructor started at the beginning of the textbook and explained it. By then I really did understand most of the concepts, and I was becoming more and more confident. On Friday, the last day of the cram course, the instructor gave us the "green light" exam. It was a scaled-down version of the test, two and a half hours instead of six hours, and designed to predict within ten points, up or down, what a would-be broker would score on the actual Series 7 exam. At the end of the two and a half hours, the instructor collected our exams. Then she ran them through a scanner right there at the front of the classroom. As soon as she ran a test through, she called up the guy, gave him his score, and had a few words with him. We had been told that she would advise us on whether she thought we were ready to take the test the next day, or whether we should wait and take it later. She didn't announce anything out loud and I couldn't hear anything she said to anyone, but it seemed like quite a few of the guys in front of me were walking out looking dejected. I started to worry all over again.

She called my name. I put on my jacket, walked up to the front, and saw my test stuck most of the way into the slot in the scanner. The instructor pointed to the little window that displayed some numbers in green light. The number was 78. The green light was predicting that I could score as high as an 88 on the test . . . or as low as a 68. I spoke quietly to the instructor. "What do you think, should I take the test tomorrow?"

She looked at me as if I were crazy. "Of course," she said. "You had one of the highest grades in the class. This is really good. You'll do fine tomorrow."

I stopped at the Harvard office on my way home. I told the Bald Shadow and his guys that I had scored a 78 on the green light test, and they were impressed. "You're home free," the BS said. I picked up Melanie at her school and we had a long, slow walk home. For the first time in a month, I didn't feel like I should be rushing home to study more. I was relaxed. Either I was going to pass the next day or I wasn't. I felt like I had done all I could do. "You know," I told Melanie when we went out for pizza that evening, "if I had studied this hard in college. I could have been Phi Beta Kappa. I could have been a doctor or a lawyer." I said someone had told me that a higher percentage of people pass the New York bar exam than the Series 7. I didn't tell her, however, that from what I'd seen, most of the people taking the Series 7 wouldn't have been able to get within shouting distance of the front door of a law school.

I went to bed early that night, before eleven o'clock, hoping to be well rested and fresh the next morning for the test. I tossed and turned all night, and kept waking up. I just couldn't stop thinking about the test. I thought about getting up and studying, but decided that would be stupid. I got up at six-thirty, showered, looked over some of my notes, kissed Melanie good-bye, and headed for the subway. It was a raw, rainy day, and the sullen, sodden, Saturday morning crowd on the subway was even more depressing than during the week. The test was at a public school in a dingy area of the Lower East Side. The test was supposed to start at nine o'clock, and we had been told to arrive plenty early, so I got there at about eight-forty. There were hundreds of people there already, waiting in the rain and cold. The queue went around the block. It probably was easier to get into Fort Knox; I had to produce two forms of identification and be checked off on a list. Inside, I found the classroom where I was supposed to take the test, and put some freshly sharpened pencils, a blank pad of notepaper, and a calculator on the desk chair in front of me. The calculator was a really basic one; we weren't allowed to bring in the ones that figure amortization.

The actual test, taken on a computer screen, is a blur now. The first part lasted three hours, from nine to noon; then we had an hour for lunch before coming back for the second session from one to four. A proctor was supposed to be watching us, but he disappeared. I remember thinking how easy it would have been to cheat on the test, to copy off someone else's screen. I finished the morning session a few minutes before noon, and ate alone, quickly—a corned beef sandwich—and fretted about how everyone said the second half of the test was supposed to be a lot harder.

It didn't seem that way. I finished the afternoon session twenty minutes early, turned in my answer sheet, and left. "If I failed," I told Melanie when I got home, "I didn't fail by much." The results were supposed to come out on Wednesday or Thursday the following week. I expected to come home from work and find a note in the mail telling me whether I had passed or not. I imagined opening that envelope. At work I tried not to be distracted, and outside work I enjoyed all the free time that had been devoted to studying. On Wednesday afternoon I was dialing away as usual in the Bald Shadow's little group when I became aware of the Queen of the Cold Callers standing next to me. She had a sour look on her face. I hung up—after some guy's secretary hung up on me—and looked at her expectantly.

"So, did you really study for the Series 7?" she asked in an accusatory tone.

Oh, no, I thought. *She knows my results. I must have failed.*

"Yeah," I kind of choked out. "Sure, I studied for it. Of course."

"Well," she said, pausing, milking the moment as the BS and all the other guys hung on every word. "Well, anyway, you passed." And she turned on her heel and walked away. No smile, no congratulations, no nothing. After a few quick high-fives with the guys, I trotted after her. She told me I had gotten a 74. I called Melanie, perhaps as happy as I had ever been, and gave her the news. Pretty soon calls started coming in for me. My mom and dad. An aunt and uncle. A couple of college friends. I felt like a hero, like I had cured cancer or something.

The guys in the BS's little group seemed genuinely happy for me. The BS did, too. He stood up, grinned, shook my hand, and said, "Let's go to lunch to celebrate." The BS taking me to lunch wasn't just huge, it was enormous. The BS never went out to lunch. I imagined a little French place, white tablecloths, good wine, cognac and cigars afterward. He took me to Burger King. We got into a line, me in front of the BS. I started placing my order when the kid at the next cash register looked at the BS. "Can I take your order, sir?" he said. The BS moved right over to the next register, placed his order, and paid for it. I dug my wallet out of my pocket and paid for my own Double Whopper. I was stunned at how rude and cheap the BS was, but nothing could spoil my mood that day. I acted like nothing was wrong. We scrunched in at a little table and tried to make small talk, as best as the BS could, over our burgers and fries. "You're really on your way now," he told me. "This is a big step, getting your license. Your license to steal." It was the first time I had heard the phrase. But not the last. I didn't think much about it at the time, however, because I didn't really know what he meant. That evening I told Melanie about the BS not paying for my lunch. "He's an asshole," I said.

A couple of days later, the BS tried again. "Hey, you know, I took you to lunch the other day, but I didn't get a chance to pay for yours," he said, as if he had just thought of it. Clearly it had been gnawing at him. "Let's go again today, to a better place." This time we went to a dumpy Italian joint where you were supposed to ladle your food out of steam tables. It was okay, but it was a far cry from the little French bistro I had in mind. It was a buffet: pizza, lasagna, some other pastas, rolls, salads. We got our trays and started moving through the line, and somehow the BS got ahead of me. We ended up paying separately again. It was as if he knew that buying my lunch was the right thing to do, but when it came down to actually paying the money, he simply couldn't do it. "He's a prick," I reported to Melanie that night.

After I passed the Series 7 exam, Harvard gave me a raise to the magnificent sum of $4.50 an hour. With my license, I could talk to clients and I could work as a qualifier. But the Bald Shadow already had one qualifier, and another cold caller who had passed his Series 7 a month before I did. There was a talent logjam. I was a little worried, but things sorted out quickly.

The qualifier had been part of a group with four other qualifiers who were trying to become Harvard brokers. This involved some heavy-duty training sessions, mostly role-playing, under the direction of the Queen. She wasn't even a broker. This didn't make a lot of sense to me. Why was she training brokers? No matter. She drilled the BS's qualifier and the other four would-be brokers on how to talk to clients, how to open accounts, and how to pitch trades. When she decided trainees were ready, they had to do presentations for the Branch Manager. One by one, they would go in the conference room with the Branch Manager, talk a little about themselves, and then make a series of pitches to one of his assistants while he watched. The assistant would play the role of the guy who was being asked to open an account with Harvard. If a would-be broker's presentation went poorly, it might be over in five minutes. It was time for him to go to another firm if he still wanted to be a stockbroker. If a would-be broker's presentation went well, it might last half an hour. And it still might be time to look for another firm. The Branch Manager hired very few brokers from the ranks of the qualifiers. Sometimes he watched a qualifier present more than once. Being asked to come in and present again was seen as progress; the Branch Manager thought the qualifier at least had potential.

The BS's qualifier did well; his first presentation went on for nearly an hour. He was offered a big desk and a green chair. Another qualifier pitching the Branch Manager at the same time did almost as well, but not quite. The Branch Manager helped him find a job at a smaller brokerage house that was affiliated with Harvard. He "went down," we said, as if he were a baseball player being sent to the minor leagues. The other three qualifiers did not do as well. They were offered jobs as salesclerks. All three left Harvard to try for jobs as brokers at other firms.

With the departure of the BS's qualifier to his own desk, his old job ordinarily would have gone to the guy in our little group who had passed the Series 7 a month before I did. Instead, I stepped in on the first day after the former qualifier had gotten his new desk. The other cold caller, my competitor, came in that morning and took his usual seat, waiting for the BS to tell him to move over to the qualifier's desk. I came in and, without waiting for anyone to say anything, sat at the qualifier's desk, closest to the BS's green chair. I started giving orders to the new cold caller who had joined us, and he did what I told him. I made suggestions to the other qualifier. He was a good guy, but he just wasn't as aggressive or ambitious as I was. He was younger than me, his clothes weren't as good, he was from Kansas or someplace and had a soft little accent. Somebody told me he had scored really high when he passed his Series 7, in the high 80s. But that didn't matter to me, or anyone else. Much more significant was the fact that the Branch Manager knew my name. The Branch Manager had never spoken to this guy. I simply overpowered him. When I suggested that he do something, he could have resisted. He could have tried to assert himself and become the BS's number-one boy. But he didn't. He did what I asked him to do. He worked as a qualifier, but when he wasn't busy he still did some cold calling. I never did any more cold calling. I worked as a qualifier, but soon I was doing much more. The BS never said anything about who should be his qualifier; he simply let me grab the job.

As a qualifier, my job was to take the contacts from the cold callers and do two things. First, I had to determine if they were legitimate potential investors: at least $100,000 in the market, and at least $10,000 in a single investment. Second, I had to determine whether there was any chance that they would invest with Harvard. Most contacts, even if they agreed to come on the phone and talk to a qualifier, would either not say how much they had invested or would say they did not want to do business with Harvard. They had their own brokers and were happy with them. As a qualifier, I could engage the contacts a little more, and sell them a little more. If the contacts liked my voice, if they liked my personality over the phone, if they liked what I said, I could convince them to tell me about their portfolios and to agree to look at Harvard materials that would be sent by mail. They also had to agree to talk to a Harvard broker who would call them in a few days with investment ideas.

The BS noticed that I qualified a lot of people. I gave him a lot of leads. He noticed anything that helped his business. Leads were good for business because they were people who were willing to listen to his pitch. He would call the leads, pitch them, and try to persuade them to open new accounts with Harvard. Once they opened accounts and became clients, the BS could call them and persuade them to make trades. Every time they made a trade, he made a commission.

When most investors ask about the price of a stock, they think there's only one price. That's not quite right. There are actually two prices: bid and asked. The bid is the price that prospective buyers are willing to pay for the stock. The asked is the price that prospective sellers would like to receive for the stock. If one broker asks another the price of the stock, the answer is given bid-by-asked. For example: Ten and a half by ten and three-quarters. The difference is the "spread." If a stock is $17.25 by $17.375, the spread is 12.5 cents. If there are more buyers than sellers, the stock probably will be sold at or near the asked price. Then the asked price probably will go higher, and the bid price probably will follow it up. If there are more sellers than buyers, the stock is more likely to be sold at or near the bid price. The bid price probably will drop, and the asked price probably will follow it down. It's simple supply and demand.

But the way brokers make their money is not so simple. Until the mid-1970s, there were minimum commissions. Then the rules changed and clients could negotiate the commissions they would pay to brokers. Institutional investors, such as big pension plans, used the sheer volume of their trades to negotiate lower commissions. Retail customers, everyday individual investors, could pay lower commissions at discount brokerage houses. But most investors remained with traditional brokerages such as Harvard, which charged a standard 3 percent commission—less than the maximum allowed by regulations, but twice or more what the discount houses charged. So if a client bought 500 shares at $20 each, the client actually had to pay Harvard $10,300. The commission is divided between the brokerage house and the broker. At Harvard, the broker's usual payout—the percentage of the gross commission that the broker received—was 45 percent. At some firms it was higher, at some it was lower. At some, more productive brokers got higher payouts—50, 60, even 70 percent. Lower producers at smaller firms might get as little as 35 percent.

Just as many investors think there's only one price for a stock, they may think that brokers get paid solely according to their commissions, based on a percentage of the value of the trade. Again, that's not quite right. On many trades there is a hidden commission, especially when the broker has acted as a "principal" in the trade. In most trades, the broker acts as the investor's "agent," which means the broker arranges the transaction between the investor and some third party, whether a buyer or seller. When the broker acts as a principal, however, the broker is one of the parties directly involved in the transaction. In a stock purchase, for example, a broker who acts as a principal sells the investor stock that was owned by the broker's own firm rather than by some third party. Many brokerage firms own inventories of stock so that they can serve as "market makers," setting prices and facilitating trades. Market makers help ensure the liquidity of a stock. The more market makers for a stock, the easier it is to find buyers and sellers.

However, brokers serving as principals at firms acting as market makers raise the possibility of what amounts to hidden commissions as they buy stock low and sell it high. Here's an example, painted broadly. A broker calls a client and recommends that the client purchase a certain stock that is trading "around ten." The client says okay, he'll buy 500 shares. He expects to pay $5,000, plus $150 for the broker's 3 percent commission. Meanwhile, the stock is trading at $9.75 by $10. The spread is a quarter, and the broker sees it as easy money. Acting as a principal, the broker buys the stock from the market into his firm's inventory at $9.75, and then immediately sells it to the client at $10. The client pays exactly what he expected: $5,150. What the client doesn't know, however, is that the stock really only cost $4,875. The broker pockets the $125 hidden commission and ends up making $275 on the deal. It may not seem like a lot of money, but it means the broker is getting more than 5 percent of the trade rather than the standard 3 percent printed on the confirmation of the trade that the client receives in the mail a few days later. Figure that hidden commission many times over, many times a day, on trades large and small, and it's easy to see how brokers can play the spread to boost their incomes. For brokers who act as principals, the bigger the spread, the better the hidden commission for them. The only tip-off for an investor that a broker might be pocketing a hidden commission from the spread is a note typed somewhere on the trade confirmation notice, often in fine print, that the broker "acted as a principal."

8

It's Our Money Now

One of the many things I learned at Harvard was that stock brokers don't really execute the trades. Every brokerage house has
a trading department, and the actual transactions are carried out by
floor traders. They're still called floor traders, even if they sit at computer screens instead of roaming around on the floor of an exchange.
When a client approves a trade, the broker calls the firm's trading
department and passes the order to a floor trader, who actually makes
the trade happen. There are many different types of trades. One of the
most common is the "limit order," which is an instruction from an
investor to a broker to buy or sell a specific amount of stock at a specific price. If the broker cannot get the specified price, the trade is not
executed. Another common type of trade is the "stop order," which is
an instruction to execute the trade when the stock price hits a specified level. It is often used to curb losses; an investor tells the broker,
"If it falls to this level, sell it."

Unless an investor specifically asks for a certain type of order, the
trade will be treated as a "market order," which is the most common
type of trade; the broker is supposed to execute the the trade as soon
as possible, at the best possible price for the client. The Bald Shadow,

along with every other broker I ever met, never suggested that a client place a stop order or limit order. Too much hassle. Too much detail. Rather than spend a lot of time focusing on the details of one account or one trade, he wanted to get on to making the next sale. The Bald Shadow executed his clients' market orders as soon as possible at the best possible price—but it was the best possible price for him, not for them.

The BS often worked with the Harvard floor traders to get bigger hidden commissions. I was stunned the first time I saw him do it. The BS called a client and urged him to buy a certain stock. Naturally, Harvard was a market maker in the stock. The BS probably wouldn't have been touting it otherwise; Harvard had to be a market maker in the stock for him to snare his hidden commissions from the bid-asked spread. But the client never heard about that. The client heard only the BS's usual masterful selling job.

In this particular instance, the stock was trading at a shade under $60, and the BS convinced the client that it was a bargain. He was confident it was going to be back above $60 very soon. "It's a steal," he kept telling the client. Larceny was about to occur, all right, but the client was going to be the victim, not the thief. Eventually the BS wore the client down, and the guy said okay, he'd buy the stock. The BS talked him into ordering 2,500 shares. At $60 a share, that was a big order, a $150,000 purchase. The straight 3 percent commission would be $4,500. Pretty good for a quarter of an hour on the phone. But the BS wasn't satisfied with that. He was always looking for the extra edge. "He'd squeeze a nickel till the buffalo shits," one broker said admiringly.

The BS called the floor trader to place the order to buy 2,500 shares of the stock. The BS asked the floor trader for the price. It was $59.75 by $60. The spread was only 25 cents per share. Since Harvard was a market maker, the floor trader could buy the stock at the lower price, and then sell it to the client at the higher price. For a 2,500-share trade, that 25-cent spread would have created a hidden commission of $625 for the BS. Not bad. But not good enough for him.

"With a half," the BS ordered the floor trader. That meant he wanted the trade to have at least a 50-cent spread. "Work the stock," the BS urged the trader. So the trader waited. The stock went to $60.50 by $60.75, still a 25-cent spread. The trader waited. The stock kept moving gradually, up to $61.25 by $61.50, still only a 25-cent spread. The trader, patient, kept waiting. Finally, a couple of hours later, the stock got to $62 by $62.50—the 50-cent spread the BS wanted. The trader swung into action. He bought the stock at $62 for Harvard's inventory, and then had Harvard sell it to the client for $62.50. Instead of $150,000, the client paid $156,250 for the stock. On top of that, his straight commission—the 3 percent printed on the confirmation—was $4,687.50 instead of $4,500. From the 50-cent spread, the Bald Shadow racked up $1,250 in hidden commissions that the client didn't know about. Altogether, if the BS had done his best for the client, the client would have gotten his 5,000 shares for $154,500. Instead, because the trade was held up a couple of hours, the client paid $160,937.50.

When the client received the confirmation of the trade in the mail a few days later, he went ballistic. I happened to answer the phone when he called. "I ordered this goddammed trade at $60, and here it comes at $62.50. That cost me six grand," the client said, struggling to control the anger in his voice. I wondered what he would have thought if he had known why he paid more, or how much the BS really made in commission that wasn't listed on the confirmation. I passed the call to the BS, who acted nonplussed. He listened. He let the client vent. He said he didn't understand how this could have happened. He sympathized. He offered semi-plausible half-explanations. The stock moved fast. Extremely fast. He had told the client the stock was going to go up fast, and it did. Maybe the floor trader had some problems. He'd heard that the man's baby had been sick recently.

Maybe there was a mechanical error. A computer glitch. Whatever the reason, it shouldn't have happened. The Bald Shadow was sorry. That's not the way he did business, especially with a good client. They had a history together. They'd made a lot of money together in the past. He'd check it out, see what the problems were. He'd see what had happened, find out who had screwed up. He might not be able to do anything to fix this trade, but he'd try. If he couldn't fix it, he would do everything he could to make it up to the client at some point in the future. Next time a really good inside tip came along, he'd call the client first. The BS calmed the client down. He told the guy what he wanted to hear. By the time they rang off, they were pals again.

I was impressed with the way the BS had blunted the client's dissatisfaction. But I wasn't surprised that the client had complained. I should have been. Later, after I had worked for the BS for a few weeks, I realized how rare it was for clients to complain, no matter what their brokers did to them.

The Bald Shadow, I learned, was a master at managing his clients. Or controlling them, to use his word. Other brokers watched him carefully and tried to pick up tips. Since he was such a difficult guy to talk to, some of them approached me to learn about his business. After the BS opened an account, how soon did he come back to the client for a second trade? Was it big or small? How soon for a third trade? How quickly, and in what amounts, did he try to increase the size of the client's trades? When did he ask for the client's whole portfolio? I didn't mind all the questions. For one thing, these brokers were showing me respect. For another, talking about the BS's business forced me to analyze it and take away for myself what I thought was important. One fact that obviously was not important was how much money the BS made for his clients. No one asked about that.

Brokers also collected hidden commissions on so-called specials. A special is a stock that a brokerage house pushes by offering its brokers extra-large commissions, much more than the usual percentage. At Harvard and many other brokerage houses, I came to learn, specials were usually stocks that were owned in-house, that were part of the firm's own institutional portfolio. But Harvard was not in the business of holding a portfolio. Harvard was in the business of selling. Harvard's interest was in unloading the stock for more than it had paid, the faster the better. Typically, these specials were large blocs of stock that Harvard had purchased for less than the current, publicly posted price. The seller was often another institution, maybe an investment house but maybe a pension fund or insurance company that wanted to unload some its holdings in a particular stock but didn't want to drive down the price by dumping a big chunk on the market all at once. Sometimes the Branch Manager would advise the brokers at the morning meeting of the day's specials. But sometimes Harvard would unveil one of these purchases in the middle of the day, and announce it over squawk boxes on the brokers' desks. It was like the old Blue Light Special: "Attention Kmart Shoppers."

The squawk box would crackle out: "We're working such-and-such stock at $24 with a $25 print." The $24 was what Harvard had paid for the stock. The "print" was the price that would be listed on the client's confirmation order. The dollar was a hidden commission. Naturally, Harvard's brokers never told their clients that Harvard owned the stock, or how much Harvard had paid for it. Instead, Harvard's brokers would call their clients, singing the praises of this particular stock at $25. It was a great company, it was going places, the analysts said this or that. In truth, it didn't matter what the company was like. It didn't matter how the stock had performed. Substantive analysis, technical analysis, forecasts—none of that mattered. The only reason that Harvard brokers told their clients they should buy the stock was that they could make bigger commissions for themselves, more money in their own pockets at the end of the day. Clients would buy the stock at $25, never knowing that they were paying $1 in hidden commission. Suppose a client bought 1,000 shares at $25 each, with a $1 hidden commission per share. At 3 percent, the straight commission on $25,000 was $750. Pocketing the special's $1 per share in hidden commissions, the broker pulled in another $1,000. Straight commissions were good, but they weren't the way to make the most money.

I asked the BS lots of questions, trying to show him I really admired how he ran his business and that I would do anything I could to help him. I was eager to move beyond qualifying. I wanted to sell something. I asked if I could pitch a trade to some clients. He was leery at first, but finally let me try. He told me what stock to try to get them to buy, and then gave me a few names and numbers. He was emphatic about one point: he did not want them moving their shares from one stock in their portfolios to this new one. He wanted them to send in new money to make the trade I was pitching. At first the BS had me calling only smaller clients, guys who didn't trade very often or very big. They typically had $200,000 or less in their portfolios. A $300,000 individual portfolio was hefty in the mid-1990s. Million-dollar portfolios were rare back then, but the Bald Shadow had several, probably more than any other Harvard broker. We called those investors "whales."

After a while, the BS started asking me to call his bigger, more active clients. He liked to keep in touch with the heavy hitters on a weekly, if not near-daily, basis. They were mostly aggressive risk-takers who saw themselves as sophisticated investors. They weren't thinking that judicious investments over the years would pay for their kids' college or make sure they had a nice retirement. They were thinking that razor-sharp investments made often and quickly would help them move from being merely very wealthy to fabulously wealthy. One day the BS asked me to call a whale. The guy had close to $4 million in the market, a monumental account. But the BS was always looking to persuade him, like every other client, to invest even more. The BS told me to get the client to buy a certain stock that was selling at $10.

"How many shares should I get him to buy?" I asked.

"Shoot for 50,000," the BS said, laughing. That would be a $500,000 order.

There was no way that I, a snotty-nosed kid, would get this crusty old whale to fork over half a million dollars. The BS didn't think I could do it. I don't think the BS believed he could do it himself. I think that's why he asked me to make the call. He would have been pleasantly surprised if I got any order at all. Something like 5,000 shares, $50,000, would have been a big success. I called the client and told him all the reasons he should buy the shares. The pitch wasn't all that different from what I had learned as a cold caller. If he had an objection, I had an answer. I would not take no for an answer. Finally the whale said, "So if I was to buy some, how much should I buy?" I knew I had him. He was going to place an order. The only question was how big. I told him 50,000 shares. He laughed so loud it hurt my ears. "That's ridiculous," he sputtered. I told him it wasn't ridiculous, and then I told him why: based on his portfolio, considering what he was worth, looking at the market in general, this company's prospects in particular, and so on. I just kept coming at him. He finally said yes. The next day he wired the $500,000 into his Harvard account.

The fact that I scored this trade impressed a lot of people. I tried to mention it casually, in an offhand way, but I made sure people knew about it. Word spread through the board room. Rob Burtelsohn got a $500,000 trade. Who? People started coming up to me asking for the details. I had never met some of them, but they acted like we were old friends. More brokers came up to me than cold callers. The BS was certainly impressed with the trade. The gross commission was Harvard's standard 3 percent, $15,000. The BS's 45 percent added up to $6,750. I got my $4.50 for that hour. Sure, it occurred to me that this wasn't quite fair. I would have liked to have had some of that

$6,750, considering I did all the work. But I never complained. I was learning. My time would come.

After that trade, the BS talked to me more, explained more, showed me more about his business. It was as if, finally, I was really an apprentice broker. Sometimes he made me feel like more of a junior partner. His top priority, I came to learn, was in building his book—bringing in more money under his management. That's why he worked so hard to open new accounts. And that's why he was always after existing accounts to invest more, to expand their portfolios. The more he had under management, the more trades he could do, and the more commissions he could earn. He told me something I thought about every day I worked as a stock broker, whenever I started calling clients. "Remember," the Bald Shadow told me. "When they send in that money, it's not theirs anymore. It's ours. It's ours to make money with. We're never giving it back to them."

I called my dad that evening and told him about the big trade, and he seemed impressed. He was happy for me, and that made me feel good. He wanted to know more about my job and how things worked at Harvard. I gave him some of the basics, but it was all vague stuff, and always positive. There was a lot we didn't talk about—he never said anything, but I knew he disapproved of cold calling—and there was a lot that I found myself too embarrassed to talk about. I certainly didn't tell him about hidden commissions or daily specials or the way the Bald Shadow was teaching me to deal with clients. I had always looked forward to talking to my dad about every aspect of my work, no matter what it was. But there was a lot I just couldn't bring myself to tell him about the business until years later.

As I learned his business and was able to do more, the BS started taking a little time off, especially whenever he had a new girlfriend. Sometimes the weekend stretched to Friday or Monday or both. The BS started taking days off during the middle of the week, which he had never done before. It was certainly noticed in the office that he was away, and it was certainly noticed that his business was still going—

and that I was running it. The BS would call me in the morning and leave instructions: Call these ten guys. Tell them to sell that stock and buy this other one. When the BS was gone, I sat behind his big desk, in his green chair. I wore his headphones, and when I went to the men's room, I strode through the rows of desks with the phones around my neck like a stethoscope. As a cold caller, I had all but run to the restroom and back. I wanted to keep my contact tallies up, and I didn't want anyone to notice that I wasn't at my desk. Wearing the BS's headphones, I took my time walking through the board room to the restroom. I wanted everyone to notice the headphones. When one of the brokers in the training program quit, I went over to his desk and took his headphones so that I would have a pair every day, not just when the BS was missing in action. Nobody ever asked me to put them back. Bicycle messengers still earned more than me, but I didn't care. Nobody thought I was a cold caller anymore.

9

Tony Galoshes

The Bald Shadow wanted to sell his clients shares that would go up, but not because he was interested in making money for them. If their shares went up, he figured, they would be more likely to listen to him and do what he recommended. He would recommend that they invest more and trade more. In fact, he followed only a handful of companies, usually five or six at most. He was always in the process of dropping one or two companies from his list of favorites and adding one or two others. He usually chose stocks in which Harvard made markets and that were carrying the biggest spreads so that he could take advantage of the hidden commissions. He would call clients who owned the stocks that he didn't want to follow anymore and urge them to buy the stocks he now liked. He always had a couple of "buy" recommendations to keep his business humming along. I never heard him tell a client that the client's portfolio was fine right where it was.

The BS did very little research to decide what companies he wanted to follow. Literally tons of reports on companies came across his desk from Harvard's research department, from independent industry newsletters, and from the companies themselves. He threw almost all of it away without ever looking at it. He would glance at some of the reports from Harvard's own analysts, and absorb just enough information to sound like he knew what he was talking about.

I never read any of that stuff. The BS would tell me what he thought I needed to know about a company. Clients should sell that stock because there's a chance the company will be sued by a competitor. Clients should buy this stock because we think a product still in research and development is going to be a big success when it comes out in a year or two. The BS was a great salesman because he really seemed to believe whatever he was saying. He made me believe it, too. I found that the more I believed it, the better a salesman I was. The better the story, the easier it was to believe.

I learned to add little flourishes. "I can't tell you exactly how I came to know this," I'd tell a client, "but I have reason to believe that this new product still in research and development will capture a significant market share as soon as it becomes available. It's the sort of product you'll see on the cover of *Time* magazine. When that happens, when everybody is talking about the product, wouldn't it be great to be able to tell people that you bought shares in the company two years before?"

Another broker who sat near us liked to pitch prospective clients by making them feel they would get a real inside deal if they opened an account with him. He'd start pitching a stock right away, and toss around names of important, plugged-in people who were supposedly buying the stock. His idea was that if some really savvy investor was buying the stock, then this prospective client would want to buy it, too. It was sort of the same theory that some bettors use at a racetrack; if the guy next to them cashes a couple of tickets, they make the same bet he does in the next race. This broker soon realized, however, that most of the prospective clients had no idea who he was talking about if he mentioned some famous fund manager or investment advisor.

A lot of times he threw around the Bald Shadow's name; if the BS was buying, then the client should, too. Pretty soon he started using any name at all. "Listen, I just found out this morning that Rob Burtelsohn is buying this stock very heavily, but he's trying to keep it quiet," the broker would tell the client, winking at me. After a while he started making up names, the more outrageous the better. One rainy day a guy wearing rubber overshoes walked by his desk as he was making a pitch, and I heard the broker tell a client, "Listen, Tony Galoshes is heavily into this stock, and thinks it could double by the end of the year."

While I was persuading clients to move their money around within their accounts—and generate a commission for the BS every time they did—the BS himself concentrated on opening new accounts. There was always a pile of leads on his desk that had been generated by cold callers and qualifiers within the previous two weeks. He would try to make five, six, sometimes seven presentations to leads every day. Over the course of a month he would make more than 100 such presentations to leads—people who had told a qualifier that they had the requisite amount of money in the market, wanted the printed material from Harvard, and would be interested in speaking to a Harvard broker. The BS would call them and try to persuade them to use Harvard, and him, to buy whatever stock he was pushing at the moment. When he was successful, the client would say okay and send in the money. The vast majority of leads never opened accounts. Most of them had brokers and were probably too polite to hang up on the cold caller and qualifier. It was easier for them to give in and agree to look at the Harvard brochure in the mail and talk to a broker who would call later. They had no intention of ordering stock through Harvard. Consequently, a one-in-ten success rate was considered very good when pitching leads to open new accounts. Any broker who opened ten new accounts in a month was doing well. The benchmark was 100 new accounts in a year. I was told several times that every Harvard broker who had ever opened 100 accounts two years in a row had put up at least $1 million a year in commissions.

The BS knew how important it was to open accounts. He had a big book, hundreds of clients, but he was never satisfied. He called leads every day, religiously, even though it was exhausting work. The BS would psych himself up for these calls, like somebody who was about to go out and give a speech in front of 200 people. Which, in a way, he was. Cold callers, qualifiers, even other brokers would lurk around our desks to overhear the BS's pitch as he tried to open accounts. I certainly paid attention, not only to the BS's presentations, but to other big producers as well. I tried to pick up on what worked. I listened to the way they used their voices.

I saw that pitching for a new account was not all that different from cold calling. One basic rule was the same: never hang up. The Bald Shadow would talk and talk, go on and on, until the prospective client either hung up on him or opened an account. It wasn't like he had another, better personality on the phone. He still had no personality. He was polite, but flat. He never said anything witty or charming to a prospective client. But he never shut up, either. He was a bulldog. He just kept talking—about why the prospective client should invest in the market, about why he should invest with Harvard, about why the BS would be the best broker for him, about what companies the BS would help the client invest in.

The BS liked to pitch standing up at his desk. Wearing his headset, he held the client card in one hand and a pen in the other. Sometimes he'd bend over and make a note on the card in his crabbed but neat handwriting. I'd try to see whether a card had my handwriting on it. Sometimes I could tell it was a prospective client that I had qualified. *I remember that guy,* I would think. *I'll bet he opens an account.* I considered it a personal success when the BS opened an account for a client I had spoken with. I was feeding him good prospects. I was doing my job well.

We cold callers and qualifiers talked a lot about the securities business, but we never talked about how brokers could do a better job for their clients. We never talked about how to research companies, or how to chart stocks and do a technical analysis. We mostly talked about how brokers sold stocks to their clients. We debated what made a good salesman. Sometimes cold callers and qualifiers asked me for advice. "Never hang up," I would reply with a shrug. I really didn't have a better answer. One day I asked the Bald Shadow: "How come you're such a good salesman? How come you are able to open so many more accounts?"

I expected the BS to blow me off. He ordinarily didn't have much time or interest in navel-gazing contemplation or philosophical discussions. All he wanted to do was make money. But he surprised me this time. He reached into the bottom drawer of his desk, fished around a little, and came up with a cassette tape. A date was written on the tape, about ten years earlier. "This is me when I was starting out," he said. I took the tape home and played it that night. The tape was a recording of the BS on the phone with prospective clients, trying to get them to open accounts. It was his voice, maybe a little younger and thinner, but otherwise it sounded nothing like the BS who I heard open accounts every day. He was terrible. He stumbled around. He said "Um" and "You know" a lot. He didn't have much to say, even about the small brokerage firm where he was working then. The BS I heard every day was smooth, articulate, authoritative, and always quick to counter a prospective client's misgivings and steer the dialogue where he wanted it to go. He had a good vocabulary and used it well. His thoughts were organized, and he expressed them clearly. His diction and grammar were good, and he gave an impression of scholarly reserve. He sounded like a professor. On the old recording, however, he stumbled and mumbled. He slurred a couple of words, mispronounced one, and often let his voice trail off at the end of a sentence so that it was hard to hear him. I wouldn't have bought anything from that voice over the phone. On one recorded call I actually heard the BS let the client get off the phone. The client said he just couldn't decide at the moment, and the BS said maybe he'd call the client again someday. He hung up. Astounding. I took the tape back to the office the next day and handed it to the BS.

"You weren't very good back then," I said.

"I stunk," he said. "But I just kept doing it. Over and over and over." That was all the advice he gave me. It was all I needed. I was a much better salesman at that point than the BS had been when he was starting out, and I still had a lot to learn. It gave me confidence for the future. The BS was not a natural salesman, but through sheer determination he had turned himself into a good one. I was a natural salesman. With even a little bit of determination, people would soon talk about me the way they talked about the Bald Shadow. I was going to be a legend.

One broker at Harvard already was a legend. He had a reputation as the all-time greatest account-opener in the history of Wall Street. The story was that he had once opened an account with a taxi driver who was driving him to the office. Qualifiers who had been around a while told me he was awesome on the phone. It was his voice, they said. If you heard his voice, you had to open an account. It was almost hypnotic. Naturally, I was eager to hear the guy pitch. But he was never in. Supposedly he was sick, some sort of long-term illness. He did come in once in a while—he looked okay to me—but I had a hard time hearing him pitch. Every time he was on the phone, so was I. One day I saw him pick up the phone and I made a point of getting off my call. I walked over to where I could hear. He was opening an account. But his voice didn't sound so extraordinary. Neither was his pitch. He approached the prospective client pretty much the same way everybody did. But fifteen minutes later, when he hung up the phone, he had the new account.

"His voice didn't sound so hypnotic to me," I told one of the other qualifiers.

"That's because you didn't hear it on the phone," the other guy told me seriously. "It's only when you hear it on the phone. Besides, it worked, didn't it?" It did work. The guy would come in once or twice a month for an hour, open three accounts, and then disappear.

There was a story about the Bald Shadow and his commitment to the pitch, and his determination never to give up. I never had the nerve to ask him about it, but a number of brokers swore to me they witnessed it. Apparently it had happened a few years earlier, in the afternoon. The BS hadn't been feeling well, but he hadn't done his pitching for the day. He put on his headphones, stood behind his desk, and started calling qualified leads. During one pitch, he began feeling more and more nauseous, but wouldn't cut off the call. He thought the guy was going to open an account. At one point the BS said, "Excuse me for a moment, please," to the potential client. He leaned over, opened his top right-hand desk drawer, moved his wraparound mike aside without taking the headset off, and vomited into the desk drawer. When he finished, he wiped his mouth with a tissue, readjusted the wraparound mike, pushed the drawer shut, and resumed his pitch. Five minutes later, after he had nailed down the new account, he meticulously filled out the necessary forms, put on his suit jacket, tightened the knot on his tie, and went home without a word to anyone in the office. The next morning, he came in to find that overnight the Branch Manager had gotten rid of the old desk and replaced it with one just like it. One of the secretaries had taken everything out of the old desk's drawers—except the top right-hand drawer—and put it all away in the new desk just as it had been in the old. The Branch Manager knew how to keep a good account-opener happy, and how to send a message to other brokers.

The Branch Manager had a general rule against qualifiers making pitches to try to open accounts. A potential lead was like gold, and far too important to risk losing because of the bumbling of a novice. But some brokers quietly allowed their qualifiers to make pitches and try to open new accounts, and the Branch Manager looked the other way. The Bald Shadow didn't allow his qualifiers to make pitches. He wanted his qualifiers to concentrate on qualifying, on helping find good solid leads. He wanted to make the pitches to those leads himself. He didn't want them wasted by a qualifier who wasn't as good at opening accounts as he was. The idea of letting any prospective client get away drove him crazy. The Queen, whose duties also included training qualifiers to make pitches, made a point of telling me that the Bald Shadow did not want me opening accounts. That drove me crazy. I had my license. I was a registered stockbroker in name, but not in practice.

If the Bald Shadow did not want me opening accounts, he should have told me himself. I began looking for an opportunity to defy the Queen and try opening accounts myself. One day when the Bald Shadow was away, I looked through his qualified leads, the stack of cards representing prospective clients waiting to be called by a Harvard broker. The top card was a guy in Arizona, someone I had qualified. He had seemed like a nice guy. I dialed his number, his secretary passed me to him, and I reminded him of our previous conversation. "I hope you received the information about our firm in the mail, and that you had a chance to look it over," I said. I started pitching him on a stock, trying to get him to open an account. He listened, said a few polite things, and then told me firmly that he had a broker he was happy with, and that he would not be opening an account with Harvard. I kept talking. He finally said he had to go, and hung up.

I picked up the next card. It was somebody the other qualifier had talked to. I stuck that card on the bottom of the pile and picked up another card I had given to the BS. I called that lead and the same thing happened. The third card was for a doctor from Minnesota. I was telling about the stock when he interrupted me. He said yes. He told me to buy him $10,000 worth. I took down the necessary details and got off the phone quickly, so excited I could hardly breathe. I was already standing up to do the pitch, just like the BS did, but I jumped up and punched my fist into the air. "Yessss!" I shouted.

The other qualifier and the cold caller had been aware of what I was doing on the phone, and had been watching and listening with the kind of fascination they might have shown for someone sticking his head in a lion's mouth. It was exciting and entertaining, but it was also dangerous. I was breaking the rules, doing something I wasn't supposed to be able to do even if I could. Now they stared at me with their mouths all but hanging open. My hand was actually trembling, the only time that had ever happened to me, but I managed to fill out a new account page for the BS's books the way I had seen him do it. Every new account had to be filed with the Queen. I filled in the form, handed it to the cold caller, and instructed, "Take it in to her," just as the BS would have told him. I could tell the cold caller didn't want to do it. He was afraid of what might happen. Maybe the Queen would kill the messenger. He took the form in, dropped it in her in-basket, and hightailed it back to our desks.

I sat and waited. It only took about five minutes. The Queen came storming across the board room, waving the form. She started hollering at me when she was still twenty feet away. "What are you doing? You can't do this! You're not qualified to open accounts! Who authorized this? Who do you think you are?" I started getting worried, though, when the Queen said she was going to take the form to the Branch Manager and get me fired. She lashed me up and down, promising she'd make sure I never worked anywhere in the securities industry. That made me nervous. Maybe I had made a mistake. I didn't think she could really keep me from getting a job as a broker somewhere else, but she might be able to keep me from getting a desk at Harvard. I asked her to talk to the Bald Shadow first. I tried to give her the impression that he had allowed me, even encouraged me, to try to open an account.

"Did he specifically tell you to call this lead?" she demanded.

"Just talk to him before anything else," I said, as if I was offering advice that was good for her.

She clicked away in her stiletto heels. I was on the phone to the BS as soon as her back was turned. Luckily, he was home. I told him what had happened, and how I needed his help. "You've got to tell her you told me to do it, or I'm screwed," I said. It was one of the few times I ever heard him laugh out loud.

"Hey, congratulations," he said. "It only took you three pitches to open a new account? This is great!" I think the BS was pleased at my audacity, but I think he was more pleased at knowing he could turn over even more of his business to me. I could open accounts, which was the hardest and most important thing he did. The BS promised to smooth things over with the Queen and, if necessary, with the Branch Manager. And I suppose he did. The next day I saw him in her office, and she never said another word to me about opening accounts. I just kept doing it.

10

The Bond Play

More than anything else, the morning meeting reminded me of the roll call that starts every shift in a big-city police department. The brokers, like the cops, carried in their coffee in paper cups or their own mugs. They tried to look relaxed, competent, and confident. Not too eager—as if the meeting was for everyone else's benefit, not for their own. They didn't need the information everybody else needed. They wanted everybody else in the room to think they already knew what was on the day's agenda, and more.

The Branch Manager was in all his Napoleonic glory at the morning meeting. He would stride brusquely to the front of the conference room, so erect that I swear I would have said he was six feet tall even though I knew he was hardly five-three. He would barely acknowledge, with a curt little nod, the handful of the biggest producers among the brokers sitting up front. He'd walk past me and other qualifiers and cold callers as if we didn't exist. We were not worthy of his time or energy, not even a flicker of his eyebrow in recognition. Like the roll-call police sergeant who reviews assignments for the day and tells his officers about news—a series of break-ins here, a suspected rapist sighted there—the Branch Manager would talk about what Harvard wanted the brokers to do that day, including the listing of specials. Many brokers worked only on specials. They didn't want to waste their time making trades that didn't carry the extra inside profit on top of their regular commissions. "The straight commission is for chumps," one broker told me. "Anybody who works just for commission ain't gonna get rich, and ain't gonna make it around here."

Once in a while the Branch Manager mentioned individual trades that had made a lot of money for the firm, or singled out brokers who had had particularly big days. A typical day for the average broker was $2,000 in gross commissions. At the 45 percent payout, that meant $1,100 for the brokerage, and $900 for the broker. If a broker did $20,000 or more in gross commissions, the Branch Manager might allow himself to admit, "Not a bad day," which was his highest praise.

I suppose Harvard clients, and all investors who rely on stockbrokers, liked to think of their brokerage firm looking out for them. They liked to imagine that brokers and analysts worked hard to identify good investments: undervalued companies, or companies that are about to start doing so well that their shares will zoom. Maybe some brokers at Harvard were like that. If so, I never met them. In fact, the welfare of the client was never discussed, even by the management. Never once did I hear the Branch Manager talk about his brokers doing a good job for the clients. Never once did the Branch Manager, or anyone else, talk about buying or selling shares to benefit their clients. Never once did the Branch Manager, or anyone else at Harvard, talk about investing in a company because its stock might rise and we might make some money for clients.

The Bald Shadow, as a broker who generated $2 million or more in gross commissions a year (an average of $8,000–$10,000 per day), was one of the brokers most often honored by the Branch Manager's recognition at the morning meeting. Another big producer was a broker named Gordo. One morning the Branch Manager abandoned his customary iciness and, for him, positively burbled praise. Gordo, he announced, "had a good month . . . yesterday." He had pulled in just over $90,000 in gross commissions in a single day. The Branch

Manager smiled, for the only time anyone could remember during a morning meeting. He not only nodded toward Gordo, but raised an arm to him in a gesture as if to say, Stand up, take a bow. Gordo played it cool. He shifted from his seat as if he were going to get up, but didn't. Instead he just gave a little half-nod of thanks, a little shrug as if to say no big deal, a little smile that said he was the best and knew it. Besides, he didn't need to take a bow. The more than $40,000 he had earned personally that day was all the applause he needed.

When the Branch Manager made his announcement, there were gasps and moans in the room, and a smattering of applause from one or two of the younger, less successful brokers that quickly died out in embarrassment. The entire room was eerily silent as the Branch Manager outlined how Gordo had made so much money in one day. A few brokers actually made notes, which I had never seen before. When the morning meeting ended, the brokers didn't immediately scatter as usual, ambling back to their desks amid good-natured insults and locker-room comments. On this morning, they took their time, lingering to talk to the Branch Manager and Gordo, to ask more questions about how he had made so much money so quickly.

It was simple, really. Things had been tense in Bosnia, and there was a lot of talk about the United States sending troops. Experts were warning of war and higher oil prices, and the financial markets around the globe were nervous. Analysts were predicting a big drop in the stock market. Investors were pulling money out of stocks and putting it into traditionally more conservative, safer investments during times of crisis, investments such as bonds, cash, and gold. Gordo stumbled onto a way to play upon all that apprehension and generate some quick commissions out of it.

Gordo identified a certain series of U.S. government bonds that were highly leverageable. In other words, you could buy a lot of bonds without putting down very much money up front. Gordo asked his clients to buy $50,000 worth of these bonds—for which they would have to put up only $12,500 in cash, plus a commission. Gordo had prepared a list of the clients he was going to call. They were some of his wealthiest clients, those who had the biggest investments in the market. They were among the most trusting clients, those who valued Gordo's advice most highly. They were also among the most conservative, the most concerned about losing any of their money, and that made them ripe for this scheme—which, as it turned out, all but guaranteed that they would take a significant loss in a very short time.

Gordo started calling his clients, explaining that the bond was a good play. Oil prices were going to skyrocket, and so were interest rates. The market could crash. Gold was fluctuating. Cash was safe, but too safe. This was an opportunity to make some quick money if the bond market jumped when—he was sure to emphasize "when," not "if"—a shooting war erupted in Bosnia and the world financial markets went crazy. A surprising number of clients went for the deal right away. They readily agreed to put up $15,625, including commission, to buy $50,000 worth of bonds. Some of them had to sell other positions to come up with the cash, which was a bonus for Gordo: another commission. When the clients received their confirmation statements in the mail, they would see that they had paid a 6.25 percent commission—which was what the government allowed and which did not seem unreasonable, particularly considering the good service they thought they were getting from their ever-attentive broker. What they didn't realize was that the 6.25 percent was not on the cash they put down, but instead for the entire $50,000—a total commission of $3,125 on top of the $12,500 they actually paid toward the bonds. I wondered how many of those clients would have felt differently had they known that one of every five dollars they spent on the bonds went to Gordo.

Gordo told the rest of us how he had talked some of his more reluctant clients into making the bond play. He preyed upon their conservatism, upon their fear of losing money, upon their faith in the bond market during times of turmoil. He played upon their egos, assuring them that it was the smartest thing to do, a bold move that would later prove how clever, how astute, how prescient they had been. One of Gordo's cold callers told me Gordo had gone so far as to describe the investment to a couple of clients as "the Bond Play," in a tone of voice that made the poor unsuspecting investors feel like they were part of some secret, sophisticated conspiracy that was beyond the ken of the ordinary investor, who was ignorantly wasting his money in lesser investments with lesser brokers.

Gordo sold thirty investors more than $1.5 million worth of bonds that day. They had put up $453,750 in cash to make those purchases—$93,750 of it in gross commissions, $42,187.50 net for Gordo. Over the next couple of days, I heard murmurings throughout the board room about other brokers trying to emulate what they, too, were invariably calling the Bond Play. But no one else had nearly as much success. By then the war drums were not beating as loudly in Bosnia, anxiety had eased in the markets, and bond prices were actually going down slightly.

About a week later, I happened to ask Gordo's qualifier what Gordo was selling that day. He rolled his eyes. "He's calling back all those people who made the Bond Play," the qualifier said. Gordo was telling his clients that interest rates seemed poised to drop, that the immediate threat of a shooting war had diminished, and while the bond play had been the right move at the right time, the best strategy now was to get back into stocks. He was guiding his clients into stocks on which Harvard was running daily specials, so he could again maximize his commissions.

The way I figured it, the typical client in the bond play put up $15,625 and lost $4,500, most of it in commissions. I never heard of any client ever filing any sort of complaint against Gordo, for the Bond Play or for anything else.

11

On the Margin

The Bald Shadow thought that because he was rich, well-dressed, and not fat, he should be dating what he called "hot" women. Every now and then he'd have one girlfriend or another come by the office. He was always questioning whether she was the right woman for him. "So what do you think?" he'd ask me. "Is she hot?" Real seventh-grade stuff. His lack of social skills and taste led him to rely on me more and more. Once he asked me to go clothes shopping with him at Barneys. He had to have the best. Even more remarkable to me, he didn't mind paying full price. In an hour I helped him pick out an over-coat, three suits, and some other stuff. "Does this look good on me?" he kept asking. Total bill: $17,000. That was about twice my annual pay from Harvard, even after the dollar-an-hour raise when I passed the Series 7. The BS never even said thanks.

Doing pitches and opening accounts became a regular part of my day. I'd make five or six presentations a day, and open an account every second day or so. My success rate wasn't much worse than the BS's. One day I opened three accounts, and the other qualifier and the cold caller gave me a little standing ovation.

A good account-opener has an answer for any objection a prospective client might raise. I got a lot of material from the rebuttal book, a battered, photocopied booklet that listed possible answers that brokers could give to negative responses from prospective clients. I was told that Harvard had put together the first rebuttal book years before, and that other firms had borrowed it and stolen from it and added to it. Every firm had its own rebuttal book, but they all pretty much said the same thing.

The book offered up to a dozen different rebuttals for any objection a prospective client might raise to opening an account with Harvard:

"I have a broker."
"I don't have any money."
"I don't like that industry."
"I don't like you."

If a client said he already owned the stock I was pitching, the rebuttal book told me to have another stock ready to pitch. If he said he owned that, too, I'd ask him if he owned a third stock. If he said yes, I'd tell him why he ought to sell it.

Gradually I developed my own style for pitching new accounts. Unlike the BS, I occasionally used a telephone instead of headphones. Either way, though, I always stood up like he did. I envisioned myself as a teacher standing over the prospective client, who was a student who needed to be educated. I tried to make my voice say, "I'm going to teach you something." I wanted my pitch to be so compelling that the prospective client would take notes. Whether they actually took notes or not—I'm sure most didn't—I always imagined them writing down what I was saying. Some brokers always said, "This is why you should buy this stock." I said, "This is why you should own this company." I was sure that owning a company sounded more prestigious than buying stock.

I had one natural advantage over many other brokers: I assumed everyone else's attention span was as short as my own. If I started rambling on and on about the company, I figured the guy's mind was going to wander. Silence was the worst response I could get from a client. I much preferred a client to give me a totally negative response. I knew how to counter that, how to goad the client into engaging me in a real discussion. If he was silent, I imagined him holding the phone two feet away from his ear while he flipped on the TV or took a stroll over to the fridge. A lot of people I called were probably sitting in front of computer terminals, and I imagined them clicking on the solitaire screen if I got too long-winded.

My goal was to close as soon as possible. This is the name of the company. This is what it does. This is why you should own it. This is how many shares I think you should buy. At that point I wanted the prospective client to ask, "Well, what's the price of the stock?" or "How has the stock been doing?" Those were buying signals. I knew that if I engaged the prospective client in any sort of give-and-take dialogue, I was almost sure to open the account. As soon as I got any response that I considered a buying signal, I went in for the kill and started closing. And I just kept closing. No matter what the client said, I came back with an invitation to close the deal. If I was pitching a company that made some sort of medical equipment, the lead might say, "I don't know anything about all that. I'm not a doctor."

"I'm not a doctor, either," I would fire back, "but I know that doctors need this product, and that's why I think you should buy a thousand shares."

There were only two possible ways for the call to end: Either the lead hung up on me or agreed to buy the stock. I wasn't going to hang up. I learned that a lot of buyers didn't know they wanted to buy until they got caught up in what I was saying and the way I said it. It was always a rush when a lead said yes. "Here's what happens next," I would say. "I'm going to hang up here and purchase ten thousand dollars' worth of XYZ for you at market price. My assistant will get back to you later today to confirm that over the phone, and you will be receiving a written confirmation order in the mail. You need to wire in the money or send a check by the settlement date in five to seven days." It always amazed me that people would say they were going to send in money, and then actually do it. Very few people "reneged," as we called it. Only about one in twenty new accounts were reneges.

As the Bald Shadow took more time off, I began keeping his book up to date. Books, actually. Most brokers had a book that was three or four inches thick. The BS had three of them. His books were extremely meticulous and organized. He made detailed, methodical notes about each trade, and showed me how to make them.

The BS often had me call clients and tell them what trades he wanted them to make, and most of them offered little resistance. Occasionally a client would get his back up and tell me that if the BS wanted something, he should damn well call himself instead of having an assistant do it. But most of the BS's clients didn't seem to mind talking to me. I think some of them found it easier to say no to me than to the BS, so they were relieved if I called instead of him. Very few of the BS's clients called him, and the few who did were typically among his smallest investors. They wanted to talk about different stocks or their portfolios or whatever. The BS didn't have time for them. But I did.

Sometimes the BS would have me call a client he didn't want to talk to himself because he was afraid the guy was mad at him. So I'd have to listen while the client moaned about what a bad job BS had done for him on some recent trade. Sometimes I was sympathetic. "I'll talk to him and see what I can do," I told some unhappy clients. But generally I tried to turn them around, explaining what we were trying to do for them, describing our "long-term strategy" for their accounts—in reality, the only strategy was to get more money out of them—and reassuring them that the offending trade would no doubt turn out to be a good deal in the end because the company was doing this or that to turn things around. The conversations began with clients breathing fire, and ended with me blowing smoke. It turned out that most of the BS's clients liked me.

The Branch Manager didn't like the Bald Shadow's absences. The BS was a big producer, and the Branch Manager wanted to see him in the office, producing. I'd risen sufficiently in stature that the Branch Manager would usually nod at me during his twice-daily strolls through the board room, and one afternoon he actually stopped and talked to me. "So I suppose the Bald Shadow is off on some beach," he grumbled. "That goddamn guy is never here anymore."

I shot right back, "Hey, it doesn't matter. I run his business now. You know that." He just kind of harrumphed and walked away. I wondered for a moment if I had been impudent. Nah. I had been cocky, and that was good. I wanted the Branch Manager to think about me. I wanted him to make me a full-fledged broker. I thought I was ready. Unfortunately, the BS didn't think I was ready. Or at least, he wasn't ready to lose me. He liked having me there to do his work.

One day my dad was in Manhattan on business, and we met after work for drinks. He encouraged me tell him all the details, every nuance of the conversation when I persuaded the whale to make the $500,000 trade. My dad couldn't believe all the work I was doing for the BS while I was getting $4.50 an hour. I was committed to Harvard—there were still four months to go on the year I'd given myself when I started there—but my dad pointed out that I was making a lot of money for the BS, and he didn't even have to pay my lousy $4.50 out of his own pocket.

I was stuck in the Queen's classes, if they could be called that, for teaching qualifiers how to pitch clients in preparation for the big test, the presentation for the Branch Manager. I didn't think the Queen had anything to teach me. I already had opened accounts for the BS. I had made hundreds of pitches to the BS's clients, persuading them to make trades. I was better at it than she was. If she had been any good at pitching, she'd be a broker herself. But I had to go through her classes. I wouldn't get a chance to pitch for the Branch Manager unless and until she said I was ready. She held the key to his door. And she was in no hurry to unlock it. Her job was to train people. The more people she had to train, the more important her job was. If she let everybody sail through to the Branch Manager, she wouldn't have a job.

For a couple of months I spent several hours a week, usually at lunchtime, sitting in the conference room with the Queen and a handful of other qualifiers who wanted to move up and become brokers. We'd practice pitches on the Queen and on each other, over and over. We'd critique each other, and she'd critique us. She made us write out our presentations in advance, and then deliver them. I thought that was a ridiculous way to sell. Selling couldn't be scripted in advance. None of our pitches were ever good enough for her. Mine were a real problem for her because I refused to do a pitch the way she wanted.

I liked to do a quick introduction, make a very few cursory points about the company, and then start to close. She wanted us to talk more about the company. She also liked to build the whole pitch around a question, on the theory that it would draw in the client. One of her favorite sample pitches was for a firm that made educational software. "Do you know what is the fastest-growing industry in America?" she suggested we ask clients. "You don't know. I'll tell you. It's raising children. That's right. Raising children is the fastest-growing industry in America today." This amazing factoid was supposed to get clients to buy shares in the educational software company. I thought her sample pitches sucked. Her approach certainly didn't work for me.

A few times I tried it her way, and it didn't feel right. I begged her to let me present to the Branch Manager. She refused. Not yet, she said. I asked her to just let me talk to the Branch Manager, and try to convince him that I was ready to pitch for him. "You're not ready yet," she said. Case closed. I decided I had to find a way to get around her. I thought that if the Bald Shadow went in to the Branch Manager and pushed for me to give a presentation, then it would happen. The BS had that kind of influence with the Branch Manager. But the BS wouldn't do it willingly because he didn't want to lose me. I needed to find a way to force him to do it.

One of the ways the Bald Shadow built up his clients' portfolios—and the size of his own book—was by encouraging them to buy stocks on margin. Most investors' accounts with stockbrokers are cash accounts. The investor sends in cash, and the broker invests it. Some investors, however, have margin accounts that allow them to invest money they borrow from the brokerage house. For example, the Bald Shadow wanted a client to buy $100,000 worth of some stock. But the client said he could afford only $50,000. No problem, the BS assured him. Send in the $50,000, and Harvard would loan the client the other $50,000. He could own $10 worth of stock for every $5 he invested. True, the client had to pay Harvard interest on that money every month—usually a point or two over the prime rate—but the BS never mentioned that. If the client asked about it, the BS assured him that if the stock went up enough it would more than compensate for the small interest payments. *If the stock went up*. That was the operative phrase. If the stock went up, it was a good deal for the client. The BS never mentioned what would happen if the stock went down.

New York Stock Exchange regulations require investors to maintain an equity position of at least 25 percent of the market value of the securities in margin accounts. Brokerage houses often set in-house limits that are more restrictive. At Harvard, for example, the firm's rule was that a client's equity had to be at least 30 percent of the value of the securities held. A client couldn't put down $10,000 to buy $100,000 worth of stock. That would have been an equity holding of only 10 percent. However, a client could open a margin account by putting down $40,000 cash and getting a $60,000 loan from Harvard to buy $100,000 worth of stock. That was a 40 percent equity position. No problem.

But say the stock took a dive, and all of a sudden it was worth only $80,000. The client still owed Harvard $60,000, which meant his equity had dropped to $20,000—or only 25 percent of the $80,000 value of the position. Harvard's back-room computers, which kept track of all this bookkeeping, would run up the red flags. Harvard would issue a margin call on the account. That meant the client either had to sell enough stock or send in enough cash to raise the equity holding back above the firm's 30 percent maintenance requirement.

The Bald Shadow loved margin accounts for several reasons. For one, they increased the size of his book. Second, they allowed him to collect bigger commissions on the amount of money his clients could invest. Third, and perhaps most important, they gave him more control over his clients. "Control the money," he used to tell me over and over. "Control the client. Control the client relationship. Remember, it's our money now, not theirs."

The BS liked it when the stocks he bought for clients on margin went up. That meant his book went up, too. If the stocks went up enough, the equity holding would go up, too, and pretty soon he could talk the client into buying more on margin. But he wasn't overly concerned if stocks went down, even when it meant a margin call. The BS saw the margin call as an opportunity to get even more money from clients. He refused to let clients sell out their positions to cover margin calls. "When you sell out your position, the only thing that guarantees is a loss," he told clients. "Do you want a loss? No? Well, the only way not to guarantee a loss is to send in the money."

The Dow Jones index was in the mid 3,000's back then. It got into the high 3,000's, within shouting distance of the then-magical 4,000 level several times, then quickly receded. During one of those fallbacks, after the BS had persuaded a lot of clients to buy on slim margins that were right at or near the minimum equity holding, the

Harvard back room issued margin calls for about fifteen of his clients. All together, they owed more than $300,000 to cover their losses. The BS was agitated. This was too many margin calls at once. He had pushed some of those clients pretty hard to buy on margin, and some of them had gone on margin just in the last few weeks. They weren't going to like it when he called and told them they had to send in money. The BS didn't want to face the music. He was afraid some of the clients would refuse to send in the money. He was afraid they would sell out their positions, thereby diminishing his book. I suspect he was afraid that some of them would tell him to sell out enough to cover their losses, and then close their accounts completely. Maybe he figured they wouldn't be as angry with me. So he asked me to call the clients and tell them they had to send in cash.

I looked at the list of names. A couple of them were clients I had qualified. I had persuaded several others to make trades, though not on margin. "I can get a hundred and fifty thousand dollars from these people," I told the BS. "I can get it today." His face lit up. I could feel our relationship changing. "I'll do it for you," I said. "But then you have to do something for me. At the end of the day today, you have to go into the Branch Manager's office and tell him that you think it's time for me to be a broker. Tell him you want me to have my own desk, my own chair, and my own cold caller. Starting tomorrow morning. Okay? Is that a deal?" The BS looked at me as if I were holding a gun to his head. I was glad. That's how I wanted him to feel. He quickly said yes, and turned away. I didn't know if he would actually go in and demand a desk for me or not. But I didn't have time to worry about it at that moment. I had a lot of phone calls to make.

That was one of the most punishing, stressful days of my life. I'm still not sure exactly how I did it, but I talked nearly all those people into sending in enough money to cover their margin shortfalls. "You want me to throw good money after bad," one client protested. *Well, yeah, maybe,* I thought to myself. But that's not what I said. By noon I had commitments for $100,000. Right around then the Branch

Manager walked past. "Hey, guy. Howya doin'?" he said. It was maybe the fourth or fifth time he had said hello to me.

"I raised a hundred thousand this morning," I said.

He never asked me how I raised it, or for what. He understood that Harvard had $100,000 that afternoon that it didn't have that morning. That was all that mattered.

"Good work," the Branch Manager said, and he kept going.

By four-thirty in the afternoon I had commitments for $171,000 in margin calls. The checks were in the mail. The BS had been following my progress all day, periodically looking anxiously over my shoulder at the list, and the numbers that I scrawled next to each name for the amount that the client had promised to send in. $5,000, $10,000, $20,000. I knew he was adding them up. When I hung up after my last call, I spun my chair around and tossed the list onto the BS's desk. "Okay," I said. "Do it."

"In a minute," he mumbled. The next time I looked up, he had gone home for the day. I asked him about talking to the Branch Manager the next day, and he put me off again. And again the day after that. He never did speak up for me, as far as I know. After a week, I quit asking.

12

On the Market

I expected to be called in to do my presentation for the Branch Manager any day. And I expected to do so well that I would be offered the crown jewels, the key to the city—a job as a broker right there at Harvard. True, it was still a long shot. But there were a handful of brokers there who had come up as cold callers. Once in a while someone had to make it, if for no reason other than to perpetuate the program, to continue holding out to young cold callers the faint hope that they, too, could make it to the top. Without that hope, who could Harvard ever entice to work as a cold caller?

Always attuned to what was going on in the board room, I became even more sensitive. One day the Branch Manager called in a broker who had not been producing much for a couple of years. They talked in his office for a few minutes, then the broker walked briskly back to his desk and started packing up his stuff. A ripple went through the board room. He was being sent down to a smaller brokerage. Maybe they were making room for me. His desk was in the middle of the board room, not the greatest location. I intended to end up by the windows, like the Bald Shadow. But I told myself it was an okay place to start.

Nothing happened. I asked the BS about my prospects, and he shrugged. He just wanted me to shut up and make money for him. Instead, I was getting to be a pain in the ass. I'm sure he realized that one way or another I was going to leave him eventually, either to my own desk at Harvard or to be a broker at some other firm. I bugged the Queen about getting a presentation in front of the Branch Manager, and she kept telling me she didn't think I was quite ready. I called Larry and asked him to meet me for a drink. He listened, nodding, as I poured out my frustrations. I told him that Harvard wasn't giving me a chance, and that I was thinking of going somewhere else. Did he have any suggestions? He told me that his firm was always looking for aggressive young brokers. He told me that his firm was different from Harvard, but in good ways. It was smaller, but it was leaner and hungrier. It was possible to make even more money than the big Harvard brokers did. He told me I could work with him, and he would show me the ropes. One thing he didn't tell me, and which I didn't learn until months later, was that his firm had a standing practice: any broker who recruited another broker got 5 percent of the new broker's commissions during the first year. If I did a couple of hundred thousand dollars' worth of commissions in my first year at his firm, which I fully expected to do, Larry would pocket $10,000.

The Bald Shadow must have known that I was looking around. He didn't want me to leave, but I think he thought I was more likely to get a desk at Harvard than to take a job somewhere else. He did something that must have been very difficult for him. He started talking about paying me more money, out of his own pocket, to stay at Harvard and keep running his business. He wasn't interested in working *with* me; he wanted me to work *for* him. "How much do you think he'd pay you?" Melanie asked me. I guessed about $150,000. That was a big number for us. I was making less than $10,000 a year. Melanie made less than $40,000 a year as a special education teacher. By staying with the BS we would triple our income. We could get married, buy a house, maybe start thinking about a family someday. If the BS had come through with a job for $150,000, I probably would have taken it.

I talked a little to my dad and a lot to Melanie about whether I should leave Harvard, without going into a lot of the details. My dad listened thoughtfully, as always, and said there was something to be said both for a high-paying apprenticeship and for getting started on my own as soon as possible. Then he said, "You probably don't realize it yourself yet, but from what you've told me it sounds like you've pretty much made up your mind. You've just got to get in the right frame of mind where you can leave without looking back. Some people never learn that. They spend their whole lives second-guessing themselves, and wondering 'What if?' over and over."

Melanie patiently listened, many times, almost every evening for several weeks, to my fretful analysis of my career at Harvard. She said all the little signals and signs around the office, such as getting a chair or a headset or having the Branch Manager utter my name, reminded her of the way the Chinese used to read wall posters to figure out which way the political winds were blowing, or the way Kremlinologists would study the body language of Soviet leaders reviewing parades to determine who was gaining or losing power in Moscow. She always listened to me and commented or asked a question, usually looking for details about how a person in the office looked or sounded. She rarely offered an opinion. But finally she did.

She said that if the BS offered me a job, I should take it. She thought $150,000 was a lot of money. It was more than her parents, one a college professor and the other a high school principal, had ever made together in a single year. "Sure, it's unfair that you're doing so much of the work and he's making so much of the money, but look at all you're learning," she said. "It's only a matter of time, maybe a couple of years, before he retires or turns the business over to you. You'll get your own desk there when you're ready for it. I think if he offers you a job for any reasonable amount, we should take it."

But the Bald Shadow didn't offer me a job for a reasonable amount of money. He didn't offer me any job at all. He kept saying we had to sit down and talk about the job, but we never did. I can't say I was surprised, even though it probably would have been the best investment he ever made. He was going to make close to a million and a half that year; I knew because I had made several hundred thousand of it for him. But I couldn't get a free cheeseburger out of him, so how could I expect $150,000 a year?

Yet I was still reluctant to leave Harvard. Right to the day I walked out the door, I was hoping I'd get a desk. To me, Harvard was the pinnacle of the business. Larry's firm was relatively tiny, and had a reputation as a scrappy, hustling little shop where the rules sometimes were bent. That didn't bother me, not after what I had seen of the way the Bald Shadow and other top Harvard brokers conducted their business and treated their clients. It seemed to me as if bending rules was a normal part of being a stockbroker. Melanie wanted me to stay at Harvard, but didn't object when I began rationalizing a move to Larry's firm.

"Even if I got a desk at Harvard, I'd be the low man on the totem pole, number eighty out of the eighty in the board room," I told her. "I'd have to scrap and scrape my way up. The stairway to the top is much shorter and clearer at Larry's firm." Larry told me had made $300,000 in commissions his first year there. He had become a vice president his second year, and a senior vice president his third year. He was a dominant force in the office. I didn't see anything wrong with being a big fish in a small pond. I toyed with the idea that I might build a bigger business and make more money at Larry's firm in two or three years, and then be able to go back to Harvard as one of the top guys. I decided to go in for an interview with Larry.

It wasn't much of an interview. Instead, it was mostly Larry trying to convince me that he was a big shot, and that I should come and work there and be a big shot, too. He showed me around. Larry had his own office because he was a senior vice president. His office was just off a smaller, considerably less impressive board room than Harvard's. There were forty desks crammed into the board room, none of them as nice as the big brokers' desks at Harvard. These desks were old and worn. Instead of matching green chairs, there were all kinds of office chairs, all sizes, all colors, all shapes. It looked like some of them were broken. Computer screens were stacked here and there. There was none of the neatness, the uniformity, the orderliness of Harvard. At Harvard, you couldn't see any wires. They were hidden. Here, there were wires and cables snaking around everywhere. In a couple of places the wires were held down on the floor by duct tape, but the tape was coming loose. If I took the job, I would be moving from Harvard to the securities-industry equivalent of a junior college. From that moment on, I thought of the firm as Junior College.

Larry introduced me to the office manager and told him that Junior College should hire me. In the scheme of things at Junior College, Larry was much more important than the office manager. Larry was a revenue center. The office manager didn't produce anything. Any competent office administrator could have done his job. When he talked to brokers who wanted to work at Junior College, he could probably veto a candidate he thought totally inappropriate. But he would need a pretty good explanation if the broker who recommended the candidate decided to appeal to the office manager's bosses, the two partners who ran the firm. The more productive the broker, the more influence—just like at Harvard, I thought.

Larry left us, and the office manager explained a little about how Junior College handled its brokers—how they wrote up their "tickets" to order trades, how they got paid, and so on. He told me about some of the stocks for which the firm was a market maker. That was always a big selling point for recruiting brokers, I came to learn; the more the firm acted as a market maker, the more opportunity there was for skimming hidden commissions out of the spread between the bid and the asked prices. The straight commission, the one that clients knew they were paying, was 5 percent at this firm, the maximum allowed, compared with Harvard's 3 percent.

He told me that much larger commissions were built into IPOs, the initial public offerings for which Junior College was known. The firm specialized in taking small companies to the market, he told me. Somebody with a small company and a big idea would come to Junior College—or vice versa–and propose that some money be raised to help the company grow. Junior College would act as an investment banker, and arrange to sell stock in the company to the public. That's where Junior College's stockbrokers came in—they sold the shares to the public. Usually the IPO would sell $15 million or $20 million worth of stock. The majority of that went to the owners of the company, but Junior College took a hefty chunk as its fee for overseeing the IPO. Brokers handling IPOs always made big commissions on them. It all sounded good to me, in theory. I really didn't have a clue how it all worked in practice. The Bald Shadow didn't sell shares in IPOs. Nobody at Harvard did. The office manager told me that Junior College had several good IPOs coming, and maybe I could get "a piece" of them. I didn't know exactly what he meant by that, but I figured someone would explain it to me when I needed to know.

My interview, if it could be called that, seemed to be over. The office manager showed me where I would sit in the board room. The chair was not new. It was some sort of cheap fabric, with no arms, not at all like the sleek green swivel armchairs at Harvard. The wooden desk was old and scarred. It looked like the kind of desk that might have gum stuck under it. I didn't care. It was mine. I was getting a desk. We shook hands and he told me to start on Monday morning. My new desk was not far from Larry's office. He saw me shake hands with the office manager, and came out to congratulate me. He introduced me to a few other brokers in the board room. They smiled and were friendly and shook hands. It seemed like they were impressed that I had been at Harvard. It occurred to me that Larry hadn't told them I wasn't a full-fledged broker. But they must have figured it out for themselves. Or maybe they thought I had gotten myself into some sort of trouble at Harvard and was forced out. No broker from Harvard would willingly move to Junior College.

The office manager at Junior College had told me I would be getting a draw of $3,000 a month. My commissions would go to covering the draw. I could keep whatever commissions I earned beyond $3,000 a month. He made it clear that most brokers earned back their draws and switched to straight commissions within three or four months. Those that didn't were gone.

The day after my Junior College interview, on Thursday morning, I went into Harvard and told the Bald Shadow that the next day, Friday, would be my last. I would have liked to walk out on him then and there, but I needed the $4.50 an hour. He was so angry that he wouldn't speak to me. It was the most bitter, contained rage I had ever seen. He could have made things very tough for me by saying, "Wait a minute. Stay here. Work with me. I'll pay you a hundred and fifty thousand dollars a year." The fact that he didn't say anything like that made it a lot easier to leave, and helped me believe I was doing the right thing. The biggest surprise came on Friday, an hour or so before I left for good. The Queen came over and spoke to me. "You shouldn't leave," she said, a chill in her voice. She wasn't pleasant. She didn't pretend that she liked me, like some people do when a colleague leaves a job. "You're making a mistake," she said. She really seemed to mean it, but I wondered if the Branch Manager or BS had told her to come and talk to me. I decided she probably took it upon herself. She might have seen my departure as a black mark against her as a trainer. I was the class of the field, and it could be bad for her if it was perceived that she (a) didn't think I was ready to move up, (b) let me get away, (c) drove me away, or (d) all of the above. None of the choices spoke well for her at Harvard. "You should stay," she said. "You'll get a desk one of these days. You're almost ready."

"Too late," I said with as much satisfaction as I could. "I'm gone."

I wanted to celebrate that weekend. Melanie, cautious as usual, didn't like to spend money we didn't have yet. I was pleased with the $3,000, and figured it was no big sin to run up our credit cards a little. She didn't feel the need. "There's no rush. I know you're going to make a lot of money in your life," she said. But I did talk her into going out and looking at apartments. Our lease was ending, and I wanted to be closer to Wall Street. I saw an ad for a building being renovated in Gramercy Park. Melanie thought it would be too expensive, so I went and looked at it without telling her. I fell in love with a one-bedroom on the fourteenth floor; it had a walk-in closet, and there was a little balcony with great views to the south, all the way down to Wall Street. I liked that. The rent was $1,900—too much for us, Melanie and I had agreed. I signed a lease anyway. When I told her, I was afraid she'd be upset. And maybe she was, but only for about five seconds. She wanted to live there, too.

"We'll make it work somehow," she said.

"Don't worry," I assured her. "In a few weeks I'll be pulling in commissions and making a lot more than three thousand a month."

13

First Blood

During my interview, I had been struck by the physical differences in the offices and the furniture at Junior College. But I thought maybe I would get used to it once I started working there. I didn't. I hated my rickety chair and my scratched-up desk. At Harvard, all the brokers had the same desk, the same chair, the same computer. Junior College was a hodgepodge. That was what I remembered as the chief difference. Until the day I started work, that is. My first day, I was struck more by the differences in the people. Harvard, I realized, had been very genteel, very polished, and relatively old. Most of the Harvard brokers were in their thirties, some in the forties, and a few even older. They all dressed well, and were well groomed. They spoke well, and were polite. I hadn't realized it when I was there, but Harvard was a heavily Jewish firm.

At Junior College, the brokers were much younger, nearly all in their twenties. Only a handful were Jewish. Instead, Junior College had a virtual United Nations of white, black, Asian, and Latin brokers. Most of the white guys seemed to be Irish or Italian, and wore their ethnic stereotypes aggressively. They were loud, profane, and crude. It seemed as though few of them knew how to tie a necktie properly, or where to get a decent haircut. Their clothes looked cheap, even the suits. Some guys didn't even wear suits, and I saw a couple of brokers in corduroy. Junior College brokers sweated openly, and sometimes smelled like perspiration or booze or whatever spicy food they had eaten for lunch.

The women in the office were different, too. Junior College had even fewer women brokers than Harvard—two or three, out of fifty-some brokers—and they dressed and acted more professionally than most of the male brokers at Junior College. But while the female clerks and secretaries at Harvard were well-spoken, well-groomed, and dressed in an understated, professional manner, the secretaries at Junior College looked and sounded like they were on their way to a dance party in New Jersey or the outer reaches of Queens. They had teased-up "big hair," cracked their gum, spoke with nasal accents, called the brokers by nicknames like "hon" or "dear," and wore tight, revealing clothing set off by cheap, dangling jewelry. It was obvious that some of them regarded the office as a happy hunting ground where they plotted to bag a broker for a husband so they could retire to the soap operas and bonbons. One fellow broker told me to pay attention when a particularly buxom secretary went to the restroom; she always came back with erect nipples showing through her tight sweater or sheer blouse. "We think she's putting ice on 'em so they stand up nice when she takes the long route back to her desk," the guy told me. "Advertising."

Maybe there was suddenly a spate of publicity about Junior College during my first few weeks at my new firm, or maybe I just noticed it because I was now working there. But I began seeing lots of stories about Junior College in newspapers and magazines. Most of the coverage was negative. *Barron's* seemed to have a story on Junior College almost every week. Often it was a story in which the reporter would describe a Junior College initial public offering; how the company seemed to have little or no earnings, scant revenues, problems with its technology or management, no prospect for growth—and its shares would have gone from $10 to $20 or $30 within a few weeks. *Barron's* seemed to indicate that this was typical for a Junior College IPO, and that there was something fishy about it.

The companies that Junior College took public were called "micro-caps" because of their relatively tiny market capitalizations—the total amount of money their stock was worth. Most well-known, decent-sized American companies had market capitalizations in the hundreds of millions, and often in the billions. In contrast, a typical IPO under-written by Junior College might raise $15 million or $20 million worth of capital. The owners would get a few million off the top, Junior College would take a million or two for putting the deal together, and the company would have $8 million to $10 million to spend on research, production, marketing, distribution, capital improvements, and other growth strategies.

My new colleagues, the other brokers, explained all this to me, but I really didn't understand how Junior College worked until I became part of a deal. "I've got a deal coming soon," Larry told me. As a senior vice president, Larry could choose the brokers who would help him when he was in charge of a deal. He liked to work with eight or ten other brokers at a time, two or three of them big pro-ducers who were making $300,000 in gross commissions a year, and the rest younger guys who were making $100,000 to $200,000 a year. He emphasized that they didn't work "as a group." Securities regulations prohibited brokers from working in groups; the danger was that cooperation became collusion and resulted in stock manip-ulation. Later, I saw first-hand how brokers working as a group could indeed cheat clients.

Larry had a deal coming—he was in charge of retailing shares of an IPO to the investing community, in other words—because a Junior College investment banker liked him and respected him. This partic-ular investment banker specialized in IPOs for computer companies, and he threw a lot of his retail business to Larry and a handful of other senior vice presidents. My first deal at Junior College was a classic example of how the firm and its brokers worked.

The IPO was for SmallTech (not its real name), a tiny company with no money but a good idea for a product that would speed up the operating systems for hand-held computers, which were barely off the drawing board in the mid-1990s. The investment banker had arranged for the company's owners to do an IPO underwritten by Junior College. The goal was to float two million shares at $10 each. The banker asked Larry to oversee the selling of one million shares to the public. Another chunk of the shares was distributed to other institutions to sell, and the rest was divided up among the owners of SmallTech, the investment banker who brought the deal to Junior College, and other managers at Junior College.

Larry allocated the one million shares among a dozen other brokers, including me. We all wanted more, of course, because that meant more commissions. On everyday trades, Junior College normally charged a 5 percent gross commission that was divided between the firm and the broker. The "payout," the share of gross commissions that went to brokers, was 50 percent at Junior College, compared to 45 percent at Harvard. On IPOs, however, brokers typically were paid a flat fee, set in advance, which was called a "selling concession" rather than a commission. For SmallTech, the concession for us brokers was twenty-two cents a share, and it was net rather than gross, so I got to keep it all instead of splitting it with Junior College. At the meeting in his office where Larry told each broker how many shares he would get, I could almost hear the mental gears grinding as guys multiplied the number of shares by twenty-two cents. I did it, too. "You'll get sixty thousand shares," Larry told me. My own brain went grind, grind, and came up with $13,200. Some of the guys were moaning, but not me. I was impressed.

Over the next few weeks, because of politicking in the office and begging from other, more senior Junior College brokers who wanted some of the IPO shares to sell, my slice of the IPO dwindled to 20,000 shares. I would rather have had the original 60,000 I was supposed to get, but I didn't complain. Instead I burned the new figures into my brain: If I could persuade enough new accounts to buy all 20,000 of the shares on the day of the IPO, the twenty-two-cent concessions would earn me $4,400 on that one day.

I didn't have any old accounts, so I had to open new accounts for the SmallTech IPO. I was surprised, then, to see the other brokers who had hundreds of existing accounts working almost as hard as I was to open more new accounts for themselves. They told me they would allow some of their existing clients to invest in the SmallTech IPO, but only if they felt like they owed those particular clients a favor, or if it was necessary to keep those accounts and prevent the clients from taking their business somewhere else. "IPOs are too valuable to waste on existing accounts," my new colleagues told me. Not when they were the best enticement for opening new accounts. Those new clients gave us more money under management in our books—and more opportunities to make bigger and better commissions down the road. I picked up the phone and started trying to find future buyers for the 20,000 shares of SmallTech that were allotted to me.

The way I worked at Junior College on that first deal was a lot like the way the Bald Shadow worked at Harvard, except on speed. The whole process was faster, more condensed. I acted as my own cold caller and qualifier, using the same kinds of lead cards that were distributed to cold callers at Harvard:

Hello, Mr. Jones, my name is Rob Burtelsohn. I'm calling from Junior College, a brokerage firm that was founded thirty-six years ago. You've probably heard of my firm. We specialize in bringing small and medium-sized companies to the market,

*often as the underwriter. We specialize in IPOs for emerging
companies. We've got an upcoming initial public offering that
presents a rare opportunity for investors. I've been allocated
a limited number of shares for this IPO. Let me present the
idea to you, and if you find the idea as compelling as I do, there
might be a chance for you to participate . . .*

I'd go on to describe SmallTech briefly. Some other brokers stretched
that part out, talking about the guys who had founded the company, a
little history, something about the product, what else the company
might do in the future. I did it in one sentence. The prospective client
didn't care about the company, the people who started it, or the products they made now or might make in the future. He didn't want to
know any of that. At that point, if he was interested, all he was thinking
about was the big neon sign blinking off and on in his mind: IPO! IPO!
IPO! He knew something about IPOs. He had read and heard about
IPOs, about little stocks that came roaring out and shot up like gey-
sers. But he didn't know how to get to be part of it. Maybe he had
asked his broker about getting in on some of those IPOs. His broker,
who probably worked for one of the old-line, traditional wire houses,
no doubt told him that it was impossible for a small investor like
him to get a piece of an IPO like that; all the shares were parceled
out behind the scenes to insiders, investment bankers, institutional
investors, and a few mega-rich individuals. Now, out of the blue, here's
Rob Burtelsohn on the phone offering him the very opportunity that
his longtime, trusted broker told him he would never see. At last, he
could get a piece of an IPO. But the only place he could get it was
from me.

Within a few weeks, I had made perhaps 10,000 cold calls and had
qualified maybe 200 of them. Some Junior College brokers didn't
bother qualifying potential clients; they'd pitch to anybody who let

them. I thought it would save time and energy to qualify investors the same way I had done at Harvard. I wanted investors who had at least $100,000 in the market, and $10,000 in one single investment. At Harvard, the rule was that to open an account, the new client had to agree to a trade worth at least $5,000. A client couldn't open an account at Harvard with a $2,000 trade. At Junior College, in contrast, a client could open an account with a $500 trade. I didn't mind opening an account with a $2,000 trade, or sometimes even less, but I wanted the investor to be somebody who was likely to invest a lot more later. I did not want "pikers"—small-time clients.

"Can I assume you have half a million dollars in the market, and are willing to put twenty-five, fifty, or a hundred thousand dollars into a single idea?" I would ask. Most potential clients would say no, their portfolios were not that large.

"Well, then, can I assume that your portfolio is fifty to a hundred thousand dollars, and you are willing to put ten, twenty, or thirty thousand dollars into a single idea?" If the potential client said yes, he was qualified and became a lead. If he said no, I thanked him for his time and tore up his card. If a potential client had all his money in mutual funds, no matter how much it was, I thanked him for his time and tore up his card. I didn't want anybody who didn't have at least $100,000 in the market and wasn't willing to invest at least $10,000 in a single stock—even though I couldn't give him $10,000 worth of the SmallTech IPO. I was looking ahead, to building my book by getting my hands on the rest of his portfolio in post-IPO trades.

When I qualified a potential client and he became a lead, I didn't ask for a commitment right then. I asked if I could call back in two or three weeks and make a presentation, after the guy had received a Junior College brochure and other general investment information sent out by the firm. Most of them seemed to think it wouldn't hurt to get some stuff in the mail, and it wouldn't hurt to hear more about an IPO. It wasn't costing them anything—not yet, anyway. I adopted the Bald Shadow's tickler system for reminding myself when to call leads and pitch them on opening an account. As far as I know, no other broker at Junior College ever did that. Those who sat near me saw that I had stacks of cards with dates on them, and that I systematically used them. They knew I had been at Harvard, and started asking me if that was something that was done there. A few other brokers adopted my system.

My patter as a cold caller, qualifier, and pitchman got better and better. Some words or phrases seemed to work really well. *Compelling. Idea. The opportunity to participate.* One trick I used frequently was to ask, "So, what kind of investor are you? Are you a growth investor?" Nobody ever told me he wasn't a growth investor. By offering an IPO, I was giving him the chance to prove it. As I talked I stood at my desk and paced a little, looking down, imagining the prospective client sitting at a little school desk copiously taking notes on everything I said. I envisioned him getting the Junior College packet I would send out to him, tearing it open eagerly, and then sitting down and reading it thoroughly.

I worked hard. Pitching is exhausting, like being onstage in front of an audience, except you're doing improvisation instead of following a memorized script. I tried to space out my pitches, so I didn't do more than three or four in a row. I'd intersperse cold calling, which was not as demanding, or do pitches right before and after lunch or some other work break. I'd pitch from home in the evening, calling leads on the West Coast. Many leads didn't remember talking to me two or three weeks earlier. Why should they? They probably got lots of pitch calls like mine. After all, they had given me information about their portfolios over the phone, and agreed to let me call back. If they'd done it for me, they'd probably done it for 100 other cold callers going through stacks of lead cards just like mine.

I wasn't offended if qualified leads didn't remember me when I called back to make my pitch. I tried to use it to my advantage. "Have you heard anything about SmallTech?" I would ask. This often struck a small chord deep in prospective clients' brains. The only way they could have heard of SmallTech was from me and my cold call two or three weeks earlier. SmallTech sounded familiar. Yeah, they would say, they had heard something about it, even if they couldn't remember where they had heard about it, or what they had heard. I came to learn that even if people who regarded themselves as sophisticated investors did not remember a stock's name, they would often say they had heard of it just so they would look like they were in the know. Knowledge is power, and I was in the empowerment business. When a prospective new account said he had indeed heard of SmallTech, I would say, "I'm not surprised you've heard something. There's been quite a buzz among people who really know the market."

Then I'd make my one-sentence presentation about the company, and start closing. I looked for words that clients might respond to. Some clients liked the concept of *faith*; I would ask if they had faith in the market, faith in technology, faith in American business. Some liked the word *confidence* better. I would try out words, looking for one they would respond to. I never asked about politics, but if I sensed that a client liked the current president or current government economic policies, I might try to use that by pointing out how it was a good atmosphere for investment and growth. If the prospective client didn't like the president or the government economic policies, I might note that thank goodness, Americans could still take a stand and vote with their wallets for good old-fashioned entrepreneurship and conservative business values—by investing in the company I was promoting.

Unless asked, I didn't need to talk about where the stock market was heading or my philosophy of investing. Most prospective clients didn't want to hear that from me. "What is the price of the stock going to be when it is first offered?" they wanted to know.

"How much will it would go up the first day?"

"How much of it can I buy?"

I was careful to avoid specifics. I didn't know much, but I did know it was illegal, and unethical, for a broker to promise a client that a stock would go up a certain amount. A prospective client would ask what the stock would do the first day, and I'd say, "Well, all I can tell you is that the stock is vastly oversubscribed right now. I feel that I could sell twice as much stock if I had it available to sell. I have a lot of money chasing not a lot of stock."

No matter how appealing the pitch, no matter how attractive IPOs were, some prospective clients automatically said they could not invest. No way. Impossible. It could not happen. My response was "Of course it can happen." I developed my own rebuttals tailored to the SmallTech offering. A common reaction was "Well, I don't know anything about that computer technology stuff." I'd fire back, "You know, I don't know much about it, either, but I do know that people who use computers every day are excited about this new technology, and that's all I need to know. Now, I think you should buy five thousand dollars' worth. What do you think?"

I took my best Harvard moves with me to Junior College, and refined them. When a prospective Junior College client committed to buying a certain amount of SmallTech, our relationship changed. We were no longer prospect and salesman. We were client and broker. We were a team. "Mr. Jones—John, may I call you John?—please call me Rob," I would say. Everything after that was *we*, him and me, a team, working together to make him rich. We talked about how *we* thought the market was doing. *Our* philosophy and strategy for *our* investments together. What *we* had heard about these little IPOs. How much SmallTech *we* would buy. How much money *we* wanted to make together.

I asked about the new client's other investments, what else he owned, to get a better idea of his investment style. "So I don't waste time in the future, can you tell me a little more—only if you think it's appropriate at this point—about your portfolio and your investment goals? Maybe you can mention one or two stocks you're holding now to give me an idea of your investment style." Most would tell me about three or four investments. Some would reel off a list of six or eight stock holdings. I would scribble them all down.

In truth, my new client's investment style wasn't all that important to me. I wanted to know what he owned so I could get him to sell it someday. I was anticipating the day when I'd call him with an idea, he'd say he didn't have the money, and I could say, "Hey, look, I know you have twenty thousand dollars' worth of IBM in your account with Harvard. Can IBM offer you a return of ten or twenty percent in a month? Can IBM double in a week, the way this IPO can? Sell that dog IBM and buy what I'm pitching."

I didn't look at the rebuttal book while I was pitching, but I kept a copy nearby and often perused it, looking for quick answers to specific objections. One I liked to use a lot was in response to prospective clients who said they had been in the market before and had been burned. They had lost money, and didn't want to invest. I would sympathize, and reason with them. "You got burned," I said. "I know how that goes. But listen, did you ever eat a piece of pizza and it was too hot, and it burned the roof of your mouth? You did? Sure, it happens to everybody. But you know what? You didn't stop eating, did you? You didn't stop eating pizza, did you?"

Any response from a prospective client was good, from my point of view. I didn't mind if a prospective client thought my arguments and reasoning were ridiculous. If a guy laughed at me, I laughed, too. We both knew it was a ridiculous argument. We had a bond, even if that bond was laughing at me. That tiny crack in the prospective client's reserve was often all that I needed to get him talking—and, more important, listening.

Many clients said they didn't know anything about microcap companies and didn't trust IPOs. Too risky. I had a wonderful response for that: "You know, somewhere along the line, a few people had an opportunity to invest in the IPO of another little company not much bigger than this one. Its name was Microsoft. Sure, some IPOs don't work out, but a lot of them do. I'm not saying this stock is the next Microsoft. But who's to say it's not?"

I tried to sound professional, authoritative, like the Bald Shadow. I tried to speak like him, but with what I thought was the natural warmth in my voice, that little hint of fun and excitement. The BS never seemed to convey any warmth, and especially no fun and excitement. He no doubt would have been shocked at the pushiness of some of my fellow brokers at Junior College when they made their pitches to prospective clients.

Some of them were maniacs to begin with, and they totally bought into Junior College's high-energy, in-your-face approach to doing business. If a prospective client took objection to the pitch, some brokers actually got argumentative or sarcastic. One guy who was particularly aggressive with clients had a favorite line when they became feisty in response. "Hey, there, billygoat, pull those horns back in," he would tell them. A couple of guys occasionally got angry at prospective clients who wouldn't agree to open accounts with them. I once heard one of them cursing a lead.

One Junior College broker went crazy whenever a guy said he had to talk to his wife. When this happened, I always tried to put down my phone and watch and listen. It was quite a show. "Wait a minute!" the broker would shout. "You gotta ask your wife? What are you, a woman? Who wears the pants in your family? Does she ask you to pick out her dresses? Why can't you make your own investment decisions? Aren't you the man?" Usually the prospective client was gone by then, no longer prospective. But if the prospective client gave him some lip right back, the broker would stand up and grab his own crotch. "Hey, man, you need what I got in my hand right now. Balls!"

After the genteel, polite atmosphere at Harvard, I felt like Dorothy telling Toto they weren't in Kansas anymore. I remained polite. Pushy, maybe, but always polite. I figured a lead who had been offended only had to make one phone call to the SEC to file a complaint. Why risk it?

I thought about calling some of the Bald Shadow's accounts and trying to steal them away, but I decided not to do it. I didn't want to piss off the BS. I imagined that he could be a formidable enemy. Besides, I thought I might want to go back to Harvard as a broker someday.

After a couple of months at Junior College, I still hadn't made any commissions and I was feeling as if I had taken a step backward. Harvard had been the big leagues. Junior College was the low minors. I was confused and frustrated. I still saw myself as more of a Harvard guy than a Junior College guy, but it was difficult to maintain the illusion when the broker sitting at the next desk was trying to pitch a client and eat a pastrami sandwich at the same time. "Why can't these guys at least be polite? They're so unprofessional," I grumbled to Larry one night over drinks.

"Listen, you dope," he said. "This firm would rather have some hungry young guy from Staten Island than some Ivy Leaguer. Those overeducated guys think too much. Here, we just make money. If you want to sit around and think, go someplace else. If you want to work hard and make money, this is the place you can do it no matter where you're from." He was right, of course. It was unrealistic to think I could have it both ways—the prestige and class of Harvard, along with the excitement and opportunity at Junior College. Maybe someday I would have both. But for now I was at Junior College.

When I started working at Junior College, I was hoping that the SmallTech IPO would come soon. It didn't. There was one delay after another. "The deal's on hold," Larry would report. I never understood why there were so many delays, except that it appeared that bringing a company to the market was a complicated procedure. Lots of paperwork, lots of requirements, lots of arrangements and negotiations. Meanwhile, Larry kept us brokers psyched up. And he kept us selling. He gave us rosy reports from the company about what its product would do, and brought in the founders of the company to tell us about it. They were good guys who really believed in what they were doing, and they helped us believe in it, too. I found that after getting a briefing from the company, I was always more effective at selling the stock.

By the time I had been at Junior College for two months, I had persuaded fifty-eight clients to commit to buying 200 to 500 shares of SmallTech and opening accounts with me at Junior College. I purposely kept the shares in that 200 to 500 range. I didn't want small-time investors, pikers who would sweat over an investment of fifty shares. And while I wanted big investors, I didn't want a few new accounts to snap up my whole allocation. I probably could have sold my entire 20,000 shares to a half-dozen savvy investors. But I didn't want a half-dozen new accounts. I wanted fifty or sixty new accounts. The more accounts, the more growth potential for my book, for my business. Besides, if an investor was smart enough to know Junior College's history and the history of this kind of IPO, that investor would probably be happy to buy the shares at $10 and sell them the first day at $11 or $12.

But I didn't want my new clients to sell out SmallTech on the first day, even if it meant they would get a 10 or 20 percent profit in a few hours. I didn't want them ever to sell. I wanted them to keep their SmallTech, and buy more of it. And I wanted them to buy more of other stocks, too, so I could build up my book. So when I was pitching a potential investor on buying 500 shares and he said, "Hey, why not five thousand?" I would tell him I wasn't even sure if I could get him the 500. I promised to get him as many as I could, however. I wanted to keep the new clients hungry, eager to buy more stock. I told them that if the stock bolted out of the gates and started going up fast, they might want to consider buying more then. It seemed to me like that was what was going to happen, and I was confident that my new clients were going to make money—if the deal ever came. As the weeks and months dragged on, some of my investors lost interest. I'd call them back to make sure they were still going to open an account, and they'd act like they didn't remember me, or they'd say they had changed their minds. Sometimes I had to sell them all over again. Sometimes they hung up on me and I had to go back to the lead cards to line up more purchasers.

While I was waiting for the SmallTech deal to happen, I was offered another piece of business, another IPO, this one being run by another broker, also a senior vice president at Junior College. Larry had introduced the guy to me in a bar after work, and I had told him I was desperate to get my career going. He took pity, apparently, because the next day he gave me 500 shares of the IPO he was managing, this one for a small company that provided services to the petrochemical industry. I called back a couple of my more promising prospective clients for SmallTech, two guys who seemed to have the most money and the most interest in investing big in IPOs. I told them about the petrochemical deal, and they went for it. I sold one guy 300 shares and the other 200 shares. I told them that the shares would probably be issued at $8, might open at $9 or $10, and could conceivably go straight to $11 or $12. "It's only a tiny deal, but it will introduce you to me and my firm and what we can do for you," I told the investors. The shares did indeed go to $12 the first day, and then made a gradual climb over the next few weeks. The two guys hung onto the stock, and said they were more interested than ever in me and in the SmallTech IPO. I made just a little over $500 in commissions on the two sales, which wasn't much. But it was a big deal to me, my first commissions on my own. In a way, I was more relieved than happy. But it was also a confidence-booster. I figured that after SmallTech came out and made a profit, I'd be able to get a lot more money from those two clients.

• • •

I had one more deal before SmallTech went public. A broker who was supervising an IPO had suddenly taken ill—the word was that he had AIDS—and resigned. He had not yet allocated the two million shares to any brokers, so the office manager took over the chore. He decided every broker in the board room could have up to 50,000 shares. The office manager said the deal was coming within a few days, so there wasn't a lot of time to make dozens of calls. Instead of booking a few hundred shares with lots of new clients over a period of weeks, we should book as many as we could over the next few days, including big sales to individual clients. The office manager didn't want the firm to be stuck with unsold shares when the IPO came.

The IPO was for a company that had a product that supposedly used magnets to relieve a particular foot condition, tendinitis or something. Very New Age. I never really understood what the company did. But that didn't put me off the IPO, or selling the company's stock. I called one of my prospective new SmallTech accounts, a guy who owned used car lots out west someplace. He was a potential whale, I thought, based on what he had told me about his investment history and philosophy. "Hey, Mack," I said, "this new IPO is coming out at three dollars. You should buy fifty thousand shares." I figured, why not start by shooting to sell the whole allotment?

"I got no money," Mack said.

"Okay, Mack," I countered. "Buy forty thousand shares at three dollars."

"I told you," he said. "I got no money."

"Mack, all right, listen," I said. "You should buy thirty thousand shares at three dollars."

He paused for a couple of seconds and then said, "Okay. I can do that."

In less than two minutes, he had gone from not having any money to giving a stranger $90,000. *I love this guy,* I thought to myself. I was elated when I hung up the phone and began filling out the forms, but still found it hard to believe that a man I had never met was about to sit down and write a check for $90,000 to buy shares from me for a company he had not heard of until I had called him a few minutes earlier. I told the other brokers sitting near me in the board room, and they got all excited; $90,000 was a huge trade by Junior College standards. They gathered around my desk, high-fiving me and whooping about the big trade I had just rung up. Some of the brokers took me out for drinks after work. I had a couple of bourbons, and was feeling full of myself. I told them that I was going to call the client back right there, from the bar where we were drinking, and talk him into buying the other 20,000 shares. I actually tried to get the guy, and it was probably lucky that I only reached his voice mail. He might have thought I was being too pushy, and canceled the whole purchase. Two days later, to my amazement, a check for $94,500 landed on my desk. The $4,500 was the gross commission. At the 50 percent payout, my net commission was $2,250. All for one phone call. I felt like I was on my way.

The magnetic-healing company's IPO came the following week. The shares came out at $3 and bumped up to $3.50 on the first day. Mack sold a big piece of his 30,000 shares that first day, which earned me a mini-scolding from several other brokers. Junior College brokers expected new accounts to hang on to their IPO shares and help push up the price even further. "Other brokers are going to be less willing to share IPOs with you in the future if they know you are going to let your clients sell out the first day. It undermines the stock price. We want our clients to always buy, never sell," one colleague told me. I wasn't overly concerned. I still had $60,000 of Mack's money in my book. I was building a business. The deal had given me a good foundation for a long and lucrative relationship with Mack, and that's what it turned out to be. Lucrative for me, anyway. He lost money on his investments while I made money on the commissions.

14

SmallTech

The SmallTech deal still hadn't come after four months. A couple of times the word from Larry was "It's gonna be next week," and once he had us all fired up with "It's gonna be tomorrow." But it wasn't. Each time, the deal was postponed for one reason or another. I was still getting a $3,000 monthly draw, but the agreement giving me a draw was for only six months. I was getting worried—maybe Junior College would kick me out in a couple of months—when Larry walked by my desk and, without stopping, said, "The deal will be next week, Wednesday or Thursday." I had heard it before, but I was nonetheless pumped up. By then I had commitments from 82 new accounts for my 20,000 shares. I had overbooked them, the way airlines do, in anticipation of some people changing their minds at the last minute.

My 82 prospective new accounts going into the IPO was enormous by the standards of Junior College. When I started at Junior College, I had challenged the other brokers who would be selling the SmallTech IPO to a competition: who could open the most new accounts. We put a blackboard on the wall and kept running totals. My eighty-two new accounts blew them away. The next closest was sixty-seven. I remembered the rule of thumb at Harvard: open at least 100 new accounts two years in a row, and you were sure to earn at least $1 million a year in commissions. I was well on my way to 100 new accounts after only six months on the job. I figured that I had made nearly 500 cold calls to get 7 leads to open each new account— more than 40,000 calls in all.

I kept a list of my new accounts, with two columns. One column listed how much stock each new account had said he wanted to buy. The other column listed how much stock I would let each one buy. In all, I probably could have sold those 82 accounts close to 100,000 shares, compared with the 20,000 I had to parcel out. But that was okay. I wanted my new clients to be hungry, and to have some leftover money when I came around offering them more SmallTech stock after the IPO. I wanted them to buy the shares at the opening, and then buy more later.

Each of my 82 prospective accounts got a call from me in the week before the IPO, advising that it was coming. None of them bailed out definitively, but some were pretty shaky.

"I'm buying a boat," one told me.

"I think my wife is about to divorce me," another reported.

One guy had amnesia; he didn't remember anything about me or SmallTech despite our four previous conversations. I couldn't reach several people. I figured that even if half didn't buy when the IPO came, I'd still have 40 new accounts, more than enough to sell my 20,000 shares and still have orders for more shares.

My prospective clients had heard me tell them on previous occasions that the deal was imminent; some of them had heard it three or four times. As always, some of them asked why there had been delays. I had been telling them all along that the delays were good news, not bad news, and I tried to reassure them again. "No, the delays have let the company get all the details straightened out, and have helped really build up the interest. I think there's more demand for the stock now than there was when I first told you about it. I'll get you as much as I can in the first offering, but in the meantime I'll let you know as soon as anything is available if you want to buy more once the stock opens," I told them. I was learning how to put spin on anything to help make a sale. When some of my prospective clients wanted to think that the IPO had been delayed solely because there was so much interest in it, and so much demand for the stock, I didn't correct them. I welcomed their pleas that I give them as much of the stock as I could.

In truth, I really didn't know why the deal had been delayed. Looking back, there might have been some administrative or organizational problems within the company, problems that kept the IPO from getting full and final approval from the regulators. The founders might have been squabbling among themselves over how to divvy up the big pile of money they would get from the IPO. No doubt there were delays when the preliminary prospectus was sent to the SEC, and the SEC asked questions or suggested changes.

Perhaps some of the delays were because Junior College was under investigation for its handling of previous IPOs. Junior College was always under some kind of investigation or another. And it's entirely possible that the delays were solely due to Junior College's strategy—widely reported in the business press—of delaying IPOs just to make investors think the company had problems so that the value of the shares would be driven down at least temporarily. The theory, according to some in the media, was that a lower issue price meant the stock would go up faster when it was finally issued—and create bigger profits for Junior College from the large chunk of the IPO reserved for the firm. I personally saw no evidence of this, and found it hard to believe that Junior College or any brokerage firm would stoop to that kind of manipulative subterfuge.

At least one of the delays might have occurred because Junior College didn't think the market conditions were optimum. IPOs for small companies like this almost never came out on Mondays or Fridays; those were slow days in the market. And right up until the IPO actually happened, it might be postponed if the market was having a bad day. It didn't take much for the market to have a bad day back then. The Dow Jones had to be down only forty points for Wall Street to consider it a bad day. Back then, NASDAQ had a bad day if it was down more than five points.

This time it seemed as if the IPO was really going to happen. That's what Larry told us. He said the regulators had signed off, and it was now up to Junior College to decide when the stock would actually be floated. Larry punched his computer keyboard, and up on the screen popped the symbol for SmallTech. It showed zero price and zero volume, but just seeing it on the screen got me and the other brokers excited. We started whooping and punching each other in the arm, talking about what numbers would be up on that screen for volume and price in the next few days, and about how much money it was going to make for us.

I not only tried to firm up my prospective clients' commitments to buy the IPO's new shares when they were issued, but I also tried to get them to commit a specific amount to buying in the "aftermarket"— to buy more shares of SmallTech after it was issued. "If it's an incredible deal at ten dollars, it's going to be almost as good at eleven or twelve dollars," I told them. "If you can't get all the stock you want at ten dollars, you can still buy more once it's issued. If the stock goes up to thirty or forty dollars, you're not going to be thinking you wished you had bought more at ten. You're going to be glad you bought more at twelve." It was and is illegal to "second-trade" for clients, to execute one trade for them only if they promise to make a certain subsequent trade in the future. I was careful not to link buying shares of the IPO to buying more shares after the IPO, at least not explicitly. I never made any promises that if a client would invest a specific amount in the aftermarket, I would get him a bigger share of the IPO. But on my own, without spelling it out for the clients, I doctored my lists to favor clients who expressed more interest in the aftermarket. When a client who wanted to buy $5,000 worth of shares in the IPO told me he would also buy $20,000 worth of shares in the aftermarket, I scratched out the 500 shares I had next to his name for the IPO and wrote in "1,000." If he was going to be one of my bigger accounts, I wanted to do right by him. When a client who said he wanted to buy $5,000 worth of shares of the IPO told me there was absolutely no way he could buy any shares in the aftermarket, I scratched out his 500 shares and wrote in "200." I wanted to use my allocation wisely.

By Monday of the week the IPO was finally supposed to happen, I had all my ducks in a row. I just needed it to actually happen. The other brokers were ready, too. We were all pumped up, but with nothing to do. We shot baskets on the mini-hoop in a corner of the board room, and played H-O-R-S-E for $5 a letter. One of the guys taught me to play liar's poker with the serial numbers on dollar bills. Another started showing me how to play blackjack—the other brokers couldn't believe I didn't know all these gambling games—when one of them, a big, good-looking guy named Michael, a former college All-American quarterback who was married to a former Miss Georgia, suddenly said, "Hey, let's go to Atlantic City."

Within an hour five of us were in a big white limo rolling down the Garden State Parkway. I had been in limos a few times, for weddings and proms, but this was different. We drank from the car's bar and watched Clint Eastwood videos on its TV, talking about gambling. Michael and a couple of the other brokers were old hands, high rollers, at Atlantic City, and they told me that we were comped at one of the resort hotels that night. Free rooms, free food, free drinks. We blew into Atlantic City, piled out of the limo and into one of the casinos, and hit the blackjack tables. The other guys all used their credit cards to get at least $5,000 worth of chips apiece. I got $500, and was afraid that would max out my card. At the tables, I was scared and nervous about gambling, but did what the other brokers told me. I bet when they said to bet, I folded when they said to fold, and I doubled my bet when they said to double. We gambled for a while, then took a break for dinner and drinks. We had a private dining room. Shrimp cocktail, lobster, champagne, filet mignon. Butlers in uniforms with white gloves served us. It was my first taste, literally, of the extravagant life, of the kind of life I wanted for myself, and it just made me hungry for more. I was drunk, not so much from the wine and liquor but from the whole atmosphere and experience. We had cognac after dinner, then went back to the tables and gambled for a few hours more, until about two in the morning.

We took a private elevator up to the suite. I had never seen a room like this. You could have put a bowling alley in it. Maybe eight or nine lanes. Everything was marble and ceramic and mirrored. There were gaudy statues, a wraparound couch, a balcony overlooking the ocean, a big-screen TV, and a whirlpool bath large enough for all of us guys to fit in for a nightcap and cigar. One of the guys turned the TV onto CNBC, and we pretended to watch the stock prices rolling across the screen. But we weren't, really. None of our accounts included any of the stocks rolling across the screen. I still didn't even own any stocks myself. I was a stockbroker who had never owned any stock.

That night at Atlantic City I ended up winning about $100, and I was riding high. Free cash. I saw it as a good sign. Money was coming my way. I would be making a lot more in a couple of days, when the IPO came. Michael won a grand, and gave most of it away in tips. A couple of the brokers lost heavily, or what seemed heavily to me, between $2,000 and $3,000 each. But it didn't seem to bother them. They joked about it. The next morning, riding back to New York in the limo, the two brokers got into a contest, seeing who could be the first to make up his losses with commissions. They got out their cell phones and started calling customers. I learned that this was a tradition for Junior College brokers who had lost money in Atlantic

City. A few months later I returned to Atlantic City with a couple dozen Junior College brokers on a firm outing, and on the way back it was an incredible commotion: a busload of hungover brokers all shouting at each other to shut up, and then over the din on cell phones trying to persuade their clients to agree to trades.

After that first trip to Atlantic City, we took the limo straight back into the office that day, Tuesday, but just goofed around, waiting for the IPO to come either the next day or the day after that. When I got home that evening, Melanie wanted to know all about my Atlantic City adventure. I told her everything, except about making $100. My dad went on gambling and golf trips to Las Vegas with some old buddies once a year—it was a tradition—and when he got home he always told my mother that he broke even. And that's what I told Melanie.

We sat around all day Wednesday, waiting for the SmallTech deal to come. I killed time, I grumbled. For the umpteenth time, I noticed how uncomfortable my chair was, how scratched my desk was. Was the deal coming or not? Thursday morning was more of the same, until just before noon when Larry strolled by my desk and said, "The deal is coming just after one o'clock." At a few minutes before one, we brokers all gathered around the computer on one guy's desk, watching the blinking screen that had the SmallTech symbol but zero for the price and zero for the volume. One o'clock came and went. 1:04. 1:06. I fidgeted and muttered. Suddenly, at 1:07, a number popped onto the screen replacing the zero for the price. It was $10.50 bid by $11 asked. Okay. The opening price was $11. That meant that brokers had been placing orders to buy the stock even before shares were actually available. The shares, which were being issued at $10, were already up 10 percent.

We stared intently, as if willing the price to move. After another minute, it did: $10.75 by $11.25. "Shit," I said almost under my breath. "It's flat." A couple of other guys looked at me like I was nuts. I guess I was thinking it would click right up to 11 and then 12 within seconds. But it didn't happen like that. It took minutes, not seconds. $11.50, $11.75, $12. "The Street's taking it," one broker said, his voice cracking with excitement. He meant that institutional investors and other brokerage houses were snapping up shares of SmallTech. Whether because they believed in the company and its product or they believed that a Junior College IPO was sure to go up on the first day, it didn't matter to me. All that mattered to me was that I could start calling my prospective new accounts and tell them that every $100 of SmallTech they had committed to buy was already worth $120.

"All right," somebody said, breaking our reverie. "Let's go to work, you guys." I hurried back to my desk and nervously began making phone calls to my eighty-two accounts. I wasn't sure that they—any of them—would really send in the money. I felt as if I had been dragging them through the mud for months with this deal; maybe they were sick of me and sick of hearing about SmallTech. If I couldn't book the IPO stock, I'd have to try to palm it off on other brokers. If that happened, my Junior College career, and my career as a stockbroker, would be over by the end of that afternoon. Even worse, what if my new clients said they would indeed buy the stock, but then didn't send in their money by the settlement deadline a few days later? In that case, I would either have to find someone else to buy the stock, or I would own it myself, personally.

I couldn't believe how well it went. I reached maybe two-thirds of my new accounts, about fifty of them, and all but two reacted positively and said they would send in the money. And why not? With the stock at $12, they were up 20 percent. That was a pretty good profit for a couple of hours. Of the two clients who said no, one said he had just been in an auto accident and couldn't think about SmallTech at that moment. The other, the guy getting a divorce, said his wife had frozen all his bank accounts and all he had was the money in his pocket, which he hoped would be enough to get drunk on that night.

Every time a client agreed to a trade, I scribbled down the details—wrote a ticket—on an order form. When I wrote my first ticket for the SmallTech order, I jumped up from my desk and literally ran it down the hall and then down the stairs to the trading department, where I turned it in to a clerk at a window. The trading department would execute the trade, and then send a confirmation form back to my desk.

Meanwhile I ran back upstairs, called another client, wrote another ticket, and ran it back down. Pretty soon I was running back down with three or four tickets at a time, then five or six. When another broker saw me heading down and handed me his tickets, I took them down. Next time he went down, I handed him mine. I was writing tickets and running down the stairs as fast as I could. "I could have done even more business if I had practiced running stairs to get in shape," I told Melanie that night.

Most of the clients expressed disappointment that they weren't getting more stock, but I reminded them that the IPO was vastly oversubscribed, and that I had pulled some strings just to get them a portion of the shares they would have liked to have ordered. "Hey, I know you told me you wanted two thousand shares," was my typical response, "but I had to fight to get you three hundred. You can always buy more shares in the aftermarket. They're around $12 now. How many do you want?" Most of my new accounts were greedy. They could have taken their tidy quick little 20 percent profits and run. But no. They had IPO fever, and they were ready to invest more.

A few clients did want to sell out. I tried to talk them out of it, and in most cases I was successful. First I tried to persuade them to buy more, and some did. If they still wanted to sell, I tried to persuade them to hold what they had, and some did. "Just hang on another day, and let's see what happens," I urged. "One more day. If it goes up another dollar or two, you'll be sorry you sold. You're ahead anyway.

You're playing with the house's money at this point." If they still wanted to sell, I appealed to their sense of ethics and fairness. "This wasn't part of our plan," I said. "We were going to play this game together as a team, but now you want to take your ball and go home." In the end, only a handful of my new clients sold out, and I quickly placed their shares with other new clients.

When the stock went up to $12 so quickly, I had high hopes that it might run like a wild dog. I could see it hitting $20 that first afternoon. Other IPO stocks had doubled on the first day. But SmallTech didn't. The stock stayed around $12 most of the afternoon. "We're not done," I kept telling my clients. "I think we should buy more . . . if we can get it." The idea that the stock was still hard to get was enticing, and most clients said they wanted to buy more. With a dozen other brokers telling their clients the same thing, and getting the same enthusiastic response from their clients, it became a self-fulfilling prophecy. The demand drove the stock up. By the end of that first day, SmallTech closed at $12.50. Some of my clients actually called me during the day, and even after the market closed, asking if I thought SmallTech was doing to continue to go up, and whether I thought I could get any more stock for them. My answers, of course, were yes and yes.

15

The 50 Percent Broker

I probably learned more about being a stockbroker during that first afternoon of the SmallTech IPO than I had ever learned about anything in any other month of my life. One of the most important things I learned was that the Junior College trading department was a profit center, and making money from hidden commissions was part of the traders' jobs. Their own income depended on how much they earned for the firm by trading the spread. I knew all about spreads and hidden commissions, or I thought I did, from Harvard, and watching the Bald Shadow tell the trader "with a half" to make sure there was a fifty-cent spread—and thus a fifty-cent hidden commission—between the bid and asked prices.

At Harvard, the BS and other brokers sold shares in any company they wanted, not just stocks for which Harvard made a market. At Junior College, I sold only stocks in which the firm was a market maker, buying and selling the stock in and out of its own account. By making a market in SmallTech after the IPO, Junior College's trading department could set the bid and asked, buying shares for $6 and selling them for $6.25 or $6.50 or whatever it could get for them. The client who bought shares at $6.50 never knew the firm had bought them for $6, and that the price included a hidden commission that was split between the firm and the broker.

What I didn't realize until the first day of the SmallTech IPO was that Junior College's trading department did this automatically. Unlike the Bald Shadow, I didn't have to say "with a half" or issue any other instructions. The Junior College traders made a significant part of their own income from commissions hidden in the spread, so they routinely skimmed off the twenty-five or fifty cents, which in turn meant higher commissions for me. I saw this immediately on that first day when I began getting confirmations of the trades I had made in the aftermarket. I was overjoyed. I was going to be making more money than I thought; not just the 5 percent standard commissions, but also an additional nickel or dime or quarter or half-dollar on every share I sold.

It didn't occur to me that this was unfair to my clients. It was the way things were done. There was nothing illegal or unethical about it, as far as I knew. Everyone did it. Apparently customers didn't know or care. At least, they never complained. Indeed, the Junior College way of handling spreads, as a routine part of business, seemed a lot cleaner to me than the Bald Shadow's way of ordering trades held up until he got the hidden commission he was looking for, even if it meant the stock price went up and the client paid a higher price. Spreads were part of an open and free market. If my clients didn't buy the stock with a hidden commission, somebody else's clients would, and they would get the benefit when the stock went up. I would have been doing my clients a disservice by not letting them buy shares if I thought the spread would be too high. And I would have been keeping money out of my own pocket.

On my last trade that first day, one of my clients instructed me to buy him 1,000 shares of SmallTech. The price was $12 bid by $12.50 asked. I put in the order, and when the confirmation came back it showed that the client bought the shares at $12.50 and would pay

$12,500 plus a 5 percent commission of $625. The client's trade confirmation showed that it cost him $13,125. There was no way the client could know that he was paying a $500 hidden commission—fifty cents per share. Instead of a net commission of $312.50 (50 percent of $625), I actually netted $562.50 (50 percent of $1,125). I had no complaints about that, and didn't think the client should, either.

Another thing I learned that first day was the way that other Wall Street firms, even the big, well-known brokerages, the wire houses, dabbled in speculative microcap IPOs such as SmallTech. The more experienced brokers at Junior College were constantly monitoring the trading screens to see which firms were buying and selling shares in SmallTech. If Merrill or Lehman or another big brokerage was on either the bid or the asked, they were ecstatic. It was an indication that "the Street," meaning other brokerage houses, was showing interest. That meant more volume, more liquidity, and more demand for the stock. It also meant the stock was probably going to go higher, at least for a while. When Junior College was the only firm making a market and we were the only brokers buying and selling the stock, it was harder to keep up the demand and the price.

Sometimes firms whose names I didn't recognize were on the bid or the asked. "Who are these guys?" I asked the other brokers. They explained that these were trading firms, smaller brokerage houses that were merely jumping in and out of the stock, scalping quick profits of an eighth or sixteenth of a dollar. Those firms had come to expect that Junior College IPOs would go up the first day or two, and they were just nipping in and out, skimming quick profits here and there. The trading firms were helping demand and liquidity at the moment, the other brokers told me, but in a day or two the other Wall Street firms probably wouldn't be interested anymore and would disappear from the screens.

• • •

Going into the SmallTech IPO, I believed I would be selling shares, and that was it. It turned out to be much more complicated. What were being issued, and what I was selling my clients, were not single shares of the company. I was selling "units" that included two shares of common stock and four warrants. Each warrant was in effect an option allowing the holder to buy a share of SmallTech common stock at a specific price after some future date. In SmallTech's case, at the time of the IPO, the unit was valued at $10. The two shares of common stock within the unit were valued at $4 each. The warrants were valued at 50 cents each and could be converted to a share of common stock for $2.50 if the common stock remained above $5 for any thirty consecutive days. It was a way for SmallTech to encourage investors to participate in the IPO, and to raise more money later and reward those IPO investors if the stock did well.

After the first tick of the IPO, when the $10 units were floated, clients had a choice of what they could buy. They could buy units, common shares, warrants, or some combination. All three prices moved independently, but in relation to each other. That first afternoon, I was concentrating on selling units, but I heard other brokers near me talking about warrants. I was confused. At the end of the day, one of the younger brokers showed great patience in explaining that I could "strip out" the warrants from the SmallTech shares in Junior College's own inventory. As long as Junior College's trading department had 1,000 units in inventory—or I could convince another of my clients to sell 1,000 units—I had the possibility of selling up to 2,000 common shares and 4,000 warrants instead of 1,000 units. Or some combination of shares and warrants. It was a revelation to me. Suddenly I had a lot more to sell. All those clients who had said they would be interested in buying in the aftermarket suddenly had more to buy.

Warrants carried big commissions, 30 percent in the case of Small-Tech. For each warrant I sold for 50 cents, I got 15 cents. I didn't tell my clients how much I was getting when I started pitching warrants to them on Friday, the day after the IPO. I don't think they would have cared if I had told them. I was sure that some of them didn't understand what warrants were. Part of that was no doubt due to my clumsy explanations. But part of it was that they simply didn't have the patience or interest in knowing what a warrant was. They only wanted to know how much they could invest, and how much they could make as the price of SmallTech continued to go up.

After closing at $12.50 on the first day, the SmallTech unit price bumped up slowly but steadily on Friday, the second day of trading, to close at $14 for the weekend. I couldn't see any reason it wouldn't keep going up, and nobody at Junior College told me otherwise, so I kept calling clients and urging them to buy more. Knowing about the hidden commission from the spreads, I had all the incentive I needed to keep flogging the stock. I quickly got used to the idea that if I sold 1,000 shares my gross commission would be the usual 5 percent plus at least $250 and maybe $500, depending on whether the spread was a quarter or a half-dollar.

Virtually all the 20,000 shares of the IPO that I had booked were still in my book, and now worth $280,000. With the portfolios of Mack and the two small accounts I had opened previously with the 500 shares of the petrochemicals company IPO, I suddenly had more than $350,000 under management. That was the start of a business. I began to see how I could make a lot of money at Junior College— much more, and much faster, than I could have made at Harvard.

At the end of the day on Friday, I tallied what I had earned from the SmallTech IPO. First there was the twenty-two-cents-a-share concession on the 20,000 shares of stock I sold to new accounts: $4,400 net. In the aftermarket, adding up all the additional 5 percent commissions, plus the spreads on the common stock and the warrants, I had rolled up $33,644 more in gross commissions, which at 50 percent netted me $16,822. I had earned more than $21,000 in two days of work. I regarded those two days as my first as a real broker. I counted on a lot more days like those.

The new month, in terms of commissions, started the next Monday, four days after the SmallTech IPO. I didn't know what to expect. Maybe that two-day IPO flurry was both the beginning and the end of the SmallTech excitement. I really didn't know whether I'd be able to make any more trades, especially since essentially all I was doing was calling my clients over and over and asking them to buy more Small-Tech. It was my only strategy, and I didn't know if it would continue to work, or for how long.

I shouldn't have worried. It took me only four days to make $25,000 more in gross commissions. By the middle of the month, when I got my paycheck for $21,000 and change from the first two days of the IPO, I was past $35,000 in gross commissions for the new month. The SmallTech price kept going up, and I kept selling more and more of it to my new clients. My gross commissions for the second month were $46,000—$23,000 for the firm, $23,000 for me. In six weeks I went from being nearly broke to being one of the top 1 percent of earners in America.

When I got that next check, for $23,000, it still seemed hard to believe I was making that kind of money. I stopped by the bank to make a deposit, went to the gym for a workout, and then waited at home for Melanie. "They gave me the money again," I told her. Until then, it seemed like that first month had perhaps been a one-time thing. But it wasn't. It was as if a huge load was lifted from Melanie and me. We wouldn't have to scramble around to make the next month's rent. We wouldn't have to look through the pockets of the coats in the closet to scrape up enough money to pay for the dry cleaning. We could go the movies and out to dinner without worrying about whether we'd be able to eat lunch the following week.

Melanie had a great attitude about all the money I was suddenly making, and kept it from going to my head too much. She didn't treat it as real. Now that I was making big money, I figured I would make big money the rest of my working life. I didn't see anything wrong with starting to spend as if I would always be a big earner. Melanie, on the other hand, thought of our sudden boost in income as a windfall. She wanted to put it away, save it, and create a nest egg. She made me see the wisdom of not making any big new financial commitments, like moving to a bigger, fancier apartment. But she didn't object to my spending some of the money on relatively minor luxuries.

Up until then, I had been getting my shoes shined only once a week or so from the shoeshine guy who came through the office every afternoon. I became a daily customer. There was also a guy who came around once a month or so and hand-tailored shirts for the bigger brokers. I had him take my measurements and ordered two shirts from him, boldly striped numbers with the white collar. They cost $150 apiece, but I only wore each one once. They were too tight, too tailored. I liked my shirts nice and roomy. For the first time, Melanie and I started to think about financial security. We also talked about a vacation, a new car, new clothes, maybe some jewelry, some art. But we didn't rush out and buy anything. "Let's just leave it in the bank for a while," we agreed. Funny, looking back, one thing we never discussed in my early days as a broker was investing in the stock market. To me, that was still something for other people, for clients, not for people like us.

Besides, most of the Junior College brokers I worked with had lost money in the market. The bulk of their investments had been in the same companies they had helped to take public. They bought them on the way up, like they told their clients to do, and then held them on the way down, like they told their clients to do. I didn't think that would happen with SmallTech, but I wasn't prepared to risk my own cash to find out. I thought it was dangerous to have both my business and my personal finances tied up in the same investments. If Small-

Tech's stock collapsed and all my clients lost their money, I would have to rebuild my business. But at least my own money would be safe. Losing both my clients' and my own money would have been a double whammy. I didn't like the idea of losing their money, but I really hated the idea of losing my own.

16

New Issue Whores

During the next few weeks, I sold SmallTech shares almost exclusively. I called back clients who had purchased shares in the IPO, and sold them more. I called back clients who had purchased shares in both the IPO and the aftermarket, and sold them more. I called back leads who had turned down the IPO, and sold them SmallTech for the first time. I didn't say, "I told you so," but they got the message: They would have made money if they had listened to me. And I kept cold calling, and kept pitching SmallTech to leads who qualified. It was easy during those first few weeks because SmallTech kept going up—no big dramatic jumps, just a nice steady climb. A quarter-point, a half-point a couple days later, another quarter-point the week after that. When it dipped a quarter or a half one week, it was back up a point or two within a couple of weeks.

I loved my job. It was easy. I was selling shares in a company I believed in. The stock climbed through the teens and into the twenties in those first weeks. I saw no reason it wouldn't go to 50, 60, or 70, like some Junior College technology stocks had in years past. As a true believer, I found it easy to convince clients to hold the stock, and buy more. Usually all I had to do was tell them I thought the stock was going to keep going up. That was enough to persuade them to hold or buy.

On a number of occasions clients called me and asked me to sell some or all of their SmallTech, and instead I talked them into buying more. A few times clients told me to sell because they had doubts about the company: SmallTech really only had one product, right? SmallTech really hadn't sold anything yet, right? SmallTech was still in the process of getting government approvals, right? The owners of the company hadn't really said what they were going to do with the IPO money, right?

"Give me an hour," I would tell the wavering client. I'd call the company, talk to one of the co-founders, and then get back to the client with reassurances straight from the horse's mouth. The owners said three more products were in development and would be rolled out soon. The owners expected to make their first sales soon, and had revised upward their revenue forecast for the next year. The owners said government approval was imminent. The owners had big expansion and marketing plans for the IPO money; they weren't simply putting it in their pockets. I would reassure the client, and then work on persuading the client to hold or buy. I'd remind my clients of stories about people whose $10,000 investments in unknown startups had turned into millions. Why not SmallTech? Why not my clients? I saw myself being known far and wide as a broker who made lots of money for his clients. My business would thrive.

Looking back, I never thought that I might have been gathering and disseminating and using insider information that wasn't available to the general public. Nor did it occur to me that the company managers might have been misleading me to build up interest among investors—and line their own pockets when the share price went up. In my youthful ignorance, I really believed everything good and positive about SmallTech, and that I was doing what was best for my clients. I never envisioned what would happen if SmallTech's one product flopped, or if the owners of the company decided that they really would prefer to put their IPO money in their own pockets instead of reinvesting it in the company. Without realizing it, what I was doing was not so much right for my clients, but right for Junior College. If nobody ever sold a stock, that stock would never go down in value. If clients only bought, the stock would go up, and they would buy more. And every time they bought more, Junior College and its brokers would earn a commission, and the amount of clients' money they controlled would increase.

My book grew to more than 100 clients through the summer. I kept selling them SmallTech, but it began to get harder. Part of the reason was that the original units in the IPO were being broken up, so there was more to sell: two shares of common stock and four warrants for every unit. Plus the share price had performed well enough to exercise the warrants and convert them into common stock. A single unit became six shares of common stock. There was a lot more SmallTech stock around. Six months after the IPO, the stock peaked at $38. Along the way, when clients wanted to sell out, I still tried to talk them out of it, but not very hard. I let them sell, unlike some of the other Junior College brokers, who did everything they could to talk their clients out of selling. Some of the other brokers would grumble at me about allowing my clients to sell; they were afraid it would hurt the share price. "Your clients should be buying, always buying. You should never let them sell. If you let them sell, you're not doing your job," one fellow broker told me in a tone of voice that was somewhere between unfriendly and downright menacing.

After hitting that peak of 38, SmallTech began dropping. Within a month it was down to 30, and the month after that 25. I kept expecting it to bounce back, and kept selling clients on buying more. I had made some crude graphs showing how the SmallTech price had gone up and up, slipped back a point or two, and then gone up and up again. I referred to these as "my charts," and gave them great gravity when speaking to my clients. "My charts show this is the pattern," I told clients. "Three or four steps ahead, one step back, three or four steps ahead. This is one of those steps back. It's a perfect time to buy, according to my charts."

I believed all this. I didn't know any better. I didn't realize until later that one of the reasons that the share price dropped back was that some big holder—maybe one of the owners of the company, maybe Junior College, maybe anyone who had a significant stake in the company—had begun selling sizable chunks of SmallTech stock. If I had read my charts correctly, I would have seen that the steps backward were occurring more frequently, and that the rebounds upward were not coming as quickly. It didn't occur to me that people who had the biggest stakes in the company were taking their profits, getting out while the getting out was good. I still envisioned SmallTech becoming a force in its technology niche.

As the stock slunk down to 15, then 14, I was having more trouble selling it, and more trouble persuading clients to hold on. When it stumbled to 10 on the one-year anniversary of the IPO, I had a brief flurry of success in convincing existing clients that this was a buying opportunity. The first blush was off the rose, I told them; the early profit-takers, the nonbelievers, they were cutting and running. Those of us who believed in the company should be buying now, I told them. Some did. But many didn't. And when the price lurched down into single digits, I became more insistent, and more aggressive in arguing with clients who wanted to sell. My job wasn't fun anymore. If I couldn't talk clients out of selling, I at least tried to keep their money in my book. I didn't want them cashing out, taking their money to some other broker at some other brokerage. I decided to start recommending other stocks. The Bald Shadow was always recommending three or four or five different stocks. If I did that, it would be easier to keep my clients from cashing out.

For a while I thought I really would be able to build a business like the Bald Shadow's, selling blue-chip stocks to lots of different clients. But that wasn't feasible at Junior College. The company was set up for microcap IPOs and their aftermarket, not for trading blue chips. It took a lot of money, a lot of buying power, to make markets in high-volume blue-chip stocks. It also took a lot of manpower in the trading department, lots of traders who could quickly handle lots of trades. With that high volume of trades, wire houses could afford to have lower profit margins, including lower commissions. Junior College and other small brokerages had neither that kind of money nor that kind of man-power. They would be overwhelmed if they started handling those kinds of trades. They had to pick their spots, and trade lower volumes with higher margins.

The first time I tried to put one of my Junior College clients into a blue-chip stock, I got an irate call from the trading department. "Whaddya doing?" growled one of the fat Irishmen who worked there. "We don't handle this shit." He explained, if that's the right word, that Junior College charged its brokers additional fees for any trades involving stocks for which the firm did not make a market. Not only would I lose my hidden commissions from the spread, but depending on the trade, I could end up paying money out of my own pocket to put my clients into non–Junior College stocks. Junior College bro-kers traded the stocks that Junior College had taken public, and that was pretty much it.

Junior College wasn't about serving clients. Neither was Harvard, or any other brokerage, for that matter. They were all about making money for themselves. But Junior College was different in being so blatant. Unlike Harvard and the big-name, traditional wire houses, Junior College wasn't interested in customers who called their brokers and gave them instructions or asked their advice: Buy this. Sell that. What's your recommendation on this or that? Junior College didn't want to sell blue-chip stocks. Blue chips had a huge volume; millions of shares traded every day. With that kind of liquidity, the bid-asked spread was tiny—a sixteenth of a dollar, a thirty-second. Mere pennies. It wasn't worth the trouble, especially when the typical blue-chip stock traded for $30, $60, $100, or more.

An investor could spend $10,000 on 100 shares of a blue chip, and if the spread was a sixteenth of a dollar—6.25 cents—his hidden commission would be $6.25 for the whole deal. Junior College was more interested in low-liquidity stocks, the microcap companies that it had taken public, and for which it made markets—and controlled the spreads. Junior College liked stocks that traded for $2.50 with a 25-cent bid-ask spread. If an investor bought $10,000 worth of that stock, the hidden commission could be $1,000.

I quickly abandoned the idea of building a Harvard-style business within the walls of Junior College. It wouldn't work. I'd go broke. If I was going to make good money—keep making good money—I would have to do it the Junior College way, at least while I was at Junior College. I began looking at other stocks in companies that the firm had taken public previously, and for which it still made markets. Those stocks had decent spreads—an eighth of a dollar, a quarter, even a half sometimes—that would allow me to keep making good money.

Most of the other Junior College stocks weren't in any better shape than SmallTech. Typically, they had their IPOs, roared up the charts for a while, and then gradually sank back. Pretty much everything I was selling was stagnant. But it wasn't hard for me to believe the positive stories about those companies that I got from other brokers, and from the managers and owners of those other companies. I believed in these other companies the same way I had believed—and still believed, at that point—in SmallTech. With a fistful of new stocks and new stories, and the conviction to sell them, it wasn't hard to convince my clients to take my recommendations and buy another Junior College stock. Even those who had bought more SmallTech when it was in the mid-twenties were surprisingly eager to take my recommendations. They were down at the moment, but because the stock had gone up so much they still regarded it as a winner. And they regarded themselves as winners for picking it. Maybe they rationalized their current negative position by telling themselves they should have sold out. In any case, they were happy to buy other Junior College stocks from me. None of the stocks I was recommending were moving significantly, except for SmallTech, which was moving down. But my business continued to be solid as I took my clients in and out of microcap stocks in which Junior College made markets.

After notching gross commissions of more than $30,000 in the month of the SmallTech IPO, and more than $40,000 the following month, my gross monthly commissions were $35,000, $12,000 (I took two weeks of vacation in the Hamptons), $33,000, and $29,000. Half of that was mine. It was an amazing amount of money. The only thing more amazing was how quickly I got used to it, and saw myself as a big producer, a heavy hitter. I was troubled by the trend, however. My commissions had gone down steadily since the IPO.

"I need a new IPO," I told Larry.

"So do I," he said grimly.

There were no IPOs coming from Larry or any of the other senior brokers who had given me pieces of their deals in the past. My connections were running dry. However, one group of brokers at the other end of the board room seemed to have one IPO after another. I'd see and hear the excitement in their group as an IPO came out and ran up. I'd see and hear them crowing about their big trades, their fat commissions. I'd see and hear them celebrating in the bars after work. It was making me crazy.

I resorted to scrambling around, sucking up to other senior vice presidents, all but begging them for pieces of their IPOs. I had better luck than some of the other young brokers who didn't have longtime connections, maybe because I was regarded as a rising star, and acted like one. The rule at Junior College was that if a broker generated $400,000 in gross commissions over any twelve consecutive months, he was named a vice president. With close to $200,000 in commissions in the first five months after the SmallTech IPO, I had a good chance, and a lot of the senior brokers in the firm seemed to know it.

By scrambling and schmoozing and doing whatever I could, I snared little pieces of several IPOs from other senior VPs at Junior College over the next few months. One day when I was busy opening accounts for an IPO, I got a call from a woman. "We have mutual friends," she said. "They told me to call you. They said you're a hot young broker." She didn't tell me who the mutual friends were, but I didn't care. She wanted to do business, and I needed clients. The woman introduced herself as Naomi. "My father is a prominent doctor on Long Island," she said. "He has always been an active investor, but his longtime broker recently passed away, and he's unhappy with the brokerage firm's choice as a replacement. So my dad has asked me to scout around and help him recruit a new broker. Are you interested in meeting me and talking about his portfolio?"

Of course I was.

We met in one of those yuppie bars on the Upper East Side. Naomi was drop-dead gorgeous. I told her about Melanie, just to make sure there was no confusion, and then started pitching her. I didn't have any women clients, but I figured I'd take anybody who had the money to buy shares. Even women. I started pitching her on the IPO I was working on. We talked about other stocks, but Naomi kept bringing the conversation back to the IPO, and said both she and her dad, the doctor, might want to buy shares. We had a couple of drinks, I gave her my card, and she said she'd be in touch. The next day, I told one of the older brokers about how a client had turned the tables and cold-called me. I thought it was funny. He waved his hand in dismissal. "You dumb shit, you don't get it, do you?" he said with a grimace. "She's a whore."

I was dumbstruck. Naomi was a prostitute? She seemed so nice, so normal. I confessed that I had never personally known a working girl, but Naomi certainly didn't fit the image in my mind. Besides, she had flirted a little, but she had never mentioned sex. "Not a prostitute whore," the other broker said. "Not a sex whore. She's a new issue whore." He explained, as if talking to a child, that new issue whores, men or women, were people who did everything they could to get as much of an IPO as they could. "But instead of investing in the company, buying the stock and holding it, and buying more in the aftermarket, new issue whores sell out early, in the first day or two. They take their profits and run," the other broker told me.

That was not good for brokers like us for two reasons. One, it didn't build our business. I opened all those new accounts on IPOs thinking I would keep the new accounts as clients, and gradually get them to invest more with me, to give me more of their portfolios, and to build my book. Two, it hurt the share price. I didn't want anyone selling unless I advised him—or her—to sell because it would hurt demand, and lower demand would hurt the share price. The lower the share price, the less I could sell, the lower the commissions, and the lower the spreads that created hidden commissions.

"This Naomi broad doesn't have a daddy who's a doctor who needs a broker to manage his huge portfolio," the other broker told me. "She called you for one reason, and one reason only—because she thought you might get her a piece of an IPO." I found it hard to believe that Naomi was that kind of person. I still found it hard to believe when she called me at my office the next day and said she wanted to buy $50,000 worth of the IPO.

"If it looks like the stock is going to do well, Daddy might want to buy a lot more. I think he mentioned the figure of two hundred thousand dollars," she said. I was wary, but I wanted to believe her, that she and her dad were aftermarket whales. I think I also wanted to prove the other broker wrong. But when the IPO came, I was still a little suspicious, a little cautious. I told her all I could get for her was $5,000 in the IPO, but there would be plenty more available in the aftermarket. On the first day, when its value leaped to almost $7,000, I called Naomi. "Do you and your dad want to buy more?" I asked her.

"No," she said. "Not yet. Maybe tomorrow. I'll talk to Daddy and get back to you."

The next day, when the value of her stock was nearing $8,500, Naomi called me and told me to sell it.

I couldn't believe it. "We had a deal," I protested. "We were going to be a team. You were going to buy more. Your dad was going to buy more. You were going to be in for the long haul."

"Listen, mister, if you don't sell my stock right away, and if you don't sell it at the price on my screen at this very moment, I'm going to complain to the Junior College trading department, the National Association of Securities Dealers, and the Securities and Exchange Commission," Naomi said, her voice icy.

Her screen, I thought miserably. She knew all the buttons to push. I knew I had been had. I sold her out for the listed price—no spread, no hidden commission for me. A whore had claimed another virgin.

I went back to the broker who had warned me about Naomi and confessed how stupid I had been. He told me a little more about new issue whores. He showed me Junior College's list with the names and addresses of known new issue whores. Such lists were common, and were probably shared among brokerage houses that underwrote microcap IPOs. Naomi wasn't on the list, but the other broker told me that new issue whores often changed their names and addresses, and used fake Social Security numbers or set up phony investment firms or corporations to get their hands on IPO shares. "They aren't really big investors," he said. "Most of them have tiny portfolios, if they have a portfolio at all." He said the only thing I had done right was not give Naomi the $50,000 worth of stock she wanted originally. He was sure she would have bought even more if I had offered it. He said a smart, aggressive—sneaky—new issue whore could get a piece of ten or twelve new issues a year and make a quick $10,000 or $20,000 in each of them. "Hey," he said. "It beats working."

17

Alfred's Deal

One of the ways that the Junior College board room was like a high school locker room was the way that brokers gave each other nicknames. Some were clever, but most were obvious, based on physical characteristics. One broker reminded somebody of Alfred E. Neuman from *Mad* magazine—which was about the level of recreational reading for most Junior College brokers—so everybody called him "Alfred." Despite the freckles, curly hair, and protruding ears, Alfred was a big broker, a senior vice president. He supervised an IPO every six or eight months. I sucked up to the guy, even calling him by his real name instead of his nickname, and he began giving me small pieces of his deals.

One of Alfred's IPOs was for a small software design company. Technology IPOs were hot, particularly for little companies like this that had anything to do with the World Wide Web. There was no reason to think that Alfred's IPO wouldn't come out of the blocks fast and have a nice run. As usual, I read what was handed out about the company, listened to what Alfred said about it, and attended the briefings he set up for us brokers with the founders of the company. Like most other Junior College IPOs, it had one product—well, more of an idea, actually, than a real product—and, to that point, no revenue, no sales, not even any orders. As usual, I bought the story. The little software design company sounded good. I was an optimist, especially if being optimistic could help me make some money. The concession for the IPO was twenty cents per share. "Okay, young Rob, you can have four thousand shares," Alfred told me. I was hoping for more. After all, it was in his interest to have more brokers opening more accounts, and creating more liquidity and more demand when the stock opened.

Every day Alfred came by to see me, and every day he made me promise to sell my new accounts not only the IPO shares, but also shares in the software design company after it was floated, in the aftermarket. I assured him I would sell a lot of aftermarket shares; I had done it with SmallTech, and I would do it with his IPO, too. No, I assured Alfred, I would not allow any of my new accounts to sell out his IPOs. I would have them buy more, I told Alfred. I knew that if I did let any significant number of my new accounts sell out the IPO in the first few days and take their profits without buying in the aftermarket, Alfred would never give me a piece of any future IPOs he might run. I kept badgering Alfred for more shares, telling him that if he allocated me more IPO shares I could sell more aftermarket shares, but he kept putting me off. No doubt every broker at Junior College wanted more shares. I wasn't surprised when, a few minutes after the little software design company went public at $5, Alfred told me I was actually getting only 2,000 shares.

I was pissed off, but there wasn't much I could do about it. I started calling the prospective new accounts that I had opened by cold-calling and pitching the software design company's IPO. I thought briefly about throwing some of the IPO shares to existing clients, especially ones who had been burned by SmallTech, but the other brokers told me that wasn't good for my business. I needed new accounts, new clients. All of us brokers did. New clients would help create more liquidity, not just for this latest IPO, but for all of Junior College's other stocks, too, including SmallTech.

If I had promised a new account 400 shares, I gave him only 200. My twenty-cent concession on 2,000 shares added up to only $400, and I would have given up the damn twenty cents for a few more shares of the IPO. Those were worth gold because they helped me open accounts, and helped me sell more shares in the aftermarket—where the spreads, and hidden commissions, were worth a lot more. "I'm sorry, I had really hoped to get you more shares, not fewer," I apologized to the new accounts I was opening for Alfred's IPO. But I reminded my new clients that I had warned that the new issue was oversubscribed, and in fact this was good news because it probably meant the stock would rise faster in the aftermarket, and that was a great investment opportunity for them. "Unlike the IPO, where few shares are available and they're hard to get," I told clients, "you can probably buy as many shares as you want in the aftermarket, and for only a little more money than the issue price—especially if you move quickly."

Like a typical Junior College IPO, this was a $4 IPO that jumped out of the box at $5. I'm not sure how he did it, but Alfred almost immediately had a sweet deal for us brokers in the aftermarket. It was a special that came over the squawk box: "Four dollars with a five-twenty-five print." Alfred must have withheld a big block of stock at $4, which was technically illegal. Or maybe he was selling stock from an insider, one of the company's founders, who had gotten it for much less than $4. No matter. The price on the screen was $5.25, and that's what investors would see printed on their trade confirmations. But Junior College and its brokers were actually getting a $1.25 per share hidden commission, plus the 5 percent straight commission that the client knew about. Actually, the gross commission was 30 percent.

One of the first new accounts I called was a guy who I thought might be a good long-term client for me. Maybe not a whale, but a player who would keep his money—and my commissions—moving. I gave him 300 shares of the IPO instead of the 500 I had promised earlier, but he didn't seem to mind. (That's what we brokers said; we "gave" clients IPO shares, when it truth what we were doing was allowing clients to buy them.) I called him and told him that his $4 shares had opened at $5. He had made 25 percent out of the gate. I suggested that now was the time to buy more, before the stock went up even more. "Can I put you down for a hundred thousand shares?" I asked. I liked to shoot high. No one had given me a 100,000-share order yet, but I was sure that some of the orders I got were bigger than they would have been if I had started with a more modest suggestion.

The client laughed. "No," he said, "I'm not going to buy a hundred thousand shares. Get that right out of your head."

"Okay," I said, as smoothly as I could, "how about fifty thousand shares?"

He didn't respond at all for a moment. I thought maybe he was going to hang up on me and end the relationship. Instead, he said, "How about twenty-five thousand?"

"Sure," I said, trying to mask my excitement. "Listen, I really appreciate your style, your straightforward manner. To show you how much I appreciate it, I'm going to knock a couple points off my usual commission. My bosses don't like it when I do that, but I don't care. I do it for my special clients."

He seemed to like my gesture. When he got the confirmation of the trade, it showed him paying $131,250 for the 25,000 shares at $5.25 each, plus a $3,937.50 commission—3 percent, instead of my usual 5 percent. The client never saw anything indicating that the hidden commission, $1.25 per share, totaled $31,250—half for me, half for Junior College. And I did it with one two-minute phone call. I loved this job. It was fun again, or at least it was that day.

I took the ticket down to the trading department, where one of the Irish guys, who usually only grunted when brokers handed in their trades, grunted, glanced at the ticket, looked at me, looked at the ticket, and grunted again. This was a good-sized trade by Harvard standards, but it was colossal by Junior College standards, especially with that kind of spread and hidden commission. Alfred must have been in close contact with the trading department, keeping track of the buying and selling, because within a few minutes he was at my desk, raising his spindly arms to reveal big sweat stains on the armpits of his striped shirt as he waved high fives at me.

With the big score in Alfred's IPO, other sales in the aftermarket, the IPO concession, and assorted other trades involving SmallTech and other Junior College stocks, I had $55,000 in gross commissions for that month. My share was $27,500. After withholding taxes, I figured I would be getting a check for around $16,000. Not a bad month.

But there was a problem. A rumor going around Junior College had Alfred leaving for another firm. The bosses at Junior College must have taken it seriously, because they suddenly announced that all commissions connected to Alfred's IPO and the immediate aftermarket would be held up for a month. "Apparently the bosses are afraid Alfred will walk out the door and leave the firm holding some of the IPO stock in its own accounts," a senior broker informed me. "Another concern is that some of Alfred's new accounts might renege on their trades." Ordinarily, if a client ordered a trade and then refused to send in the money for it, the broker had to eat it. It was his responsibility to book the stock somewhere else, or pay for it himself. If Alfred left before some of his accounts sent in their money, Junior College would be left with his stock, still not paid for, in the firm's own accounts. So Junior College decided to withhold commissions connected with the IPO until all the orders were settled.

I went to see the new manager who had been hired to oversee Junior College's brokers. He had been recruited away from one of the big wire houses. He was a legitimate guy, a respected broker who had become a respected manager of other brokers at the wire house. He had a good reputation. He wasn't a Junior College type of guy. He was more of a Harvard kind of guy, I thought. He was a distinguished-looking, gray-haired man, with an air of reserve. The brokers at Junior College began calling him the Stuffed Shirt, which quickly was shortened to Stuffy.

He was hired to oversee the retail arm of Junior College, the brokers, because we were being split off into a separate company from the investment bank. The owners of Junior College would remain with the investment bank. The best guess in the board room was that the owners were trying to insulate themselves from the sleazy practices, regulatory investigations, and bad publicity associated with Junior College's brokers. If and when Junior College's brokers got into trouble, it wouldn't affect the investment banking operation. Even if the retail side of Junior College was shut down, the Junior College investment bank, as a separate company, could still take companies public. They would simply place the stock with other retail brokers.

We brokers saw Stuffy as a patsy hired by Junior College to take the fall if the brokerage arm of the company got into trouble. He was an experienced manager. He wouldn't be able to say he didn't know what was going on. Especially with the money he was making. I heard that he was getting a $300,000 salary, plus 2 percent of all Junior College's retail brokerage commissions. The firm had $50 million in commissions that year, so the package added up to a tidy $1.3 million for Stuffy. At first, he came in saying he was going to clean things up and transform the firm. He was going to change the way Junior College brokers worked, and spruce up their image. He called each of the fifty brokers in, one at a time, and chatted with us, talking about how we worked, what we sold, the kind of clients we had in our books, and so on.

One of his first announcements was that we would begin selling a certain kind of bonds. We brokers thought this was stupid. These kinds of bonds were fine for a big wire house, but not for Junior College. The commissions were too small. Our clients weren't interested in staid, long-term bonds. Our clients were players. They wanted action. They wanted IPOs and microcap stocks that could double in value in weeks or days, and sometimes hours. Some of the brokers laughed at Stuffy behind his back. Most of them ignored him. He couldn't change us. This was Junior College. He could try to dress us up, but he still wouldn't be able to take us to the cotillion. We were more suited to the mosh pit. It turned out the brokers were right. They didn't sell Stuffy's bonds, and after a few weeks we stopped hearing anything about them.

Stuffy became more like us, instead of us becoming more like him. Pretty soon he was coming around telling us about specials that Junior College was running, with big hidden commissions on stock that Junior College had bought cheaply in big blocs. Or he'd tell us that Junior College itself was going to be buying big blocs of some microcap stock. "You should be selling it to your clients," he told us. If Junior College was buying big quantities of a lightly traded stock, he reasoned with us, then it would make sense that the stock was going up. What he didn't mention was that if our clients bought the stock, that would help it go up—and then when the stock had gone up all it was going to go up, Junior College would unload its stocks, probably by offering us a high-commission special. We'd sell even more of it to our clients, and pretty soon Junior College would be out of the stock with a nice position, while our clients would be up to the gills in a stock that (a) was dropping in price and (b) had no more buyers to get the price back up. Stuffy and Junior College were using us, and counting on us to use our clients, to help them make money. It hadn't taken Stuffy long to realize that we were his bread and butter. The more commissions we generated, the bigger his 2 percent cut. If he wanted to keep making his $1.3 million a year, he needed to help us do what we did best: sell, sell, and sell some more.

When Junior College withheld my big commission on Alfred's IPO, I didn't bother making an appointment with Stuffy. I didn't stop to think about what I was going to say to him. I stormed out of the board room and down the hall, and burst into his office. He looked up, surprised. I all but jumped down his throat, yelling at him, waving around my pay stub. "Goddammit, I'm not gonna take this bullshit," I hollered. "If you can't fix this, I'm leaving. I'm outta here. I'll quit, I swear to God I'll quit. And I'll take every one of my clients with me." I'm sure he was taken aback. He had probably never seen a display like this at the old wire house. But he was cool about it. He let me rant for a bit, then calmly said, "Okay, let's talk about this. Here, have a seat. Sit down. Let's see what we can do." He had a tiny little TV on his desk, always tuned to C-SPAN or one of the news channels. I had never seen a TV that small with that good a picture, and I was fascinated. He showed me how it worked, and all of a sudden I wasn't as angry.

Stuffy turned out to be a pretty good guy. "Look, the firm doesn't want to lose you," he said. "I don't want to lose you. I think you're a real rising star. You're one of the few guys I've seen at this firm who could be a successful broker anywhere on Wall Street, including at my old firm." I knew he was stroking me, but I didn't care. I loved it. I still didn't see myself as a Junior College guy. I was more of a Harvard guy who happened to be working at Junior College for a little while.

"What's your plan?" Stuffy asked me. "What's your long-term plan, not just for your career, but for your life?"

It was my turn to be taken aback. I didn't have a long-term plan. I didn't know any Junior College broker who did. Our only plan was to make as much money as we could as quickly as we could. It was a stressful job, driven by intensity and aggressiveness, where you could go from being on top of the world to down in the dumps from one day to the next—one hour to the next, one minute to the next. Brokers at Junior College worked like manic obsessives, and lived like manic obsessives, until they burned out and disappeared. I didn't know what to tell Stuffy about my long-range plans. I stammered through some answer about maybe becoming a manager at Junior College myself someday.

Stuffy smiled at me, letting me know that he knew I was bullshitting. But he kept piling on the compliments. He asked about my commissions for the year. He said it looked pretty certain that I would get to $400,000 for the twelve months, and be made a vice president. Once I was a vice president, I could qualify for a private office, maybe even a cold caller. That was up to Stuffy. He was the one who decided which brokers got offices, cold callers, and secretarial help. "Just keep doing what you're doing," he told me. "You've got one foot in an office."

I did make it to $400,000 in commissions over twelve months. One of the brokers said it was customary for a broker who made vice president to give gifts to the traders who had executed all those orders for him. I didn't mind giving a few bucks to the shoeshine guy, but I really didn't want to give gifts to the fat Irish guys who ran the trading department. Those guys got salaries and commissions and bonuses from Junior College to make money for Junior College. Sure, they helped maintain good spreads, but that was just as much for Junior College's benefit as for the brokers. Moreover, the traders were always stealing from the brokers' commissions. Say a stock was trading at $4 bid by $4.50 asked. They'd tell me it was $4.25 by $4.50. Instead of getting a fifty-cent hidden commission, I'd get only twenty-five cents. The traders would keep the other twenty-five cents for Junior College's account. They were paid a percentage of how much they earned for Junior College's account, so they were stealing from me and lining their own pockets. At least, that was how I looked at it.

I talked to several vice presidents, and they said they had given the head trader, a big, florid-faced guy who looked a little like the actor Brian Dennehy, between $500 and $1,000. Reluctantly, I gave the guy $500 in crisp new $100 bills. He grabbed them, grunted

"Good luck," and stuffed them into his pants pocket. "I'll bet he reports it on his income tax returns, too," I said sarcastically to Melanie.

I celebrated my imminent promotion to vice president by taking Melanie to Paris for five days. We were living much better than we ever had, but we weren't throwing money around like a lot of other Junior College brokers did. I had leased a car, a Mercedes, for $700 a month and rented a parking space in a garage near our building for $350 a month, so I drove myself down to Wall Street every morning. I parked in a lot near the office for $15 a day—not a lot more than I used to spend on cab rides back and forth. The car, and driving every day, was a luxury, but it made me feel better about myself, and made me feel that I had more control over my life. Instead of listening to Peruvian or Indian or Russian or country music or whatever was playing on the radio in whatever cab I happened to take in the morning, I could drive myself through the Manhattan traffic and listen to Howard Stern, who provided me with most of my news of the world beyond Wall Street. I had more control over my life.

18

Mr. Vice President

My goal for the next twelve months was $800,000 in gross commissions, which would earn me the title of senior vice president. Another, more immediate goal was to get my own personal cold caller and a private office, in that order of priority but preferably at the same time. That was up to Stuffy, now that I had qualified to become a vice president. He decided which vice presidents got their own offices and cold callers, and when.

There was no ceremony announcing my new title. My first day back from France, I called the administrative offices of Junior College. "I need new business cards that say 'vice president' for my title," I told the woman who answered the phone. She said she'd have to check on that, and promised to get back to me. I fretted for a few days about bookkeeping errors that might show me with, say, $397,000 in commissions for the year, but one morning when I came in my new cards, reading "Rob Burtelsohn, Vice President," were on my desk. I sat down and scrawled out a dozen notes to friends and relatives: "Just wanted to let you know about my promotion at work. All's well, hope to see you soon. Love, Rob." I wrote a slightly longer note to my folks, and included a stack of cards. I knew my mother would want to pass them around and brag about me, and that my dad would keep one in his wallet and another on his desk. Over the next couple of weeks, I handed out dozens of my new cards in the bars where brokers congregated after the market closed every afternoon. For over two years other young guys had been giving me business cards that said they were vice presidents at one brokerage house or another. Everybody on Wall Street seemed to be a vice president, and for more than two years I wasn't. Now I belonged. I was part of the fraternity.

Between working my own clients aggressively and grabbing snatches of IPOs such as the one run by Alfred, my business got better. All the vice presidents and senior vice presidents at Junior College were supposed to get together for dinner, on the firm, once a month. There were about twenty of us, and about half showed up in any given month for the dinner, which was usually held in a private room at some decent restaurant. Any broker who had set his own personal record for most commissions the previous month was supposedly a guest of honor at these "personal best" dinners. I went to a few dinners, including two where I was celebrated for achieving a personal best, but I thought it was a waste of time. I stopped going after deciding that I would rather be out with my own friends than sitting around for three or four hours while the managers of Junior College blew smoke up my ass. "I know I am becoming a big producer," I told Melanie. "I don't need these guys to tell me."

Headhunters began calling me. Brokerage firms were always scouring Wall Street for productive brokers who wanted to move, and stealing away each other's brokers was a time-honored practice. For the most part, brokers were among the least loyal people I had ever met. Whether by nature or nurture, whether because it was part of their personalities or a result of their training, brokers were so focused on making money that they had no qualms about moving from one firm to another at the drop of a bonus check. Time and again, I saw brokerage firms take a raw young guy, mold him into a competent stockbroker, and then watch as the guy walked away with the firm's clients for a few thousand dollars more a year. In addition, I realized that brokers were a suspicious, complaining breed, always sure that their firm was somehow screwing them or favoring someone else. And a lot of the time, they were right. Brokerage firms were no more loyal to them than they were to the firms. Brokerage houses chewed up young guys and spit them out, whether they were cold callers or qualifiers or brokers, if they didn't produce more for the brokerage than they cost. I figured I had to look out for myself in this business. It was a tough industry, and no one else was going to look out for me. I quietly began meeting with headhunters, and letting them arrange interviews for me at other firms.

A number of firms, most of them smaller than Junior College but all of them emphasizing microcap stocks in the same way, were interested in me. I wasn't interested in them. I still saw myself as a broker who was more suited to Harvard or one of the old-line wire houses where a broker who did a million in gross commissions might have $100 million under management. A 1 percent or 2 percent return on a broker's book at a wire house was considered good. At Harvard, the Bald Shadow had a 10 percent return on his book and was a star. In contrast, brokers at Junior College who did a million dollars in commissions might have only $5 million or $6 million in their books. Returns of 30 percent, 50 percent, and higher were not unheard of.

The year before I arrived at Junior College, one of the brokers had $2 million under management and made $1.5 million in gross commissions. It was hard to imagine, especially from the clients' point of view; for every $2,000 the client invested with that broker, the broker took $1,500 out of the account. Either the broker was making some spectacular decisions and getting some spectacular returns for the clients—which seemed unlikely, given that the broker was selling only Junior College stocks—or clients kept putting in more money to make up for the commissions that were being skimmed off. The other

brokers at Junior College all assumed the broker was constantly persuading clients to send in more money to cover their losses and his
commissions. "The guy must be a hell of a salesman," they would say
admiringly when we sat around in bars after work. Junior College
brokers, at least in front of each other, scorned the wire houses.
"Those brokers must be mopes," they would say. "How can they have
one hundred million dollars in their books and make a measly one
million in commissions? If I had that, I'd be turning over ten million
at least. Either they're not good salesmen or they don't work hard or
both."

I didn't want to run a Junior College–style business for my entire
career. It was a good training ground, a good place to learn the industry, but I didn't want to be constantly pushing and scrambling and
screaming and, in Junior College parlance, shooting the wounded. I
wanted to be a hell of a salesman and make $1 million in commissions,
but I didn't want to do it by bleeding my clients dry. It would be easier
to make $1 million a year in commissions if I had $100 million under
management, and that meant working for wire houses. "If I'm going
to put myself out in the job market," I told the headhunters, "I want
to concentrate on the big, respected, well-known, old-line brokerage
firms." I thought to myself, *$100 million—now, that's a real book. That's
a real business.* In comparison, Junior College wasn't a real business. It
was a scam.

When I started interviewing, I called several brokers I knew at different firms on Wall Street, guys I thought I could trust to be discreet, to
find out what they thought of different brokerage houses, to see if
they had heard of any places that were hot at the moment, and to find
out who was hiring and who wasn't. One of the brokers I had been
friendly with at Harvard—not the Bald Shadow, who probably wasn't
speaking to me—surprised me. "Why don't you come back here?" he
suggested. "I can arrange an interview for you." It hadn't occurred to

me to go back so soon, but I liked the idea. I missed the professional-ism, the mentality that said Harvard was the best, the classiest. "I'll make some quiet inquiries on your behalf," the guy promised. He called me back a couple of days later. "You've got an interview scheduled with the Branch Manager," he reported.

Déjà vu swept over me in the Harvard lobby, especially when the Queen of the Cold Callers came out to take me to the Branch Man-ager's office. It was odd to walk back into the Harvard board room. It felt like the place where I had grown up. There were so many memo-ries, but I had changed. I was a high-earning broker myself now, with my own business. But I was nervous, and I kept telling myself, "Relax. You have every right to be here." I had never even been in the Branch Manager's office before, and I couldn't keep myself from glancing around for the hook where I was supposed to hang my tongue. He wasn't there, and I couldn't decide whether to sit on his couch or in one of the overstuffed chairs in front of his desk. I was settling into a chair just as he walked in. I had been afraid he might not remember me, but he did. He greeted me by name and said, "What can I do for you?" I didn't know what to say. He knew why I was there. He was just trying to put me on the defensive, and it worked. Trying to recover, I told him that I had talked to the Harvard broker, who had suggested there might be some interest in my returning. "Let's sit over there," the Branch Manager said. I moved over to the couch, and he turned around one of the armchairs and sat in that.

He asked about my work at Junior College. "Tell me all about it," he urged. I told him how many accounts I had opened, about the IPOs I had worked on, about the number of clients I had, how much money I had under management, what kind of trading volume I did, and what kind of commissions I generated. "What about the liquidity of the stocks you handle?" he asked. I knew he was really saying that Harvard wasn't Junior College; he wouldn't have me or any other broker in his board room selling the same handful of stocks back and forth among clients in order to keep the price up. I gave what I thought was the right answer: "There are problems with liquidity for some of the microcaps, but I keep my own clients away from those." He asked about why I had come to Harvard nearly two years before. I gave him a brief recap of my history, and he seemed interested. He asked whether I had any questions, and I said, "Just one. What are the chances of you hiring me?"

He shrugged. "I'd say the chances are good," he said. I walked out flying high, nodding and waving to familiar faces. One of the Branch Manager's assistants—not the Queen, unfortunately—called me a couple of days later and offered me a job. I felt like it was a vindication, an admission that Harvard should have given me a desk a year earlier. The offer was for a draw of $6,000 a month for six months. I would not have a cold caller or a qualifier. I would be expected to open ten accounts over the six months—which was no big deal to me. I had opened ten accounts or close to it several times at Junior College during single weeks. I figured I could open fifty in six months. I would be a star.

By Harvard standards, it was a good offer to a young broker. It wasn't that long ago that I had been working there for $3.50 an hour. I thought about it for a few days and then turned down the job. The Harvard broker who set up the interview for me was upset. "I can't believe you're turning this down," he said. I thought the Branch Manager would be angry with me, as if maybe I was trying to show him up. But I don't know what he really thought because I never saw or talked to him again. Myself, I had no qualms or misgivings. It had been an easy decision. I got a better offer.

Actually, I had several better offers. The first one, from a wire house, promised me an $8,000-a-month salary for the first year. Not a draw, which I had to pay back out of my commissions, but a salary, on top of my commissions. It was hard for me to believe that a big firm would offer someone like me, who had been making commissions as a broker for a mere eight months, a salary of nearly $100,000 a year. Plus commissions. However I didn't like the manager who interviewed me. I loved his office, with the view of the Statue of Liberty over his shoulder. But he was pompous. He looked down on Junior College, and said so. He said the only reason he was offering me a job was that I had not been at Junior College very long. "You haven't been totally poisoned yet," he said. "There's still hope." He offered me a soda out of the refrigerator in his office. I figured he didn't care whether I was thirsty; he just wanted me to know he had a fridge. I turned down the soda. I told him I'd think about his offer, and a day or two later I called the headhunter. "Tell the guy thanks but no thanks," I instructed.

I interviewed at half a dozen firms. Each the interview was conducted by a guy who was the manager of that particular crew of brokers, and the interviews were all pretty much the same. They presented themselves as relaxed and low-key, and I did the same. In truth, I was energized. I was "on." I smiled, I gestured, I made witty comments, I was aggressive but friendly in my manner, confident but not quite arrogant in my bearing. I was selling my best and favorite product— myself—and I wanted to shine. I think I did. The only awkward moments, more for them than for me, were when they asked me about Junior College. Like the manager at the first wire house that offered me a job, they seemed to think it was a plus that I had not been at Junior College very long. They never came right out and said they thought Junior College was sleazy, but they said things like "We have a different kind of business here," or, "Our brokers don't work quite the same way with their clients."

As near as I could tell, their primary interest—no, their *only* interest—was in whether I could sell securities to clients. At most firms, I figured that the typical manager had to show something like $5 million a month in commissions to break even. He needed brokers to help make the nut, and then pile on the profits. No manager who interviewed me asked me about my investment philosophies. No one asked me what I knew about economics in general or securities in particular. No one asked me what I read to keep up on the market, or what research or charts I did on my own. If they asked me about a particular stock, it wasn't to find out what I knew about the company. It was to find out how I would sell it. They wanted to be reassured that I had the kind of mentality that would let me call up strangers and get them to send me substantial amounts of money. When one manager asked me how I picked the stocks to recommend to my clients, I knew the answer. "I pick stocks I can sell," I replied. He smiled at me.

Not once, never ever, did a manager ask me about making money for my clients. No one asked how my clients had done with me, whether I had made money for them. The performance of the stocks I liked was irrelevant, and so was the service I had performed for my clients. For the managers who interviewed me, and for the brokerage houses that employed them, the top priority was not making money for their clients. The top priority was making money for themselves. I began to realize that there was no real difference between Harvard and Junior College, between the wire houses and the boiler rooms. They all had the same goal: to raise capital from clients, and keep as much of it as possible by generating transactions.

Every interviewer asked the same two key questions. First, how much did I have under management? Second, what was my trailing twelve? I would tell them that my book was about $1 million at the moment, and my trailing twelve—my gross commissions for the previous twelve months—had been about $400,000. *Hmm,* they always nodded. I could tell they were impressed. Forty percent. Not bad. That was a good sign. They didn't really care about the percentage, but my 40 percent showed that I had done respectable business with a book that wasn't huge. For a bigger brokerage than Junior College, where I presumably would have a much bigger book, my percentage might not be as high, but they would expect my total commissions to be even higher.

I think I could have gotten job offers from every firm where I interviewed, if I had expressed sufficient interest. At all but one, fairly early in the process, usually after one interview, I told them I wasn't interested. The one firm I was interested in was one of the old-line, traditional, big-name wire houses, the sort of firm that is a household name, the sort of firm that advertises on business programs on radio stations and runs clever commercials during big sporting events on TV. The Wire House was a classy operation, like Harvard. My friends would be impressed if I worked there, and so would my parents and other relatives. It would be a respected, dignified job, more like a profession than the frenetic rough-and-tumble atmosphere at Junior College.

I went back for a second interview, and a third. At the third interview, the manager offered me a $75,000 cash bonus to come to Wire House. This was not unusual. When brokers who are good producers move from one firm to another, they typically get financial incentives not unlike a signing bonus for a professional athlete who goes from one team to another as a free agent. I had heard of brokers getting bonuses in the hundreds of thousands to leave one firm and join another. The $75,000 I was offered seemed fine with me. After all, I had been a broker for barely a year. My trailing twelve was all I had, because I had begun making commissions barely a year earlier. But the manager at Wire House didn't seem to care about my lack of experience, or that I had gotten that experience at Junior College instead of someplace more reputable. He figured I could make some money for him, and that's all that mattered.

Like a pro athlete, I had to sign a contract, in this case for two years, to get my bonus. If I left the Wire House before the two years was up, I was supposed to pay back a proportion of the $75,000. If I left after a year, for example, I was supposed to pay back half of it. It was well known, however, that brokers who left firms early hardly ever paid back any part of their bonuses, mostly because it was more trouble than it was worth for the firms to come after them. Besides the money, my contract with Wire House gave me a cold caller and my own office. The office meant a lot to me, after spending all of my brief career in so-called board rooms, but the cold caller was more important, maybe even more important than the $75,000 up front. "If I can get a good cold caller, somebody who works the way I worked for the Bald Shadow," I told Melanie, "I'll be a lot more efficient and a lot more productive. I'll be able to spend more of my time qualifying and pitching, the things that I do best and that give the best return for my time. I'll have a bigger, better business, and I'll make more money." But maybe the most attractive thing about the offer was that I would be leaving Junior College for a more reputable, more ethical firm.

I stuck my head in Stuffy's office. "Gotta minute?" I asked. My voice or my expression or something must have alarmed him, because he got a funny look on his face and told me to come in and sit down. He closed the door. He even turned off his tiny TV. We talked for two hours. He tried to persuade me not to go to Wire House. There was nothing wrong with Wire House, he emphasized; he had worked at a very similar place for twenty-seven years. He had done well there. He had made a lot of friends. But there wasn't the excitement of Junior College, the cutting-edge deals, the ground-floor appeal of helping little companies with good ideas make their dreams come true. I was confused, and I don't think I made a lot of sense.

"I have to go to Wire House," I said at one point. "I've already signed a contract."

"Ah, the contract is no big deal," Stuffy assured me. "The manager over there will just tear it up. You call and say you're not coming, he tears it up. They haven't given you any money yet, so there aren't really any financial issues to settle. You just walk away."

Stuffy asked about my deal at Wire House, and seemed impressed. "I can't match the seventy-five-thousand-dollar bonus they were going to give you," he said, "but if you went over there, you probably would have lost at least that much in commissions during the first few months at the new job, while you're rebuilding your business."

Stuffy had hit on a sore point. Wire House's commissions for brokers ranged from 28 percent to 42 percent, depending on the product—stock, bond, fund, whatever. I was afraid it would take me years to build up my business at Wire House. Stuffy must have sensed this, because he zeroed in. "In the long run, you'll make more money if you stay here," he said. He pointed out that Junior College had a big advantage in concentrating on little microcap stocks, especially when it came to spreads and hidden commissions. A twenty-five-cent spread means a lot more on the $3 stocks that Junior College sold than it would on the $30 stocks that Wire House sold. And my commissions at Junior College were sure to go up, he assured me, with the cold caller he was going to give me. I perked up, emerging from the haze of confusion. I was always ready to negotiate anything that could be negotiated.

"What about an office?" I asked. Stuffy spun his chair sideways a half-turn and gazed off into space, as if reviewing the floor plan in his mind. "Okay," he said after a minute. "I'll give you an office."

As long as Stuffy was saying yes, I had more requests. It was clear to me that I had some leverage at the moment, and now was the time to take advantage of it. "An office and a cold caller won't do me much good," I said, "if I'm not getting pieces of IPOs." I wanted some assurance from Stuffy that I would get a piece of every IPO that came through Junior College, no matter which senior vice president was running it. He said he couldn't make any promises, and then promptly promised me that he would make sure I got as much as possible from every future IPO. I knew he couldn't make any guarantees, but it wouldn't hurt and might very well help me get more IPO shares if he asked the brokers running IPOs to make sure I got a good chunk. A promise to try to help was the best he could do, and I believed he would follow through.

I went back to my old battered desk and uncomfortable chair, and dialed the number of the manager at Wire House. "I can't come," I told him.

He took it calmly. He didn't seem surprised, and he wasn't critical.

"I hope we can work together sometime in the future," he said. "Good luck, and stay in touch."

The next morning, Stuffy came past my desk and motioned for me to follow him. We went into one of the glassed-in offices that lined the sides. There was another broker already in one half of the office, with a cold caller sitting beside him at a smaller desk. On the other side of the office was another broker's desk and another cold caller's desk, both of them vacant. Stuffy stuck out his hand. "Welcome home," he said.

19

The Kid

Stuffy began sending me young guys who wanted to be my cold
caller. Some had been working for other brokers, and some were
fresh off the street. Most of them were losers. They had answered ads
in the newspapers for trainee brokers or Wall Street jobs that sounded
great. Then they found out that they were going to be dialers making
minimum wage. And this is what marked most of them as losers: they
stayed and tried to do the job. Yes, I had answered an ad like that, and
I had stayed and worked as a dialer for $3.50 an hour. But I knew
where I was going. I knew I had what it takes to become a broker. Most
of these cold callers were worthless to me. If they had been at Junior
College for a while and were any good, some other broker would have
locked them up by now so that they worked exclusively for him.
The new applicants were even worse. I was looking for someone who
spoke well, and most of the applicants did not speak well. Some had
heavy accents. Some didn't speak clearly, slurring or clipping off words.
Some mumbled, and some said *uh, um, like, yeah, uh, y'know, yeah, like
y'know, whatever.* A few tried to use big words and sound intelligent,
but misused the words, or mispronounced them. Once in a while a
young job applicant would come in, probably right out of college,

with a fresh haircut and a new suit. The haircut wasn't any good, and neither was the suit, but at least those kids were educated and were trying to make a good impression in the business world.

Sometimes they would be well-spoken. They could carry on a conversation without mumbling or stuttering or sounding too stupid or too smart. But when it came time to talk to rich people on the phone, they choked. They thought they weren't as good as the people they were calling up, that they had no right to talk to them. I was looking for someone who thought of himself as an equal to the wealthy professionals and executives on the phone, as somebody who was just as good as they were, but simply hadn't made his millions yet. I was looking for someone who could prod and push rich people on the phone. I was looking for someone who had the same attitude I did when I was a cold caller.

I finally found him. He simply showed up one day, answering an ad the same way I had. He was clean-cut, well-spoken, a recent college graduate, with a major in philosophy, of all things. Most important, he was a natural hustler. I started calling him the Kid. The Kid turned out to be almost as good a cold caller as I had been. One big advantage he had was that I spent a lot of time on him. It hadn't been all that long ago that I had been a cold caller myself, so it was easy to recall my own uncertainty about what I was doing, how I was doing it, and where it might lead me. I sat the Kid down on the first day and promised to help him take the Series 7 test to become a broker himself in 120 days—provided he worked hard.

"If you work hard," I promised, "I'll take care of you. I'll explain all the things I wish someone had explained to me, including how the cold calling and qualifying and pitching works, and why cold calling is so important to brokers. I'll explain the rest of the business as we go along, when you're ready." I started off by telling him how much money I made from individual trades, and how much I had made the year before, my first as a broker. His eyes widened. He was going to work out, I thought.

I tried to treat the Kid the way I wished I had been treated by the Bald Shadow and the other brokers at Harvard when I was a cold caller. When he went to get my lunch, I bought his for him, too. I sent him to the bank with my cash card a few times to get money for me, but I never had him pick up my dry cleaning. Unlike a lot of Junior College brokers, at the end of cold days I never sent him to the garage down the street to pick up my car. A cold caller would double-park his broker's car in the street outside the Junior College building, and then sit there with the engine idling until the broker trotted out and climbed into his nice warm car right outside the door.

In our first couple of weeks together, I spent a lot of time with the Kid, outlining the business and what I expected of him. I told him how and why I did things the way I did them, and criticized the way some other brokers did things. To get away from the distractions of the office, and to avoid wasting valuable lead cards, on several afternoons I took the Kid back to my apartment and practiced with him. I went over scripts of cold calls, with me playacting the part of a person who had been called and had all sorts of reasons for not wanting to talk to a broker from Junior College. It all paid off. Within three weeks, I could rely on the Kid for a dozen or more leads a day. He really got excited every time I opened an account from a lead he had given me, and I encouraged that. We developed a little high-five ceremony for the occasion. I still did a little cold calling myself, but more to help him, to show him how it was done, than to generate leads. I concentrated on qualifying his leads, pitching prospective new accounts on stock ideas, and selling Junior College stocks among my existing clients. I eavesdropped on a lot of his calls, mostly to help him but also, I've got to admit, because I loved hearing him say, "Hello, I'm calling for Mr. Rob Burtelsohn, a vice president at . . ."

Over the next four months, I showed the Kid more and more of my business. Though he technically was not allowed to speak to clients about specific securities until he had his license, he did it all the time. For example, it helped him get people who had been cold-called to agree to talk to me, the broker, if he could tell them I was going to offer them an IPO. Sometimes he cold-called people and then qualified them and pitched a stock all in the same call, even though that was also illegal. I knew he was technically breaking the rules, but I didn't stop him. It was common for non-licensed cold callers at Junior College to pitch stocks, to qualify leads, and even to misrepresent themselves as brokers. The managers had to know it was going on, but none of them seemed to mind.

Some of the brokers had trained their cold callers to give the brokers' own names and take notes so that when the brokers called back they could say, "You'll remember when I talked before, you told me about your work as an engineer. It was snowing that day. You told me you had a hundred and fifty thousand dollars in the market, and I mentioned an upcoming IPO that might be a good investment for you . . ." Usually the potential clients were impressed with the broker's memory. But this system backfired occasionally when the cold caller wrote down something wrong, or a broker couldn't read the cold caller's notes. For the most part, however, it worked. And I never heard of a broker or cold caller or anyone else at Junior College getting in trouble for misrepresentation or illegally acting as a broker.

When the Kid got his books for the Series 7 exam, he asked me to help him study. I refused. He kept bugging me about what might be on the test, and why this question or that one should be answered in a certain way. "I'm not going to help you study for the exam," I said. "I'll help you with anything else, but not that. No broker ever helped any other broker with the test. It's something you have to pass or fail on your own." That had been the attitude of the BS and other brokers at Harvard toward cold callers studying for the Series 7, and it was my attitude now. In truth, I wanted nothing to do with that exam. Studying for it had been one of the most stressful and unpleasant experiences of my life. Besides, I probably had forgotten most of what I had learned.

If I didn't need it in my current business, I forgot it. "The Kid doesn't need to know how much I don't know," I told Melanie one evening. "I'd rather he keep thinking I know it all."

When the time came, the Kid passed his Series 7 with flying colors, something like a 78. I didn't take him to lunch. I took him to dinner, splashing out for martinis and steaks and good wine and cigars afterward. Throughout the evening, I told him of my plans for him to get more involved in my business, until he was ready to get his own desk at Junior College. I had invested a lot of time and energy in the guy, and I wanted some payback now that he had his Series 7 license and could do some more meaningful work for me. After my experience with the Bald Shadow, I knew the value of having an apprentice who was a licensed broker—a "registered representative," in brokerese. The next morning the Kid was back at his desk cold-calling for me as usual.

I began working with him on qualifying and pitching. We did more playacting. Even after months of cold-calling and then passing the Series 7, some guys had trouble working as qualifiers because they couldn't bring themselves to ask strangers if they had $100,000 in the market, and then ask for some of that money. Some young guys were never able to step up to talking to people who had $100,000 in the market. In contrast, it took me all of about fifteen minutes to get comfortable with it. It took the kid about four days. He was good. I taught him my favorite responses, many of which I had borrowed from the Bald Shadow. For example, when a prospective client accused me of pressuring him to buy a stock and open an account with me, I would say, "Please don't misconstrue my enthusiasm for pressure."

"What does *misconstrue* mean?" the Kid asked me.

"It doesn't matter what it means," I told him. "All you need to know is that it sounds good, and it works." It became part of the Kid's regular rebuttal repertoire.

We brought in another small desk for a new cold caller, and the

Kid began acting as my qualifier. We went back to the playacting sessions, and I showed him how to open accounts. He had more trouble with that. He wasn't good at closing. We worked and worked on it and gradually he got better, but he was no Rob II. I found, however, that I could trust him, and I began to take a little more time off now and then, leaving him in charge the same way the Bald Shadow had left me in charge.

The Kid generally did a great job for me. However, as in any business involving strangers promising to do things for each other with large amounts of money, there were occasional problems. My biggest loss over a renege came on a sale made by the Kid shortly after he got his broker's license. When he started opening accounts in my book, I told him I would split the commission with him on the first trade in any new account that he brought in. He opened a few small clients with a few small trades, and made $100 here, $200 there.

One day he rushed up to me all flushed. "I just opened an account with a big trade," he said. The new client, a farmer in North Carolina, had agreed to buy 5,000 shares of a stock priced at $8. I was thrilled for the Kid, but I was also a little apprehensive. He was doing this through my book and it was a big trade; if the guy reneged and the stock went down, I would be on the hook. And that's exactly what happened. The stock was one of Junior College's old IPOs, on its way from a high of $20 to oblivion, and it didn't stay at $8 long. Two days later it was at $7.50, and the farmer's check was nowhere in sight.

"I'm already down twenty-five hundred on the five thousand shares if the farmer doesn't pay," I pointed out to the Kid in a way that made him realize how unhappy I was.

"I'm trying to reach the guy, but I can't get him on the phone," the Kid replied. "There's no answer, or his wife says he's out and will call back, but he never does."

Two more days went by, and the stock dropped another quarter.

I kept nagging the Kid: "Are you sure that was a good trade? Did this bumpkin understand? Did he say yeah, he'd send in forty thousand dollars?"

The Kid, at my suggestion, had been taping some of his pitches so that I could replay and critique them. (At the time, I didn't know it was illegal to tape someone on the phone without his or her permission.) The Kid dug around and found the tape of the call to the farmer and played it back for me. The guy talked painfully slowly, with a thick-as-molasses country-Southern accent, like some real Gomer. But he seemed to understand. He said he would send in the money. It sounded like a good trade. "I would have put the trade through myself, based on what he said," I told the Kid.

But still no check arrived, and the stock was down another quarter, to $7. I was on the hook for $5,000. I started calling the farmer myself every hour on the hour, and finally got him on the phone at about ten o'clock in the evening. He denied ever talking to the Kid. He swore he didn't know anything about the trade. I played the tape back for him. It was obvious that it was his voice. He denied it. "That's not me," he drawled. "And I'm not sure it's legal for you to go around tapin' people without their permission. Maybe I should ask my cousin the sheriff about that." I figured the guy must have gotten burned by a broker somewhere along the line, and had resolved to screw every broker he could for the rest of his life, starting with me and the Kid. I hung up in frustration.

Stuffy came by my office the next day. "The operations department has notified me that you have a forty-thousand-dollar outstanding trade that nobody has paid for," he said. "They need the money." I explained what had happened. I played back the tape. Stuffy was sympathetic. It sounded like a good trade to him, too. But that wasn't the problem at the moment. The problem was what to do with the 5,000 shares of stock hanging there in limbo, now down to $6 a share.

"You know how it works," Stuffy said. "If the farmer isn't going to pay for the shares and they don't belong to him, they belong to you.

You've got to pay for them. So you've got a choice. Do you want to sell them and then make up the losses out of your pocket? Or do you want pay for the shares and hang on to them until the price goes up?"

Stuffy was a broker's broker; he said "until" the shares went up, not "if." But we both knew those shares were never going up. The smart move was to sell the stock and take the hit. That's what Stuffy wanted me to do. But I wanted him to know I wasn't happy about it. I wanted him to feel my pain.

"If I sell the stock now, I'm going to have to eat a ten-thousand-dollar loss—that's net, not gross," I told him, poking my finger at him in front of his chest for emphasis. "What would you do if it was you? If you were caught in a bind like this even though you didn't do anything wrong?"

"I'd sell, and as soon as possible," Stuffy said. "Let's just get it off the books and move on." He knew that was the surest way to make sure the firm didn't get stuck paying for the bum trade. I swallowed bitterly, sold the stock, and paid for the losses with money held out of my next paycheck. I was grumpy with the Kid for several days, even though I knew it wasn't his fault. He had cost me money. He offered to share the loss with me, and I said I would take half of it out of future commissions that I was supposed to split with him. But I never did. Reneges were part of the overhead.

20

Wary Buyers

The investor on the line was a lead from one of the Kid's cold calls. I could sense that the guy was my kind of client, and that I was his kind of broker. He had a lot of money in the market. He was a blue-collar guy who had taken a small office-cleaning company and turned it into a big maintenance services firm. I had an IPO for him. I also wanted him to buy in the IPO's aftermarket. And I wanted him to buy Small-Tech. I did something I almost never did. I pitched him on all three ideas pretty much simultaneously. The time-honored rule was one idea per call, one sale per call. Anything more was at best confusing, at worst greedy. But I sensed I could do it with this guy, even though I'd been talking to him for only five minutes. "Okay, okay," he said, cutting me off. I knew he was either going to hang up on me or become a great client.

"Okay," he said again. "What do you want me to do? Which one do I do first?"

It was the perfect response, just what I wanted to hear. I made several hundred dollars in commissions off the guy that day, several thousand more a couple of weeks later when the IPO came, and many more thousands over the following months. I had relied on my salesman's sense about people, and it had paid off.

As my business grew, I was learning how to run it and how to make it grow even more. I borrowed things I had learned from the Bald Shadow or other brokers at Harvard, and tried to pick up things from the more successful brokers at Junior College. But there wasn't much most of them could teach me. To put it bluntly, most of them were at Junior College because they could never make it at Harvard or anyplace better than Junior College. Most of them were at Junior College because they didn't really belong in the securities business at all. Quite a few of them would be out of it in a short time because they weren't generating enough in commissions. Cheap clients were known as pikers, but there were piker brokers, too. They were brokers who only dealt with cheap little clients and made cheap little trades. "The wealthier the client, the bigger the trades, the more money we can make with less work," I told the Kid.

Over the phone, from the first cold call through qualifying and pitching, I learned to develop a sense about people: who might be a big player and who might not. I disciplined myself to blow off the prospective clients who seemed to be pikers. Identifying and targeting clients as buyers made me more efficient. I didn't want to waste my time on small trades. There were brokers at Junior College who were on the phone literally all day, cobbling together trades of $2,000 or $5,000, picking up commissions of a couple hundred here, a couple hundred there. I would rather go a week with no trades at all, and then make one big trade for $50,000 with $5,000 in commissions. That got the other brokers talking. And frankly, I liked to have the other brokers talking about me. Respect was important, but not because I wanted them to accept me. I couldn't care less whether they accepted me. I was more concerned that they saw me as different from them. I was someone who had been at Harvard, and could be again one of these days.

Some brokers liked to socialize with their biggest clients. I think it made them feel like they were moving up in the world. I never met clients in person. Every once in a while a client would say he wanted to come in and see me, but I discouraged that. I didn't want him to see what a dump Junior College was. Besides, we were having a good relationship over the phone. Why risk messing it up by meeting in person? Maybe he would see me and not like me. Maybe he'd think I dressed too well, or I was too young. I always had an excuse.

One of my colleagues loved to rub shoulders and break bread with clients, and he often bragged about it. "I'm going out to dinner tonight with a client," he told me one day. "You should come along. He's not only really rich, but also a really great guy. We've become friends. The guy has a string of health clubs and gyms, and sometimes we pump iron together. C'mon with us tonight. You'll enjoy meeting the guy."

"Okay," I said. "Maybe by watching you in action, I can pick up some tips about how to handle a whale."

We went to dinner, and I didn't think the client was such a great guy at all. He was really crass, with crude table manners and language to match. He seemed like a money-grubbing hustler who happened to get rich. This guy really liked action. He was more of a gambler than an investor. When my colleague went to the men's room, I happened to ask the guy how long he had been a client. "Just long enough for him to lose three million dollars for me," the guy said, laughing. He didn't seem to care. Crass or not, that was the kind of client I wanted—as long as I didn't have to go out to dinner with him.

As in pretty much any other business, the old 80–20 rule prevailed in the securities industry: 20 percent of the clients did 80 percent of the business. I tried to take care of all my clients, but I really concentrated on the 20 percent who did most of the business. I called them all the time. I became friendly with them. I developed relationships. I have to say that I liked a lot of my clients and they liked me, though I avoided meeting them in person. A couple of clients liked cars, and I would talk about the latest Lexus or Rover or Merc.

I called clients by their first names, and asked them to call me by my first name. However, one self-described good ol' boy from Alabama or someplace in the South always called me "Mr. Rob." The only other person who ever called me that was the cleaning lady I had finally persuaded Melanie to hire to tidy up our apartment once a week. The guy was so polite and laid-back, I often let him get away with more than other clients. He once called me and said, "Mr. Rob, would you mind sending me ten thousand dollars so I can take my daughter out shopping before her wedding next month?" Ordinarily I talked clients out of taking any money at all out of their accounts, but I sent it to the good ol' boy without objection.

He was one of the few who never complained about his Junior College stocks. I could count on the good ol' boy for a good talk, even if he wasn't going to buy anything. Once in a while I'd call him ostensibly to pitch something, but really just to chat. Simply talking to him picked up my mood sometimes. I found myself talking to him in the same easy manner I talked to my uncles.

Like most clients, that good ol' boy made money with me at first. I opened his account with the SmallTech IPO, and of course it went up. I asked him to buy some more, he did, and it went up some more. I had him hold it too long, though. And then when it started to drop and he wanted to sell, I put him into another Junior College stock that ended up falling, too. I felt badly when the good ol' boy ended up losing most of the money he had invested with me at Junior College. But in truth that's what happened to most clients at Junior College—not just mine, but everybody's. The Junior College brokers made money for them for a while, but they inevitably lost much of it if they kept listening to the brokers. I had been telling myself that SmallTech and these other Junior College "house" stocks could come back, that the companies still had potential. Gradually I realized that they didn't have potential. The companies for the most part had no real revenues and no real profits, and in some cases no real products. The stocks weren't coming back, and they never would. But I kept up the hope that the next IPO would be better, that it would be for a company that really would be a success.

I tried to make money for all my clients, and felt bad when they didn't. But some of them made it pretty hard to feel very bad for them. I learned that investors are fickle. When I presented a stock to a client, I was supposed to be right. He didn't need my advice to be wrong. He could be wrong on his own. But being a broker was in many ways a no-win proposition, and there weren't many clients who were willing to cut their brokers any slack. I could make nine good recommendations in a row to a client, but if I was even a little bit wrong on number ten, the client was pissed off. If I recommended a stock and it went up, I was a hero—briefly. If I got the client out of the stock too soon, I was a bum. If I left him in too long, I was a bum. If by some stroke of dumb luck I got him out at exactly the top of the market, well, that was what he thought I was supposed to do. I was just doing my job.

Many clients seemed to be driven by greed to squeeze every last penny of profit out of a deal, and they were eager to rip into me if they could have made more by buying or selling a little earlier or a little later. In many ways, being a stockbroker at Junior College was difficult for someone with a conscience. I certainly found it wrenching at times. I didn't like seeing my recommendations go down the toilet and my clients lose their money. But in many ways, the hard-edged, demanding attitude of the typical client made it easier for me to see my role as strictly a salesman. I was telling them why they should buy a stock from me in the same way that I used to tell suburban corporations why they needed security and lighting systems. The decision to buy or not was up to them. *Caveat emptor.* After all, this was a marketplace, a pure marketplace, and the first rule of any marketplace is, "Let the buyer beware."

Although I became personally friendly over the phone with my bigger clients, if I could, my strategy remained pretty much the same as it always had been with them, beginning with the first cold call. When I was pitching them something, I wasn't going to get off the phone until they bought. I didn't make them hang up on me the way I did when I was pitching a lead on a new account. But it was always up to them to bring the conversation to an end. Otherwise I was happy to stay on the phone all day, always closing the sale. "Yeah, I know, you told me you've got an office full of people waiting for you to give the presentation that was supposed to start ten minutes ago, so how many shares do you want? Five thousand?"

I fondly remember landmarks in my career as a broker. My first successful cold call. Opening my first account. Earning my first commission. One of those landmarks came after I had been at Junior College more than a year. I talked a client into selling out a position in a blue-chip stock at another brokerage, and investing the money with me in a Junior College microcap. I called him, pitched him on the stock, and listened impatiently while he told me he didn't have the money. Looking at my notes from my book, I reminded him that he had a good-sized portfolio with another firm, a wire house, and one of his biggest positions was in the blue-chip stock. He had told me this when I qualified him. "You could sell that stock," I suggested, trying to sound casual, as if I recommended that to clients all the time, and as if they did it all the time. He didn't say yes right away. He wanted to talk about it. I didn't know a damn thing good or bad about the blue-chip stock, but I made it sound like I did, and I made it sound like selling it was a very shrewd move.

"All right, I'll sell it," the client said eventually. "But I don't want to call my other broker and tell him why I'm selling it. I don't want to call him at all."

That was fine with me. I didn't want him to call his wire house broker, either. The other broker would probably talk him out of it. "Hey, I'll sell it for you," I said. I sent the client a standard form that allowed one brokerage to sell a stock held at another brokerage. He signed it and sent it back, and I sent it to the wire house and did the deal with no muss, no fuss, and an unexpected commission.

Clients rarely initiated contact with me or any other Junior College broker. They knew that if they called me, I would try to sell them something, and I would probably succeed. Maybe at the old-line wire houses, clients would sometimes call their brokers to discuss their portfolios, but not at Junior College. For most clients, their Junior College investments were a small part of their overall investment profile. The risky part, I assumed.

Once in a while a client would call and ask what I knew about this stock or that stock, but it was usually a fairly new or unsophisticated client who didn't understand what Junior College was all about, and that I specialized in low-volume microcaps that Junior College had taken public. The stock the client wanted to discuss was never one of Junior College's, so I never had anything to say about it. Junior College had no research department and no analysts. I could have looked up information on other stocks, but why bother? It wasn't a good use of my time to put my clients in non–Junior College stocks. Without admitting that I knew absolutely nothing about the stock in question, I would raise some doubts about it and then plunge right into selling the client on a Junior College stock. If he had money to ask about a stock, I had a stock for him to buy.

When Stuffy talked me into staying at Junior College instead of going to Wire House, part of the deal—along with the office and the cold caller—was his promise to make sure I got a good piece of every IPO that Junior College handled, no matter which senior vice president was running it. On the first couple of IPOs after that, I did get an allotment of new issues; not as many as I would have liked, but enough to open a couple of dozen new accounts each time, and breathe a little new life—and new money—into my book. But the next few IPOs were disappointing. I was getting meaningless allotments of new issues. On the most recent one, I had been promised 20,000 shares. I could have sold 100,000. I opened thirty accounts, thinking each one would get 500 to 1,000 shares. When the IPO came, however, I was allotted 2,000 shares. I was livid, and I marched right into Stuffy's office and told him so. "This is not what you led me to believe," I insisted. "You led me to believe I would get meaningful allotments of future IPOs." He sighed and shrugged. He had tried to get me more shares, he said. That was all he could do.

Three-quarters of the way into my first year as a vice president at Junior College, I wasn't even halfway toward the $800,000 in gross commissions I needed to become a senior vice president. I wasn't going to make it, and I blamed it on the lack of IPOs. I needed a change. I decided I needed to hook up with the one group of brokers at Junior College that was doing a lot of IPOs.

21

The Dirty Dozen

It was and is illegal for stockbrokers to work in groups. Even if brokers aren't manipulating stocks, working in groups could give the appearance of conspiracy and collusion. But at Junior College the Dirty Dozen worked as a group openly, blatantly, and enthusiastically. The leader of the Dirty Dozen was the Maniac. He was about my age, but had been at Junior College for four years—long enough to become a big producer, a multimillionaire, a senior vice president with a dozen brokers, sometimes more, working for him. I say working "for" him because of the way he dominated younger brokers. They weren't his serfs; they were his slaves, the way he bossed them around and abused them. If they didn't do want he wanted fast enough or well enough, he screamed at them, heaping on high-decibel, extremely personal insults that withered the poor guys in humiliation. Yet a lot of guys wanted to work for him. They wanted to join his group, and who could blame them? I was a big producer, putting up good numbers: $30,000 or $40,000 in gross commissions in good months. The brokers in the Maniac's group routinely topped $100,000 a month in gross commissions. It was as if he was running his own little company within Junior College. Young brokers wanted to join the Dirty Dozen because it was the surest and quickest way to get rich in a hurry on Wall Street. A little humiliation now and then was worth $1 million a year. After a few years, you could retire and go do whatever else you wanted to do in life.

The brokers in the Dirty Dozen all tried to act like junior versions of the Maniac. In fact, the guy who acted most like him was Lazlo, who became his number-one assistant, his second-in-command. Lazlo was a smart guy and a good salesmen, but most of the other brokers in the Dirty Dozen weren't the sharpest knives in the drawer. In fact, I was convinced that some of them would not have still been in the business if the Maniac had not taken them under his wing. But he did take them under his wing, and they were making big money—much bigger money than I was making at the time. I began to think about joining the Dirty Dozen. I was a better salesman than most of the Dirty Dozen guys, probably as good as Lazlo and not much behind the Maniac himself.

But I had mixed feelings. Junior College's shaky reputation on Wall Street was due in large part to the Dirty Dozen brokers. They did a lot of things that weren't right. They pushed customers too far. They talked clients into buying stock they didn't want or need, stock that they knew was on the way down. They manipulated stock prices to get bigger hidden commissions. They flat-out lied to their clients. "They're a dirty group," another broker told me one day.

"What do you mean, a dirty group?" I demanded. I pressed him for more details, but he just shook his head. He didn't want to talk about it. I would have to find out for myself what was so terrible about the Maniac and his group. I was confused. Maybe other brokers were bad-mouthing the Maniac and the Dirty Dozen solely because they were jealous.

I was certainly jealous. The Dirty Dozen brokers were set up at the opposite end of the Junior College board room, so I could easily see and hear them cheering and shouting. Their end of the room was frenetic, fast-paced, exciting. They were making money, crowing loudly over big trades, howling and high-fiving and chest-bumping each other not just when they had new IPOs, but in between new issues, too. They always seemed to have big trades coming up. Besides the specials with attractive hidden commissions that Junior College ran for the whole firm, the Maniac seemed to have frequent specials just for his brokers in the Dirty Dozen. None of us outsiders could figure out exactly how he did it, but his brokers seemed to have big days on a weekly basis, sometimes even more often. Despite my qualms, I began thinking that perhaps I should join the Dirty Dozen.

I made friends with some of the Dirty Dozen brokers, going out to lunch with them or getting drinks after work. They were mostly good guys, a lot like me: guys who hadn't done especially well in school, guys who would rather play a video game than read, guys who enjoyed the good life and liked to party, guys who liked making and spending money. I warmed to Lazlo, especially. He had some sort of Eastern European background, but we never really talked about it. I got the impression he was close to his family, but we never really talked about relatives, either. We talked—or rather, he talked—about his babes and his cars and his vacations and his clubbing. He talked about clients in vague terms, about things he had said to them or they had said to him, and about how much money he made on trades he talked them into making.

During the previous year, eleven of Junior College's fifty-some brokers had rolled up gross commissions of $1 million or more. Six of the million-dollar men, including Lazlo, came from the Dirty Dozen. "I brought in two million in new money under management into my book on the last IPO alone," Lazlo told me. "My total book is now past twenty million." That was huge by Junior College standards. The way Junior College in general and the Dirty Dozen in particular churned clients' money, he was going to have an enormous year. Even if he made only 10 percent on his clients' money, that was $2 million in gross commissions—$1 million for himself and $1 million for Junior College.

With the other brokers at our end of the board room, I had often talked about SmallTech and other companies that Junior College had taken public. We talked about their management, their products, their growth prospects, the technical analysis of the ups and downs of their shares. Lazlo and the other brokers in the Dirty Dozen never talked about that stuff. They didn't care. Occasionally they talked about big trades or big clients or how they had talked somebody into a trade, and how much commission they had earned from it without the client's knowledge. Mostly they talked about how much money they had and what they were spending it on. They seemed to spend a lot of it on luxuries, and just throw a lot of it away. They had to have the most exotic, expensive drinks. They had to buy rounds for the house. They bought Cuban cigars for $50 apiece, and then gave them away to strangers. They gave huge tips to strippers, and even more to call girls. They gambled like crazy men, not seeming to care whether they won or lost. I had not realized that bookies still existed, and that anybody could bet with them, until one of the Dirty Dozen brokers, a guy named Jimmie, had me over to his place to watch a basketball game. He kept calling his bookie, upping bets and making new bets. I couldn't keep track of all his bets, but my guess is that he lost about $3,000 just sitting there in his living room drinking beer and watching TV. And he didn't seem to care.

My night of debauchery with Lazlo, all the drinking and drugs and the strip joint and the casino, was not unusual for him, or for any of the Dirty Dozen brokers. I knew that was how they played. The next day, watching him resort to unauthorized trades and parking stock to make enough money to pay off his blackjack debts, was my first real peek into the way the Dirty Dozen brokers worked. When Lazlo bribed Travis to give him the trade confirmations that were supposed to be mailed out to clients, I knew it was wrong. But I didn't know what to do about it. It seemed so routine, as if it was a normal part of business not just within the Dirty Dozen, but throughout Junior College. The attitude throughout the brokerage house—indeed, throughout the entire securities industry, as near as I could tell—was that brokers would do whatever they could get away with.

The Dirty Dozen brokers seemed to think I somehow had helped find Travis, the mailroom guy who gave Lazlo the confirmation orders instead of sending them out to clients. They thought I had helped show them a new way to deal with unauthorized trades—what they called "wooden tickets." I still wasn't part of the Dirty Dozen, but suddenly I had honorary status within the group.

"Hey, you should move down to our end of the board room and start working with us." It became a refrain from Lazlo, Jimmie the Gambler, and the other Dirty Dozen brokers. The Maniac himself became friendly. He was just under six feet tall, blond, and handsome in a preppy sort of way. He was always impeccably dressed in expensive, stylish clothing. His hair was just so. The Maniac was particular about his skin. He always had a tan, a smooth, even tan. He took a lot of warm-weather vacations, but he never showed any sign of sunburn, and he kept the tan even in the dead of winter when he had not been away for a month. I figured that he spent a lot of time on the tanning beds, maybe even when he went to the Caribbean or wherever. Being out in the real sun would have wrecked the smoothness and made his skin at least a little red here and there. Besides the tan, he was also obsessed with the softness of his skin. He was always touching it, softly stroking the back of his hand or the side of his neck. He spent a lot of money on skin cream, and a lot of time putting it on and rubbing it in. He always smelled great.

Maniac swaggered around his end of the board room like a dictator, hollering at his guys, waving his arms. "If you haven't booked that stock I told you to sell by four o'clock this afternoon, I'm gonna nail your balls to the board room wall," he screamed. Lazlo sometimes strutted around behind, mimicking the Maniac's moves and threats, or just standing by and shaking his head, smiling sadly at the schmuck who was being berated, as if he was some loser who was being kept on for now, despite his miserable failings as a broker and, less significantly, as a human being.

One day Maniac and Lazlo came into the office, all excited. "Hey, c'mon down to the street," they told everybody. All the Dirty Dozen brokers went down, and a few of the brokers from my end of the board room went, too. I just looked out the window. Lazlo and the Maniac had purchased matching Mercedes convertibles, those sporty little ones that we used to call "mistress mobiles." The cars were identical except that Maniac's was red with a black leather interior and Lazlo's was black with a red interior. "Red leather always looks cheap to me, no matter how good it really is," I muttered to someone. In truth, envy was gnawing at me. I wanted to be making the kind of money where I could go out and buy a luxury car on a whim.

I began paying closer attention to the Dirty Dozen and the group's way of operating. It didn't take long to figure out how the Maniac and his minions made so much money. For one thing, they got a lot of deals, a lot of IPOs. Most senior vice presidents who supervised IPOs at Junior College had ties with investment bankers who brought them the deals. The Maniac got deals from investment bankers, but he and Lazlo also went out and found deals on their own. They would talk to friends or relatives or neighbors or clients or anybody they could to sniff out little companies that they could take public. They would hear about somebody trying to start a little company, get in touch with the guy, and pitch him on an IPO. Usually the guy hadn't even been considering it. "We can take you public, and you can make millions," they promised. "You personally can make millions." All of a sudden the guy was considering going public.

On a couple of occasions, I was told, the Dirty Dozen literally found deals in bars. The Maniac or Lazlo or one of their brokers would be out drinking, they'd meet a guy, the guy would say he was trying to get a company going, and the next thing you know Junior College was issuing an IPO for him. Once they took a vacation to a dude ranch in Wyoming or someplace, moose hunting or something, and came back with an IPO that called for the owner to create a chain of dude ranches throughout the West. I don't think any new dude ranches were ever opened, but in the meantime the IPO raised several million dollars, most of which was divided between the owner and the Dirty Dozen brokers.

Here's how it worked. The Maniac would bring a deal to Junior College, which would set up the IPO and underwrite it, giving the Maniac the vast majority of the shares to sell to clients. A relatively few shares would be distributed to other Wall Street firms to help build a buzz and get some publicity for the IPO. The Maniac would then allocate his shares among the Dirty Dozen brokers. They would get on the phone, cold calling, to open new accounts. They would "second trade" the new accounts, telling them that they couldn't get any shares in the IPO unless they promised to spend a certain amount buying shares in the aftermarket in the days following the IPO. Nobody in the Dirty Dozen, including the Maniac, seemed to care that this was illegal. Indeed, he encouraged it. Dirty Dozen brokers would also call existing clients and tell them about the IPO, but they would tell the existing clients that they could not have any shares when they were first issued; however, the existing clients could buy in the aftermarket, when the stock was just starting to go up.

Along with their new accounts, the Dirty Dozen brokers worked hard to set up "nominee" accounts. These accounts were usually opened on behalf of friends or relatives who did not have the same last names as the brokers, in order to avoid suspicion among securities regulators. Nominee accounts were illegal because they were not true investment accounts opened by and for investors, and under investors' control. Instead, they were opened in another person's name, but were controlled by the brokers for the purpose of manipulating the stock price. An old college buddy was always a good choice, or some distant relative who had a different last name. Jimmie the Gambler, the Dirty Dozen broker who had introduced me to the world of bookies, often had several nominee accounts lined up for an IPO. He would get a buddy 10,000 shares of an IPO at $5, and then sell the stock for the buddy when it got to $6. The broker and the buddy would split the $10,000 profit. If the buddy didn't have the money to buy the stock, Jimmie might lend it to him—but in that case the broker might give the buddy only $1,000 or even $500 of the profit instead of $5,000. Jimmie told me that a mutual acquaintance, one of my old fraternity brothers working as a bartender, had made close to $100,000 by acting as a nominee for Junior College IPOs. Once Jimmie showed me a paper bag full of hundred-dollar bills, the bartender's $18,000 share of an IPO, that he was going to drop off at the bar where he worked.

The next time I saw my old frat brother the bartender, I mentioned something about his Junior College investments with Jimmie. He told me that in the previous two years he had actually made almost $150,000 acting as Jimmie's nominee for IPOs, and that after his biggest score, nearly $25,000, he had spread the money out on his bed and let his girlfriend roll around in it naked, like Demi Moore in the movie *Indecent Proposal*. "Got the best sex of my life that night," the bartender confided.

• • •

Nominees were important for IPOs handled by the Dirty Dozen because they allowed the group to amass large chunks of stock at relatively cheap prices, and that's where the manipulation came in. An IPO would come out at $8 per share, and the broker would sell it to the nominee.

The stock would jump right up to $10, largely because of buy orders that Jimmie and the other Dirty Dozen brokers had placed even before the stock was issued. They placed those orders based on the demand they had generated for the stock in the aftermarket. The more buy orders, the higher the stock would open. Once the stock opened above the issue price—$10, for example—the broker would sell the stock from the nominee accounts back to Junior College's own accounts in its trading department. Since Junior College was making a market in the IPO stock, its trading department was allowed to accumulate blocs of stock. The Dirty Dozen brokers would keep that stock in reserve in the Junior College accounts, while at the same time building up the demand by pitching it to both new and existing accounts in the aftermarket. The stock would go up to $11, and then Dirty Dozen brokers could sell it and keep the $1 price increase as a hidden commission that clients never knew they were paying. Meanwhile, the stock kept moving higher, which made it easier for the Dirty Dozen brokers to get more orders and drive the stock up even more.

The Dirty Dozen brokers wanted to control as much of the stock as possible. If they lost control of it, if it went to investors who were not their clients, those investors might sell it to someone else who was not a client for the true market value. The Maniac and his brokers typically controlled 70 percent or more of all the shares issued in one of their house stocks. Whenever someone outside their group offered the stock for sale, the Dirty Dozen brokers snapped it up before the price could drop. The Dirty Dozen brokers did not want "their" stocks to trade for their true market value. They wanted their stocks to keep going up, and to trade for much more than their true value. The way they manipulated the prices of stocks operated much like a pyramid scheme. They did it with the tacit cooperation of the Junior College trading department. The trading department was a profit center for Junior College; the higher the commissions, the more money everybody earned: the firm, the traders, and the brokers—all at the expense of the clients.

22

Crossing, Churning, Parking

It quickly became apparent that while most Junior College brokers were happy to take advantage of big spreads and hidden commissions, there was a difference in what the Dirty Dozen brokers did. They didn't just take advantage of the spreads, they created the spreads through stock manipulation. Junior College brokers emphasized buying, not selling, the firm's house stock. That was just good business. But the Maniac tried to go further. He absolutely prohibited his brokers from selling their stock to anyone outside the Dirty Dozen or their nominees. He did not want to allow a single share to leak "out of the box" onto the open market, where there was a risk that it would be traded at its true—and much lower—market value. A trade like that would undermine the entire pyramid of the artificial market he and the other Dirty Dozen brokers had created for the stock.

By not allowing any outsiders to gauge the price of their stocks, the Maniac and the Dirty Dozen could keep the value wherever they wanted. By continuing to push the stock in the aftermarket, and playing on the temporary liquidity from Wall Street's brief fling in the first few days, the Dirty Dozen typically could push a $10 IPO stock up to $20 or $30. At some point, when the Maniac thought the market might be reaching a top—the number of buyers was drying up, in other words—he would order the Dirty Dozen brokers to start selling the blocs of shares they had accumulated from their nominee accounts at the original IPO price. I saw and heard the Dirty Dozen brokers flat-out lie to their clients about stock prices. If a stock was trading at $10 bid by $10.50 asked, they might tell the client it was at $11. The client would buy it at $11, and the Dirty Dozen broker would pocket the $1 per share that the client had overpaid. "Cuffing the quote" was what they called it. Cuffing quotes was particularly useful, and profitable, for the Dirty Dozen when they were manipulating a stock. If they knew that the share price was going to $11 because they were going to take it there, they had fewer worries about getting in trouble with the SEC if they made a trade at $11 when the price was still at $10. A client who went back into the records looking for evidence that the broker had lied to him would see that, yes, at some point during the day the stock had traded at $11.

The big problem with microcap stocks, particularly those being manipulated by Dirty Dozen brokers, was liquidity. Within a few days of an IPO, other Wall Street firms typically had taken their early profits and disappeared from the trading. They weren't interested in hanging on to the stock. They just grabbed quick profits for themselves and their clients. When they sold the stock, they typically sold it through Junior College, which was the principal market maker for the stock. The stock went either into Junior College's inventory or into the portfolios of Dirty Dozen clients. There were a finite number of buyers: the clients on the Dirty Dozen brokers' books.

While "normal" stocks listed on the big exchanges would trade tens of thousands, hundreds of thousands, even millions of shares per day, these microcaps would trade in the thousands, even the hundreds. With such low liquidity—and no legitimate outside buyers—the challenge for the Dirty Dozen was to keep their own clients buying and selling "their" stocks within this closed, artificial market. One illegal trick they used was "churning" stock, sometimes within the group and sometimes within their own books. Suppose a client purchased stock at $9 in the aftermarket, a day or two following a $7 IPO. Junior College's trading department, meanwhile, listed the prices for the stock at $10 bid by $11 asked.

The Dirty Dozen broker would advise the client to sell his stock for $10, a quick little 11 percent profit. The broker would buy the stock into Junior College's inventory at $10, and immediately turn around and sell it to another of his clients for $11, thereby earning a hidden commission of $1 and, almost as important, boosting demand within the closed artificial market that the Dirty Dozen had created. The trading department could then raise the price of the stock to $11 bid and $12 asked, and the broker could call another client who had bought the stock at $7 or $8, and persuade him to sell it for $11. The broker would then sell that stock to yet another client for $12. Again, the broker pocketed a hidden commission, and the price went up. This was not how the securities industry was supposed to work in a fair and orderly public market. This was a closed market artificially created by Dirty Dozen brokers at their desks.

The trades mentioned above all carried the advantage—for the broker, anyway—of having big spreads that generated big hidden commissions. But even Junior College's 5 percent straight commission, collected both on the sale and the purchase of stocks, could yield nice paydays for brokers when they were churning or "crossing" stocks, which was another illegal tactic common in the Maniac's group, especially on slow afternoons when there wasn't a new IPO or a special to flog. Lazlo might turn to Jimmie the Gambler, sitting next to him, and say, "Hey, I've got a client with fifty thousand dollars invested in Stock A. You got anybody like that?"

"Sure," Jimmie might say. "I've got a client with fifty grand in Stock B."

"Great," Lazlo would say. "Let's cross them."

Lazlo would call his client and persuade him to sell out his $50,000 position in Stock A and buy the $50,000 worth of Stock B from Jimmie's client. Jimmie would persuade his client to sell out the $50,000 in Stock B and buy the $50,000 worth of Stock A from Lazlo's client. In effect, the two clients swapped positions. But each client was at least $5,000 poorer because each had paid a 5 percent commission—$2,500—first to sell the old stock, and then to buy the new stock. Lazlo and Jimmie each collected $5,000 either from cash in the client's account, or by selling off some of their clients' stock. If the client didn't have any cash for the broker to collect, the client emerged from the two trades not with $50,000 worth of stock, but with $45,000. The missing $5,000 had gone straight into the broker's pocket.

I did not cross or churn or park stocks. I could have made more money if I did, but I didn't want to get complaints from my clients. I wanted to keep them happy. I wasn't afraid of losing my license. At Junior College, that didn't seem like something that could happen for merely crossing, churning, or parking stocks. In fact, I was at Junior College for about a year before I realized those practices were really illegal. Within the Dirty Dozen, it seemed like a routine way of doing business. And as near as I could tell, none of the managers at Junior College objected. They didn't seem to be particularly bothered by ethical issues or other regulatory problems for their brokers, including the Dirty Dozen. Like every brokerage firm, Junior College had a compliance officer, a well-paid executive whose job was to make sure that the brokerage and its brokers conformed to the rules. Maybe he didn't know what was going on. Or maybe he was told to look the other way. For whatever reason, the rules were routinely ignored by Junior College brokers. It was much different from Harvard, where if a broker got a complaint he was in hot water with the managers. If a Harvard broker got a serious complaint from the SEC, he was gone.

The Junior College managers did discipline the Dirty Dozen brokers internally, sometimes, sort of. There were always lots of informal complaints flying around, usually about parking stocks, which clients could spot when they received their account statements and saw that they owned stocks they had not wanted to buy. Churning and crossing were harder to pin down because clients actually approved those trades in advance. They probably would not have approved them had they known the brokers were churning and crossing them solely for the commissions, but it was more difficult to prove that. A broker could simply lie and say he was acting in the clients' best interest and giving his best professional advice.

When they saw that a stock had been parked in their accounts, most clients were quick to phone or fax to complain that they had paid for trades they had not ordered. For the most part Junior College either ignored the complaints or allowed the accused brokers to work things out quietly with the clients. Brokers usually accomplished this by giving back just enough of the clients' lost money to make them shut up and go away without making formal complaints to the Secur-ities and Exchange Commission or the National Association of Se-curities Dealers.

Brokers headed off a lot of the complaints themselves, sometimes even before the statements arrived and the clients could call in. Several brokers routinely parked stock, paid off Travis to withhold their trade confirmations, and then called up the clients and warned that their next statements would contain "a clerical error" showing that they had purchased the unwanted stock. "Just ignore that," the brokers would tell the clients. And the brokers would have another month to either sell the stock to someone else or find another client's account where they could park it.

I went out to lunch with Jimmie one afternoon when he returned to his office to find that one of his clients had called to inquire about an unauthorized trade. Jimmie's sales assistant, who was new, had referred the call to the Junior College operations department, and the operations department had nullified the trade. Jimmie had parked the stock and gotten caught. He reacted like a typical Junior College broker: He screamed at the sales assistant. How could she be so stupid? Why wouldn't she just take the message and let him return the client's call? Why was she trying to kill his business? It was a weird scene. The sales assistant merely had tried to do what she thought was her job—provide service to the client. She was learning that service to the client was not her job.

Sometimes when clients did make formal complaints, Junior College or its brokers were ordered by the SEC or NASD to pay fines or make restitution. They did this faithfully, as a cost of doing business, and always with the notice in the published report that they did so without admitting or denying any wrongdoing. Junior College usually took no additional disciplinary action against offending brokers. Once in a while, Junior College would suspend a broker for a few days if a complaint was still pending and the firm figured that the suspension might lessen the fine later. The broker would stay away from the office and trade from home. He'd come back in after his suspension with a stack of tickets for new trades that he would turn in to the trading department to execute. Nobody at Junior College batted an eye.

I witnessed a good example that sums up how different Junior College was from Harvard. One evening a broker who wasn't doing well apparently sneaked into the desk of another broker who was doing even worse, and photocopied some of the pages of the other broker's book. The other broker found out about it and confronted the thief in the board room. The thief slugged him in the face, knocking him down. The thief was shouting, "I wasn't stealing your goddam clients, I was just borrowing them!" as a couple of other brokers dragged him away and kept him from committing further mayhem on his victim. The guy whose clients had been "borrowed" and who had been knocked down complained to Junior College's managers. They gave the thief a reprimand. A verbal reprimand. And that was it. He, after all, was a bigger producer than the broker whose book had been stolen and who got punched in the face.

• • •

Most of the Dirty Dozen's clients loved the Maniac and his brokers—at least for a while. And why not? Dirty Dozen brokers would call them, promise them that their investments would go up 20 percent in a few days, and then that's what would happen. Dirty Dozen brokers would call again, the clients would invest again, and the stock would run up again. As this happened over and over, clients came to trust the Maniac and his group. I'm sure many clients must have known these were shady, unethical brokers, but I think many of those clients liked that idea. They didn't see themselves as doing anything illegal, but they were happy to have brokers who did—as long as the returns were high.

At first I thought the Dirty Dozen's clients were the sort of people who probably cheated when playing Monopoly with their kids. Then I realized that wasn't right. Most of their clients were probably regular people, no better or worse than anyone else, who became a little bit irrational when it came to investing. Or maybe a little bit greedy. I came to think that pretty much any investor would be willing to overlook his suspicions about stock manipulation if he were the one benefiting from it—even when it should have been obvious to clients that they were being misled. For instance, on several occasions I heard Jimmie on the phone lying to clients that a stock price was $8—clients themselves rarely had any easy access to up-to-the-minute prices of microcap stocks. Then, when the trade was made at $9, Jimmie would make up a story for the clients about how some big orders had come in just seconds before his trade, unexpectedly boosting the stock and forcing the clients to pay more than anticipated. Jimmie would congratulate the clients for buying a stock that was obviously heating up, and the clients would think they had just made a good move.

However, no matter how hard the Maniac and the Dirty Dozen worked to keep artificial markets thriving in as many stocks as they could—usually three or four at a time—and to bring out a new IPO every few months, sometimes a stock would start to fade. And they all

faded eventually. It was a pyramid, after all, and so far the only pyramids that haven't crumbled are in Egypt. No matter how much the
price rose, no matter how hard the Dirty Dozen brokers pushed their
clients to buy more, some clients ran out of money. When clients
couldn't buy any more stock, the price stopped going up. When the
price stopped going up, some clients insisted on taking their profits.
Dirty Dozen brokers, using every strategy from begging to threatening,
tried to persuade them not to sell. Inevitably, as the price stagnated,
more clients began to sell, which forced down the share price even
further. As the price dropped, more clients sold, at first to lock in their
profits and then to cut their losses.

Sometimes, usually when they were about to pitch a client on more
stock or a client was complaining about how much a stock had gone
down, a desperate Dirty Dozen broker would buy a few shares himself just as the market was about to close. Jimmie did this several
times. If the stock had been trading at $5, he might order the Junior
College trading department to buy him a few shares at $6. Thus $6
would be the closing price for the day, and the opening price the next
day. If Jimmie did that on that last day of the statement period, the
artificial $6 price was what the client saw on his account when the
statement arrived in the mail. By then Jimmie had probably sold out
his small position for a few dollars' loss, and the stock had dipped
back to $5. But the client didn't know that. The client looked at his
statement, saw that the stock had gone up from $5 to $6, and was
receptive to the sales pitch when Jimmie called back and said the stock
was starting to move again.

Once a Dirty Dozen stock started to slip, the fall was almost always
inexorable. Within months, it was not unusual to see a stock that had
been trading at $20 be listed at $1 or $2, with no volume. Sometimes
the companies went out of business, and sometimes they lingered in
name only, with a supposed share price in the pennies—if there had
been anyone to buy them. Many of the Dirty Dozen's clients lost all or
most of the money they had invested. But that didn't seem to matter

to the Maniac and the rest of the Dirty Dozen. By then they had a new IPO and a fresh group of new accounts with new money, eager to pour it into a surefire investment. The burned-up clients simply disappeared, sadder but not a hell of a lot wiser. They thought they had been burned by the vagaries of the microcap market and IPOs. They thought they simply had bought high and sold low. They didn't realize that much of the money they had lost had gone into the pockets of Junior College and the individual brokers in the Dirty Dozen. In effect, they had been swindled.

It helped the Dirty Dozen that the group had an inordinate number of clients in foreign countries, especially Bermuda. I don't know how the Maniac made the first connection, but he probably made some money for one rich guy over there, who then told his rich buddy about it, who then told another rich buddy about it, and so on. Kind of like a tip on a horse race that's been fixed. I could just imagine these wealthy expatriate aristocrats sitting around in their fancy polo and yacht clubs, talking about the outlandish returns on their speculation in American stocks, as if it was some wild and woolly Third World country.

By the time I started watching them, the Dirty Dozen brokers had perhaps a couple of dozen very wealthy clients in Bermuda—people who had invested between $1 million and $5 million with the Dirty Dozen. The Maniac and Lazlo were always on the phone to Bermuda, and once or twice a month one or both of them would fly over "for the day" to meet with clients and raise some more cash. They returned with armloads of vintage champagne, boxes of Cuban cigars, cartons of expensive perfume from duty-free shops, and stories of hookers servicing them in hot tubs. They also bragged about how they had talked the clients into giving them more money. The infusion of money propped up and prolonged the pyramids.

I figured that the Bermuda clients were likely to invest more because they were far away. They didn't realize the reputation of Junior College and the Maniac's group. Or maybe they did, and the distance made it easier for them to look the other way. I loved it when one client from Bermuda, who happened to be an Arab prince or sheik or something, announced that he was coming in to meet the Maniac, who was overseeing the guy's $2 million account. I saw the sheik come in, and I could tell he was surprised by the atmosphere of Junior College. It wasn't the same sort of House of Morgan or Rothschild atmosphere where he usually did his financial business. He disappeared into Maniac's office for twenty minutes, and then departed with a cordial handshake. Maniac was fist-pumping around the office, crowing about how he was going to get a couple more million from the sheik. Then a fax came in not twenty minutes after the sheik had departed. He was faxing from his limo. He wanted all his accounts at Junior College closed immediately, and the funds wired to his bank in Bermuda. Apparently the Maniac had made quite an impression.

When a stock started to fall, the Maniac typically began to sell the shares—often huge blocs of shares—that he personally controlled. Some of the shares were part of his compensation for helping to arrange the IPO; they were often awarded to him for a small fraction of the original IPO cost. Some of the shares were from his own nominee accounts. When the pyramid was at or near what he thought was its peak and the pool of buyers was about to diminish, the Maniac began to feed out the shares under his control, and when the stock price began to fall he started selling them as if he was bailing out a sinking boat.

He did this by telling his brokers he had shares for them to sell. Sometimes these shares, I came to realize, were the basis for the "specials" he ran for his group only. He bought a big bloc of stock at a $10 IPO price, watched it climb to $20, and then when it fell back to $17 he ran a special that gave his brokers a $2 hidden commission—and a 50 percent profit for himself. He never told his brokers that the new shares were his own. And most of them never seemed to be able to figure it out. Or maybe they just didn't want to face the reality that their leader was stabbing them in the back by forcing them to sell his shares at a huge profit while undercutting their artificial market. He would breeze into the office in the morning, call all his guys into a closed-door meeting, and tell them he had 100,000 shares of one of their stocks that had to be sold to clients by the close of trading that day. He would give each broker a chunk of shares to sell: one guy had to sell 10,000, another had to sell 15,000, another had to sell 7,500. If a broker argued that he didn't think he could book the shares with his clients, the Maniac turned on him with a withering fury. And the Dirty Dozen brokers took his abuse meekly.

One afternoon I was going to go shopping for a birthday present for Melanie at Steuben—she liked little glass sculptures and figurines, as long as I didn't tell her how much they cost—and I went looking for Jimmie to see if he wanted to come along. He usually was up for whatever I had in mind, from the bar to the gym to the shops, but this time he said no way. I found him at his desk, his head in his hands. I thought he was going to cry. "I don't know what I'm gonna do," he said. "Maniac says I've got to book twenty thousand shares of this stock by the end of the day, and I don't think I can do it. Nobody will buy it anymore. He says I won't get any of the new IPO if I don't do it. He says he might kick me out of the group."

Like other Dirty Dozen brokers, Jimmie was terrified of losing his job with the Maniac. They were all getting rich because of the Maniac, even if he made impossible demands, stabbed them in the back, and treated them like dirt. They had to go out and work even harder to sell declining shares to a shrinking pool of clients.

Brokers did leave the Dirty Dozen when they got sick of the pace and the pressure, but there were always plenty of other young brokers at Junior College who were interested—including me. I told myself that what they were doing must not be all that unethical or illegal, largely because they just kept doing it and nobody seemed to mind, least of all the managers of Junior College. When the Maniac and Junior began talking to me about joining the Dirty Dozen, I was flattered. But I wasn't quite ready to join them. I had been at Junior College for twenty-three months. I would wait another month, until my two-year anniversary, to decide whether I would join the Dirty Dozen.

23

Prep School

Junior College was always awash in rumors, often about who was leaving the firm and where they were going. During the time the Maniac was wooing me, rumors floated around about him leaving and taking the whole Dirty Dozen with him. The buzz was that he was going to start his own firm. He was tired of sharing his commissions with Junior College. If he owned the whole company, he could keep 100 percent. I watched for signs, and soon found them. The Maniac wasn't around as much. He was in and out a lot. I figured he was setting up his new office. It must have been somewhere nearby, because he was rarely gone for more than a couple of hours. He and his group seemed to be having more hush-hush, closed-door meetings than ever.

They were definitely leaving. I wondered if I should try to go with them. Sure, I was a vice president at Junior College. I had my own office, or half of one, anyway. The Kid was doing a lot of the tedious stuff for me. I was making a good living. But the work was slowing down. I was just pushing the same tired old stocks back and forth among my clients. I felt like my business was losing its energy, its momentum. I had no new deals anywhere on the horizon. I was getting stale, and I could see how it was affecting my business. With no new deals, things were only going to get worse. One afternoon the Maniac walked into my office. "Hey, stud," he said. "Take a walk with me."

The new firm he was starting was only a couple of blocks away, on the fourth floor of a building right on Wall Street. It was like a scaled-down version of Junior College, except the furnishings were all new. It was nice. I liked it. Everything was there, ready to go, even the computers. But no workers. We were the only people there. The Maniac showed me around, and told me about the guys from Junior College who were coming over with him: Lazlo, of course, and most of the rest of the Dirty Dozen, plus a handful of other Junior College brokers I knew and liked. I remarked that it must be expensive to start a securities trading company from scratch, but he said it hadn't cost him anything personally. Indeed, he had made money on the deal through a private placement, selling tiny pieces of the company to several of his wealthiest clients for $1 million each. He used some of the money to start the firm, and pocketed the rest. Everything in the office was new and first-class, not worn and threadbare and thrown-together like at Junior College. Between the decor, the youthfulness of the Maniac and his followers, and the way they dressed, this was more like a Prep School.

"We're going to open soon," he said. He explained that his group just had to tidy up "a few loose ends" at Junior College. When that was taken care of, he said, the whole group was going to get up, walk out of Junior College, come straight over to Prep School, sit down, and start doing business. Big business, he said. He was working on a couple of sweet new IPOs, maybe the best deals he had ever been involved in. Megabucks for all. "We'd like you to consider joining us," he said. I asked him to tell me more. He told me he would make the same offer he was making to five other Junior College vice presidents he considered especially promising. He said I would come on as a senior vice president and partner. I would get a piece of the firm, 1 percent to start but with the possibility of increasing to 5 percent within a couple of years.

A partner. I could be a partner in a securities firm. I had been a broker for less than two years. Even as he was telling me about it, I could imagine calling my mother and father and telling them. I was drawn out of this little daydream by Maniac's explanation that the job offer depended in part on how well I helped overcome one of the hurdles blocking his exit from Junior College. "Keep talking," I said. He said he had quite a few shares in Junior College's inventory. Selling those shares to clients was part of the tying up of the loose ends of his business at Junior College, which he had to do before he could leave to start another firm. All the shares in inventory, naturally, were from companies he had helped take public. The biggest chunk, about 100,000 shares, was from a company that ran a chain of karate schools. The Killer Karate shares had gone public at $3 six months earlier, rocketed up to $18 in the first few weeks, and then gradually declined. They were at $8 at the moment, but the Maniac said he "had a plan" for getting the stock back into double digits as soon as he opened his new firm.

Maniac said he had only three partnerships available for the six of us he was recruiting from Junior College. The three of us who booked the most of the 100,000 shares of the Killer Karate stock for him, selling it out of Junior College's inventory to our own clients, would join the Maniac in his new firm as partners. Without thinking, I said count me in. I figured it wasn't much of a commitment. I could pitch as much or as little of the stock as I wanted. Even if I was one of the top three, which I fully expected, I could always tell him I had changed my mind and decided to stay at Junior College if I didn't want to move with him. I shook hands and walked back to the Junior College offices.

I was surprised when the Maniac followed me into my office. "Let me see your book," he said. He grabbed the looseleaf binder that held my handwritten records for all my clients, listed all their current holdings, and logged all their previous trades. Like most brokers, I didn't like anyone looking through my book. But the Maniac just grabbed it and started thumbing through as if it were his. I began to imagine how it would be to work for—not with, *for*—this guy, to be part of his group, at his new firm. All I had done was shake hands, and now he acted like he owned me. He started making suggestions about which clients could dump what existing stock position to buy some of the Killer Karate shares he wanted to unload from the Junior College inventory. He pointed out which clients had enough cash in their accounts to buy some Killer Karate stock.

He said I could park it in their accounts, the same way Lazlo had parked stock by making unauthorized trades for unsuspecting clients and then trying to cover his tracks before they could find out about it. If need be, I could use Travis the same way that Lazlo had. And even if a few of my lousy little clients got angry and left me, so what? There would be plenty of new clients, bigger clients, full-blown whales, at Prep School when I came over there as a senior vice president and partner.

I didn't want to hear about parking stock or burning my clients. But I still harbored the thought that I could book the Maniac's stock and become a partner at Prep School without doing anything wrong myself. "Look," I finally said, trying to show only a little of my irritation, "if you give me my damn book and get out of here, I can get to work." He snapped the book shut and walked out without another word.

For the rest of the afternoon, I called clients and pitched them on the Killer Karate shares that Maniac was trying to unload. I hadn't said anything to Maniac, but I knew why he needed help selling the stock. His brokers were having trouble selling it to their usual clients. This particular pyramid was crumbling. The Dirty Dozen was choking on the stock, and needed fresh blood. Without new investors, each passing day and each downward tick of the share price was costing the Maniac money on his 100,000 shares.

I booked about 10,000 shares with half a dozen of my clients that afternoon. Most of my clients weren't interested. I must not have been at my sharpest, and maybe I wasn't as persuasive as usual—probably because in my heart I wasn't convinced that it was in my clients' best interests to buy that stock at that moment. On the other hand, Maniac had told me that the stock was going to go up again. He could have been just telling me what I wanted to hear. But maybe he was being straight. Either way, I had pitched stocks to clients in the past with fewer assurances than that. But somehow this didn't feel right. My doubts about going to Prep School were increasing. I knew the Maniac and his gang cut corners legally and ethically. But their work was so much more exciting—and lucrative. I felt like I might be getting into bed with the devil, but it was a very attractive devil—and a devil I thought I could control.

At home that evening, Melanie and I talked about it. "Do whatever you think is best," she said. She always said that; it was very supportive, but not very helpful. I woke up in the middle of the night screaming, bathed in sweat. I don't remember dreaming anything, but at that moment I knew I wasn't going to try to book any more Killer Karate stock. The next morning I went in to the Maniac's office and said, "I'm out of the competition. I won't be coming with you to the new firm."

He seemed surprised and puzzled, but didn't ask for any reasons. Instead, he just said, "Okay. Maybe you're not ready for the big time. But you will be soon. Just let me know."

I went back to my clients who had bought the Killer Karate stock and told them I had made a mistake. Those were the hardest calls I ever made as a stockbroker. I told my clients I wanted to take them out of Killer Karate and back to whatever stock they had been in. I didn't want them to think I was churning their accounts just to generate commissions, so I offered to waive my commissions. They all said no, that was all right, they would pay the commissions. They said they were glad I had called when I realized I had made a mistake. Some brokers would have kept quiet, one told me, and just hoped that somehow the stock would go up. My clients believed me, and they trusted me. It was gratifying, but I knew I had done them wrong.

I saw Maniac a few more times around Junior College before he finally left for Prep School. There was no discussion of my joining the new firm as a partner or anything else. Not joining Prep School was the best thing I ever did in my life. If I had, there's a good chance I would be writing this from prison.

Prep School got off to a roaring start when Maniac and his gang left Junior College a couple of weeks later. I was surprised to find that a couple of dirty brokers—so dirty they had been fired by Junior College for making so many illegal trades that even Junior College couldn't ignore them—had resurfaced at Prep School. I thought they had been banned from the securities industry, but here they were happily trading away and getting rich as vice presidents at Prep School.

Prep School had an IPO within a month of opening for business, then another not long after. I heard from Lazlo and a few of the other former Junior College brokers that they were making more money than they ever had at Junior College, and they were hiring brokers from other firms. Lazlo encouraged me to go see Maniac and try to join the firm. "You'll get richer than you ever imagined," Lazlo said. "Look at me. I'm probably going to make two million—*net* two million—in the firm's first year. Plus several hundred grand, probably at least half a million, as my share of the partnership. You could do the same. You're crazy not to come over." It was tempting. I wanted to make that kind of money, but I didn't want to work with the Maniac.

I ran into the Maniac at parties a few times over the next couple of years. We just kind of nodded to each other. I heard that he was making over $1 million a month. I still saw Jimmie and a few of the Dirty Dozen brokers socially, usually when I ran into them in bars or in my neighborhood. Sometimes I played squash at a club on the Upper East Side with Jimmie, and we would go out afterward.

Jimmie loved working at Prep School. None of the hassles of bosses looking over his shoulder, the way it had been at Junior College. He told me he had changed a client's life. He had talked the guy into investing his last $200,000 in a Prep School IPO, and it had gone up tenfold in a matter of weeks. The guy had called Jimmie and offered to buy him a Porsche, but Jimmie had turned him down. He had just bought a Porsche. When he ordered the car, he told me, he wrote a check for $110,000, and the Porsche salesman told him it would be ready in two days. Jimmie gave him $2,000 more in cash to have it ready in an hour.

One night Jimmie said something about a "brown bag operation" at Prep School, and I asked what he meant. He explained that stock promoters—non-brokers hired by companies to encourage people to buy their stock and drive up the price—often made under-the-table payments to Prep School brokers who talked their clients into buying the stock. The payments were always in cash, usually $100 bills, and were typically delivered in an ordinary brown paper grocery bag that was handed over in a bar or on a street corner. Jimmie told me he himself had received up to $10,000 in a bag, but he knew that payments could be much bigger than that. He once picked up a bag from a stock promoter to be delivered to the Maniac, and the Maniac had opened it in front of Jimmie and counted out $120,000. Jimmie said that wasn't the only kind of brown bag operation at Prep School. Sometimes he would pay off brokers from wire houses who had agreed to recommend Prep School's house stocks to their own clients. Those brown bag payments were typically much smaller, $2,000 or $3,000 or $4,000, Jimmie said, laughing at how supposedly straitlaced, proper brokers could be bought off so cheaply.

Jimmie said Prep School was also refining the use of nominee accounts with another trick, also illegal, that was called "spinning" IPO shares and had an extra dividend for the Maniac and his brokers. The Maniac was always trying to persuade corporate and venture-capital executives to bring him IPO deals. To help talk them into giving him the business, the Maniac began offering them big pieces of other IPOs for their private portfolios. The Maniac would give a venture capitalist $500,000 worth of an IPO, the share price would go up 20 percent on the first day, and the Maniac would sell out the account. The grateful venture capitalist would have a neat $100,000 in personal profit in a few hours, and would be much more disposed to place his next IPO with Prep School when the time came.

Maniac, Lazlo, Jimmie, and the other Prep School brokers loved to hang out after work in expensive strip clubs like Scores, Tens, Stringfellow's, and Pure Platinum. I went with Jimmie once, and he described the system of signals the brokers had with the girls. "A routine tip for a dancer is ten or twenty dollars," Jimmie explained. "If you really like her, you tip her a hundred-dollar bill. If she comes over after her dance and sits down with you and orders a drink—usually watered-down champagne, at twenty bucks for a couple of ounces—it's a signal she's available. If she lights a cigarette, she's willing to sleep with you. You give her five hundred, she meets you outside, and she goes home with you, or wherever you want to go. I like to take 'em to the Peninsula Hotel. She spends a couple of hours with you for five bills, and if you have a good time you tip her a couple of hundred more."

Jimmie told me that he did this two or three times a week. It was his social life. "Yeah, it's expensive, but I can afford it," he said. "Besides, it's worth it when you don't have to go through all the trouble of meeting someone, asking her out, getting to know her, wining and dining her, doing all that just to get laid. This costs about the same, and every time you can have a different beautiful woman who'll do anything you want."

One day Jimmie called me from Prep School and asked me to

come and see his new apartment. He actually had purchased two apartments, adjacent condos in a newly renovated building on the Upper West Side, knocked out the walls and had them renovated into a huge one-bedroom. He hired a decorator and paid her to put in marble floors and suede wallpaper. He bought a vibrating massage chair for $3,000. He bought a six-foot-tall aquarium for $10,000, and spent another $5,000 stocking it. I noticed that the fish were floating, and said something about it. "Aw, they say you're supposed to clean the goddam tank. I don't have time for that shit," Jimmie said. As near as I could tell, all the Prep School brokers were making and spending money like that. I ran into Lazlo on the golf course, and he was wearing alligator golf shoes. He told me he had moved to a big place in the suburbs with an indoor pool and a maid and butler who both lived in. He said he could screw the maid any time he wanted. I heard that the Maniac was rolling up business expenses of $50,000 a month on his platinum card, including frequent flights to Bermuda—on chartered Learjets by then—to raise more money.

Melanie and I were out to dinner one night in SoHo with some friends, a lawyer and his wife, when we ran into the Maniac and his wife. They were leaving just as we were, and he invited us to go to a bar with him. It was a posh place, and he ordered champagne, a bottle per person. My lawyer friend's eyes bugged out. "Do I have to pay for this?" he whispered to me with alarm. No worries, I said. Then the Maniac ordered an $800 bottle of cognac. When we left, we left the bottle two-thirds full on the table, along with a $300 tip on the Maniac's credit card.

A few months later the Maniac, still trying to recruit me, asked me to join him, Lazlo, Jimmie, and several other Prep School brokers for a trip to Las Vegas for a heavyweight title fight. The Maniac said he would cover the plane flight, the rooms, the fight tickets, everything but gambling losses. We flew out first-class, got there in the afternoon, and checked into one of the big hotel-casinos. The other guys headed for the tables, but I wanted to play golf. When I got back, there was a message for me to come to one of the hotel's penthouses. I showered, changed, and went up. The elevator door opened, and there were two gorgeous women waiting for me. They were wearing G-strings and nothing else. "Rob?" they asked, giggling. "Hey, everybody's been waiting for you. C'mon, we'll take you to the party."

The party was in a big room with floor-to-ceiling windows that offered a spectacular view of the Strip and the desert sunset beyond. A bartender was on duty, and a butler brought around trays of food. And there were at least two dozen stunningly beautiful women, more than one per man, lounging around talking to the guys, all of them brokers. I drank, ate, talked to both brokers and babes, and had a terrific time. There were bedrooms and bathrooms at either end of the living room, and when I went into one bathroom there were a bunch of brokers and women doing lines of coke. In another bathroom, people were taking turns using the Jacuzzi—two women and one broker at a time. I must have gotten pretty smashed, because I remember sitting on a toilet, noticing a phone right next to me on the wall, and picking it up to call my brother. He had borrowed $1,000 from me a year before, when he got out of college. I told him I loved him and to forget the debt.

Everybody got more and more drunk, and I'm sure the bedrooms were put to good use, though I didn't see anybody actually pick out a woman and disappear with her. As the night wore on and everybody got blasted, however, one broker seemed ready to leave his wife for the blonde who had been brushing her perfect breasts across his face all evening. I had arrived at the penthouse at around six in the evening. The boxing card we had come to see was scheduled to begin downstairs at eight o'clock, with the featured heavyweight title bout at ten o'clock. We never went. We just stayed in the penthouse and partied, though someone—I think the bartender—did turn on the fight on TV. I staggered back to my room around 3:00 A.M. The next day, sitting next to Jimmie on the flight home, I tried to calculate what the party had cost the Maniac. It must have been $45,000 at least, maybe more, and we didn't even see the fight.

Maniac and his brokers continued to do business at Prep School just as they had at Junior College—but without even the minimal restraints and controls that Junior College had put on them. They had several more IPOs, and each time they managed to run them up pretty quickly in the first few days. But then the share prices collapsed. With each new IPO, the runup of the share price was smaller and quicker. The fall was faster and deeper. The Street was losing confidence in the Maniac and his ability to support his IPOs. Prep School and its brokers became increasingly desperate to manipulate stocks, and went to greater and greater lengths to get money from clients. The compliance officer hired and paid very well by the Maniac seemed not to know or care that the Prep School brokers lied, cheated, and stole from their clients. When clients called to complain, the brokers and managers at Prep School refused to take their calls, and would not call them back. When clients faxed in complaints, the faxes were wadded up and thrown away. The only time a client would hear back about a complaint was if the same broker who did the wrong in the first place called to try to smooth things over—usually with more lies.

Customers ultimately complained to the authorities about how Prep School brokers were making unauthorized trades, parking stock, churning, crossing, and outright refusing to execute orders to sell out positions and close accounts. The NYSE, SEC, and New York district attorney's office all began investigations. Prep School and its brokers paid their fines, served their suspensions, and agreed to clean up their operations. Then they went right back to doing things the way they always had. I heard that sometimes when investigators were at Prep School going through records of illegal trades in one room, the brokers were in the room next door doing more illegal trades. It was literally all they knew.

Some of Prep School's brokers did get tired of the cheating and lying and stealing, and left the firm. One of them told me he quit after he found out that the Maniac was looting an escrow account that had been set up at a bank for investors who wanted to get a piece of an IPO. Prep School had promised investors that it would not accept more than $5 million in applications into the account. When the details of the IPO were worked out, investors who had put money into the escrow account would get shares and refunds, proportioned according to how much money the IPO would raise and how much they had put in escrow. But the Maniac forged documents, lied to the bank, and started taking money out of the escrow account illegally. Apparently he then used the money—more than $1 million—to buy shares and prop up the price of other Prep School house stocks that were dropping in value.

Even Lazlo tried, temporarily, to leave Prep School. A number of other small brokerage firms had started up in the Prep School mold, with a few aggressive brokers, a questionable company or two that wanted to raise money in an IPO, and a small but complicit trading department staff to make markets in microcaps. Those firms were always looking for brokers like Lazlo, and he joined one when he had a falling-out with the Maniac.

I didn't know what their spat was about, but I know that Lazlo became a wreck. One night when Melanie and I were at a bar I went to the men's room and found Lazlo in there, staring at himself, red-eyed, in the mirror. I hadn't even known he was in the bar. Usually it was difficult not to notice him, no matter how busy or crowded or noisy a place was. "Hey," I said.

"Rob, I'm a mess," he blurted out. "I don't have any friends." He looked like he was going to cry. I didn't want to get involved in this. I was just out for a drink with my girlfriend, having a few laughs with some friends.

"Aw, you've got a lot of friends, are you kidding me?" I said, trying to be jocular. "You're always the life of the party. There's nothing wrong with you that can't be cured by a fifth of Jack Daniel's and one of those women upstairs in a short skirt." He looked at me in the mirror and started to say something, but I split before he could. I didn't even stay to use the facilities. I waited until I saw him come out a few minutes later and leave the bar before I went back to the men's room.

Lazlo called me one day from his new firm, pitching one of the old Junior College IPO stocks that the Maniac and his crew had manipulated for years both at Junior College and then at Prep School. It was down to $2, and had been languishing there for months with very little trading volume. Lazlo swore to me that it was about to take off. The Maniac was going to run it up again. Lazlo expected it to be at $4 within a week, and $6 within a month. He was persuasive. I was greedy. I was also suspicious, but I should have been more suspicious. Why was Lazlo, at another firm, flogging an old Dirty Dozen stock? Didn't he have something better to sell?

"You're just trying to find buyers and unload some worthless shares," I said.

"No, no, really, I'm buying this myself," he told me. "It's going to go up, I swear it."

"How do you know?" I demanded.

His tone grew conspiratorial. "You know how these things work," he said.

I believed him, as an old friend. And knowing how the Dirty Dozen and Prep School operated, I figured I would get in and out quickly. Maybe I would sell right away, at $3 or even $2.50. I relished the chance to stick a loss on Maniac.

So I bought 5,000 shares at $2, and watched the stock move. I watched it move down. $1.75. $1.50. I finally sold it at seventy-five cents. The last time I checked, it was trading at six cents. Lazlo had tricked me. Shame on Lazlo. But shame on me, too. I should have known better, but I was a little too cocky and a little too greedy. I never spoke with Lazlo again, though I heard he didn't last long at his new firm. He and the Maniac apparently patched up their differences, because Lazlo went back to Prep School. It must have been a bitter realization for him that he couldn't make it at another firm, that the only place where he could earn big money was at Prep School, doing Maniac's dirty work. Those two guys needed each other.

Prep School lasted four years before the authorities shut the firm down and put it into bankruptcy. Court papers alleged that the firm and its brokers had cheated clients out of $75 million. Thirteen men who worked at Prep School, including the Maniac, Lazlo, and Jimmie, were indicted on a variety of securities and fraud charges. All of them either pleaded guilty or were convicted. They were fined, banned for life from working in the securities industry, and given prison sentences that ranged up to twenty-five years, depending on the charges against them and whether they had entered plea bargains. Some of the guys, including Jimmie, whose one-year sentence was one of the lightest, were remorseful about what they had done. They seemed genuinely sorry, as if they hadn't realized what they were doing and how it was hurting people. They were just doing what their bosses and colleagues at Prep School did. The Maniac and Lazlo and a number of other Prep School brokers, however, did not seem sorry at all. They were only sorry that they got caught, and that they weren't making as much money anymore.

That could have been me. I could have been one of the guys who went to jail if I had accepted the Maniac's invitation to become his partner and help start Prep School. In the years since, every time I find myself feeling a little more envious or greedy or ambitious than perhaps I should, it hasn't been hard to remind myself of how close I came to ruining my life.

24

Graduation

After two years at Junior College, I was tired of the place. I was making good money, but I thought I could and should be doing better. The star brokers at Junior College were the biggest cheats. I looked around, and the brokers with the most support from the Junior College management, especially cold callers and other administrative help, were the brokers with the most compliance problems. I felt like I was taken for granted for trying to be a relatively honest broker. Junior College kept paying its fines and doing business the way it always had. I learned that one of the top brokers at Junior College had such a long rap sheet with regulatory agencies across the country that he was banned from the securities industry in half the states. But that didn't stop him from doing business in those states—he put his sales assistant on the phone to do his business for him. And Junior College's bosses looked the other way.

"I'm sick of it," I told Melanie. "I need a change."

"You're just in a slump," she said, careful as always. "Things will pick up again. Are you sure any other firm would be any better? You're established at this firm, you're a known quantity. You know you can make good money where you are. It's sort of the devil you know versus the devil you don't."

Her view was that I shouldn't move unless I was sure the new job would be better. My view was that there were no guarantees in this business, and I wouldn't know if a new job actually would be better until I got there. When I finally told Melanie I was going to start looking in earnest, she didn't object.

Even though I had not taken a new job when I interviewed at other firms a few months earlier, plenty of headhunters were still chasing me. Once again, I began answering some of them. One headhunter put me in touch with a firm that was just starting up. The Owner was an impressive man. He reminded me of my dad, except a lot younger. He wasn't that much older than me. He had been a wire house star who a few months earlier had started his new firm—a "boutique" firm on Wall Street, the headhunter said—because he thought it would be the way to make the most money while not killing himself the way he had during his first few years as a broker.

Boutique Firm specialized in IPOs and secondary offerings—stock offerings by companies that were already public. Most of them had gone public years before, and now they were coming back to the market to raise more money for expansion. These were real, mature companies, not the fly-by-nights that came to Junior College and Prep School with one idea, no products, no revenues, and a great desire for fast money. This sounded great to me. Boutique Firm valued what I had become good at while working at Junior College—opening accounts for stock flotations. At the same time, Boutique Firm seemed relatively respectable, upscale, and legitimate. It seemed like a firm that was going to grow both in business and in reputation, and a place where I could grow, too.

I met the Owner at the Leopard, a private dining club on the Upper East Side. He told us he had an apartment nearby that he and his wife used when they came into the city, but they spent most of their time at their house—it sounded like a mansion, either on or near the water—on the North Shore of Long Island. We had a private dining room at the Leopard, with our own waiter who served only us. It was a terrific meal. I had duck. We had white and then red wine, and I remember both as being maybe the best I ever had. The Owner was smooth and charming, with just a hint of arrogance. I liked him. He was the kind of guy I wanted to be in a few years.

I talked about myself, what I had done as a broker, and what I wanted to do. I played down Junior College; it was merely a stepping-stone for me. Boutique Firm's owner understood me. I knew he would ask about my trailing twelve eventually, so I volunteered that I had generated about $400,000 in gross commissions for Junior College over the previous year. And I told him how Junior College had held me back, and how I was looking for "a new atmosphere, a new attitude," and what I needed to generate even more commissions—principally, more and better administrative support, and bigger allocations of share flotations.

It was a good dinner. "You remind me of a young me," the Owner said. "You want what I want in a securities firm. I want something that's first-class, a small place that does big deals." He said that Boutique Firm aimed to combine the class and orderliness of Harvard with the energy and excitement of Junior College. That was exactly what I wanted to hear, and I told him so. The Owner said he would be in touch. Two days later he invited me out to the Long Island mansion. We played tennis and had lunch, and he said, "Rob, I want to go into business with you." I liked that. He didn't want to merely hire me; he wanted to go into business with me. We quickly negotiated the basics of a deal. It was standard at big brokerage houses for brokers recruited from other firms to be guaranteed 30 percent of their trailing twelves for the first year. Boutique Firm was not a big brokerage by any standard—it had half as many brokers as Junior College—but the Owner said he would guarantee me a generous

$150,000 for the first year. My payout would be 60 percent of gross commissions, up from 50 percent at Junior College.

I asked for two 100 percent lookbacks, and he agreed. That meant that the firm would look back at the end of the year and pay me 100 percent of my gross commissions, rather than 60 percent, for my two biggest single months. For example, if my two biggest months were each $100,000 in commissions, I already would have been paid $60,000 for each. But at the end of the year the firm would write me a check for $80,000, representing the other 40 percent for each month.

Calculating quickly, I reckoned that even if I stayed at $400,000 in gross commissions, the higher payout and the two lookbacks would boost my net commission from $200,000 at Junior College to at least $260,000, and maybe more than $300,000 at Boutique Firm. But I had every reason to believe my commissions would rise dramatically, in part because the Owner promised that I would have two cold callers and that I would receive at least $100,000 worth of new issues for each of the five or six stock offerings the firm was underwriting every year.

The Owner said I would have a private office, and the title of senior vice president. He also offered me equity in the firm. He was the majority owner, he said, and his longtime mentor, an older guy who would act as the Managing Partner, had a one-quarter share. There would be half a dozen other partners, including me, with shares ranging between 2 percent and 10 percent. My share, as the young-est and newest partner, would be 2 percent—to start. I was thrilled. A partner. If the firm made $10 million in profits, I would get $200,000 of that.

"It's a great deal," I told Melanie that night. "I wonder what else I can negotiate with the guy, what else I can get out of him, to make it an even better deal."

The Owner had assured me that while Boutique Firm did make mar-kets in stocks, especially those of the companies whose shares it floated, the firm's trading department was not a profit center. Making markets in stocks gave us brokers the opportunity to take advantage of bid-asked spreads when they existed, and to skim off hidden commissions. After all, hidden commissions from bid-asked spreads were neither illegal nor unethical, and I was sure that virtually all retail brokers on Wall Street and beyond made a significant portion of their income by selling their clients stocks in which their firms made a market and took advantage of the spreads.

What *was* illegal and unethical was the conspiracy between brokers and traders to manipulate share prices to create bigger spreads, and thus bigger hidden commissions. This was more common at firms where the trading departments were profit centers, where the traders themselves were expected to take advantage of spreads to generate larger commissions for the firm, and for themselves. By telling me that Boutique Firm's trading department was not a profit center, the Owner was giving assurances that he didn't want or expect his traders to manipulate prices and create artificially wide spreads to generate bigger hidden commissions. I liked that. I wanted to work for a clean operation.

But I still wasn't ready to commit to the move from Junior College to Boutique Firm. I was enjoying the negotiations. I liked the fact that I had gotten pretty much everything I had asked for from the Owner, who was renowned as a hot-shot salesman. I wanted to make sure I didn't leave anything on the table. For the cherry on top of the deal, I decided to ask for $20,000 up front, in cash, to be paid the moment I walked through the door, as a compensation for the "disruption" of changing firms.

The Owner said no. He wasn't going to give me any cash up front. I argued that I was sure to lose a few days' business, and a few of my clients probably wouldn't come with me to Boutique Firm. Besides, Junior College was sure to screw me out of my last few commissions. And no doubt I would have some unforeseen incidental expenses, just in making the move. I needed $20,000 just to smooth the way. We went back and forth. He wasn't going to pay me the money. I wasn't going to come without it

I really didn't care that much about the $20,000. But I sensed that I could get it. More than anything, I think I wanted to show the Owner something about myself, what kind of salesman I was. It was like a game to me, and negotiating with him was like playing against the best. He was the old gunslinger with the reputation, and I was the young guy who had just ridden into Dodge. Several times I thought the Owner was going to tell me to forget the whole offer and hang up, but I didn't cave in. I just kept saying the same things over and over, in different ways. Finally he said, "What about ten thousand?" I knew I had him. I had won. I said no, and kept insisting on $20,000. The Owner finally offered $10,000 the day I walked in the door and $10,000 at the end of my first month. I said yes, and agreed to start in ten days.

I went home, told Melanie I had taken the job, ordered her to put the salad she was making into the fridge, and advised her to dress up. She protested, mildly at first, that it was a school night. Then she didn't want to get into the limo that I had waiting out on the street. But she finally let me drag her into the car, and I didn't hear any more objections through the rest of the evening at the Rainbow Room, the 1930s-retro restaurant and nightclub on top of Rockefeller Center. We drank champagne and ate lobster and profiteroles, and between courses we danced to the big band. I wanted a cigar but didn't want to blow smoke at her—she hated that—and she surprised me by saying she would share the cigar with me. She took a few puffs, the first tobacco of her entire life as far as I knew, and professed to like it until she said it made her dizzy. We talked that night, with more confidence than we ever had before, about what a long and happy life we were going to have together. A little giddy, after midnight we took the limo home, where we propped up the pillows on the bed and I helped her grade the papers she had brought home with her.

•   •   •

I needed every minute of the next ten days to get organized for the job change. I had a lot to do, and I had to do it as quietly and secretly as I could. I wouldn't actually tell Junior College I was leaving until I was ready to walk out the door. Brokers didn't give two weeks' notice, like the rest of the world. Brokers quit and walked. They didn't want to hang around their old firms, playing out the string, and their old firms didn't want them hanging around, either. It would just provide the brokers with more opportunities to take their clients with them.

I wanted to take as many of my clients with me to Boutique Firm as I could. I figured I'd lose 10 percent to 20 percent, which wasn't bad. Sometimes when brokers left their old firms, particularly if they'd really been working their clients over, they'd keep fewer than half. Burning their books, it was called. They would churn and cross and maybe even park stock like crazy, trying to bleed the clients dry. This usually happened only if a broker was leaving the business, or if he was sure that most of his clients wouldn't go with him anyway. Sometimes this was because he had done such a lousy job for them. Sometimes it was because the firm he was joining was so much different from the one he was leaving. Brokers leaving Junior College for a wire house, for example, probably couldn't expect to keep a majority of their clients. Many Junior College clients already had accounts at wire houses and were happy with them. They had accounts at Junior College solely for the specific purpose of playing the micro-cap stocks. Their Junior College investments were usually a relatively small, high-risk corner of their whole financial picture.

I, on the other hand, was going to a firm that, while it appeared to be much different to us as brokers, was outwardly quite similar to Junior College in the eyes of the typical investor. Both were small firms, and both specialized in stock flotations, new issues, for small companies. I figured that most of the people who invested with me at Junior College would also want to invest with me at Boutique Firm. Clients viewed themselves as investors with me personally rather than as clients of Junior College. Their loyalty was to me, not the firm.

The problem over the ten days before I moved was that I had to call each and every one of my clients, tell them about the move, and persuade them to come with me. But securities regulations prohibited me from transferring my clients' portfolios to Boutique Firm until I actually started working there. So for each client I prepared in advance the necessary forms to transfer his portfolio. This involved a lot of paperwork, filling out forms that included all of each client's individual information, plus the details of each of his positions in my book. I did a lot of this at home, or at my new desk in Boutique Firm's new office on Wall Street. I met the six other brokers, all older and more experienced than I, who were also minority partners in Boutique Firm. Most of them seemed all right; they were professional in appearance and demeanor. The exception, to my surprise, was the Owner's mentor, the older broker who had a 25 percent partnership. He was slovenly in appearance and disorganized in manner. It made me apprehensive that he was the firm's Managing Partner, in charge of day-to-day operations.

My office was on a sort of mezzanine, overlooking the small board room. I watched it fill up with young brokers newly hired by the Managing Partner, who seemed to have taken over the hiring from the Owner. I didn't like what I saw. The brokers didn't dress well or talk well. I didn't think any of them were the kind of guys that Harvard, for example, would ever consider hiring as brokers. I didn't think Harvard would have hired most of them as cold callers. They seemed louder, more profane, more vulgar, and more sloppy even than the brokers at Junior College. I took to shutting the floor-to-ceiling blinds of the glass wall of my office that overlooked them.

My long absences were noted at Junior College. I would come in at the usual time, do a few things for an hour or so, and then disappear until after lunch. I'd come back for another hour, and then leave in midafternoon. One Junior College broker walked past my desk, grinned knowingly, and said, "Trading from the golf course, eh?" It was a euphemism within the firm for looking for another job, or preparing to leave for one that had already been accepted. I hoped Stuffy hadn't sniffed out my impending departure. I was afraid he would put on a heavy-duty campaign to keep me during those last few days, and I didn't need that. Even more, I was afraid he would go through my book and start assigning my clients to other brokers.

This was a common practice. Junior College, naturally, wanted to keep those clients and their money. On a number of occasions, Stuffy had strolled through Junior College, handing out sheets from the book of a departing broker. "Joe's leaving," Stuffy would say. "Here are three of his clients who are now your clients." When I got pages from a departing broker's book, I would drop everything to call the clients. They were better than any lead from a cold caller. They were known Junior College investors.

If a client had made money with the broker, I said, "Look, you don't want to go with him to his new firm. You want to stay with Junior College. He was giving you all of Junior College's ideas. He was putting you into Junior College's investment opportunities. If you stay with him, you won't get those same ideas. You won't get the same investment opportunities. When Junior College has an IPO in the future, that firm and that broker won't be able to offer you any of it." If the client had lost money with the broker, I said, "Look, you don't want to go with him. He lost money for you. Have a fresh start with me. I'll take care of you." A couple of my biggest and best accounts were clients I had inherited from brokers who had left Junior College. I ran into one of the departed brokers once, a few months after he left, and he let me know he wasn't happy that I had taken away one of his best clients.

"You stole him from me, you bastard," the broker said.

"I didn't steal him," I said. "You left him behind."

Now the shoe was on the other foot—my foot. I was trying to keep my clients when I left Junior College. Every morning during those ten days of pre-move preparation, I sneaked my book out of Junior

College's offices. Technically, it belonged to Junior College. I'd take the book either to my new office at Boutique Firm or home to my apartment, and start calling clients. I was able to reach nearly all of them. I told them that I was moving, and that it was a great opportunity for me—and for them. I told them a little about Boutique Firm, and how it was a different firm—and better—than Junior College. There would be more stock available in Boutique Firm's offerings than there was in Junior College's, I said, which meant more opportunities for us—I still emphasized *us*—to make money. Furthermore, I was going to be a partner in Boutique Firm, which meant that I would be able to get bigger allocations of the firm's best stock offerings. Virtually every client I spoke with said he would come with me. A number of them were surprisingly personal, and congratulated me on my move.

Completing the forms that would transfer each account from Junior College to Boutique Firm was tedious, laborious work. I had writer's cramp for hours at a time. Some brokers simply sent the blank forms to their clients and asked them to fill them out themselves. Not me. I wanted to make it as easy as possible for my clients to come with me. Some brokers sent the forms in the regular mail. I used Federal Express. In the package of stuff I sent them, which included a brochure about Boutique Firm, all they had to do was sign the form I had already filled out and put it in the prepaid, addressed FedEx return envelope I had included.

The Managing Partner at Boutique Firm had promised that I would have some help from a secretary or a sales assistant in filling out the forms and putting together the dozens of packages I was sending out. But nobody ever helped me. I did it all myself. Things were not going to be as rosy as I had hoped at Boutique Firm. But it was too late to reconsider the job change, particularly for something so petty. By my last day at Junior College, there was a big stack of Federal Express envelopes, one for each of my clients, in my new office waiting to go out as soon as I resigned.

My last day was on March 15, timed to the last day of a commission period. My paycheck on April 1 would be for commissions earned between February 16 and March 15. Not that there were a lot of commissions. I had done very few trades in that last month, knowing I was going to leave. Why share commissions with Junior College? Especially since other brokers who had left told me that Junior College usually found some excuse to not pay departing brokers their commissions for that final month.

I was nervous on my last day when I walked into Stuffy's office to resign. He had talked me into staying once before, and I was afraid he would put the full-court press on me again. I came in, sat down, brushed off his small talk, and told him I was leaving immediately. Stuffy seemed surprised. He told me he had heard some rumors that I was trading from the golf course. He said he knew I had been unhappy about not getting more shares of IPOs to sell. But he had no idea that I was serious about leaving, that it had gone this far.

Stuffy asked where I was going, and I told him. He acted like he had never heard of Boutique Firm, while I knew damn well that he had. He was being dismissive, both of my new firm and of me. His attitude made it easier for me to quit. If he had been positive and reassuring, the way he was when I tried to leave for the Wire House, I would have been more tempted to stay. It was time to move on. I shook his hand, walked back through the board room, picked up the phone, called Boutique Firm, and told a secretary to go ahead and send out the FedEx packages to my clients. I hung up, and then walked over to Jake's office and told him I was leaving. He wasn't surprised, but some of the other brokers were. Several brokers mentioned Boutique Firm's good reputation already, and I caught just enough envy in their voices to reassure me that I was doing the right thing. Everyone wished me good luck, and talked about getting together for drinks later. There weren't a lot of long good-byes. I was eager to get over to my new job and get to work. I walked out of Junior College for the last time.

25

Boutique Firm

One of my clients, after agreeing to stay with me, called back a few days later and said a broker from Junior College had telephoned him and was bad-mouthing me. The client had told the broker he was staying with me, and then called me to let me know that this other broker was going after my clients. I was tempted to walk over to Junior College and confront the guy. But I'm glad I didn't. I probably would have gotten myself into more trouble than I needed. Instead, I picked up the phone.

When the guy answered, I reamed him out. Of course, intellectually I knew he had every right to call another broker's clients after the broker left the firm. I had done it many times myself. But I figured if I sent a message to Junior College, not as many of my clients would get calls from the brokers there. It helped that this broker was kind of a wimp, and I didn't like him anyway.

"You phony, backstabbing scumbag," I screamed at him. "You weasel, lying, two-faced, sneaky little shrimp." I went on like that for a minute or two, and told him what I was going to do if he called any more of my clients telling lies about me. "First, I'm going to call my lawyer and have him sue you for slander," I said. "Then I'm going to file a complaint with the NASD. Finally, I'm going to come over there and staple your tongue to your desk. And everybody in your crummy board room is going to laugh at you when I do it."

In the face of my tirade, the guy only sputtered a little. It sounded like he was going to try to offer some sort of explanation or excuse, but I slammed down the phone before he had the chance. I sat back and laughed out loud. I had never spoken to another human being like that, and was pretty sure I never would again. But it did feel good. I ended up losing about 20 percent of my clients in the move to Boutique Firm, but I don't think any of them stayed with Junior College. I think they just cashed out and quit playing the microcap market, which was probably a good move for them at that point.

Most of the clients who left me were pikers, so I ended up keeping about 90 percent of the money that was in my book. I was in good shape. As soon as I arrived at Boutique Firm, however, I set about trying to build up my book. Boutique Firm used the same sort of lead cards for cold calling that were used at Junior College and Harvard. But for some reason—dumb luck, probably—I had a couple of celebrities pop up on cards at Boutique Firm. I got Warren Buffett's card once, and I called him every day for a month without ever getting him on the phone. I cold-called a National Hockey League coach and actually got him to open an account with me. When I saw the card with his name—I'm a huge Islanders fan and watch lots of hockey on TV—I immediately wondered if it was him.

I called the number—it was in the South—and heard the same distinctive, raspy voice I heard when he was interviewed on television. He was one of the easiest accounts I ever opened. When I asked him for his occupation, he said, "Hockey coach." I wanted to keep control of the relationship and I wanted him to see me as the advisor, the professional. I didn't want to give him the upper hand by letting him know that I knew he was a sports celebrity. So I asked, as casually as I could, "I didn't know they played hockey down there. What do you coach, a high school or college team?" No, he said, showing no offense; he said he coached a professional team, in the NHL. Oh, okay, I said, as if I couldn't care less. We ended up doing a fair amount of business together over the next couple of years, and I helped him make some good money. But I never let him know how thrilled I was to have him for a client.

Not long after I arrived at Boutique Firm, the firm handled a stock flotation for a little company that had gone public a few years earlier and now needed more money to expand. I had been promised at least $100,000 worth of shares in all the firm's new stock offerings. Those allocations would help me open new accounts and build my business. It was a key part of the deal I had made with Boutique Firm and a big part of the reason I left Junior College, where I had to fight and scramble for tiny allocations of IPOs.

I didn't get $100,000 worth of stock on that first deal. I got $50,000. I tried to complain to the Owner, but he never returned my calls. I kept leaving messages, and he finally told the Managing Partner to give me $60,000 worth. In the next two stock flotations at Boutique Firm, I got $50,000 in one of them and $35,000 in the other. Promises were being broken, just as at Junior College.

The cold callers were another problem. The Kid had stayed behind at Junior College, where he got a desk and became a broker. Boutique Firm kept its promise to give me two cold callers, but the young guys they kept sending me were hopeless. There was nobody worth investing any training time in the way I had back at Junior College with the Kid. I let my Boutique Firm cold callers fly or fall on their own. It was an attitude much more like the way the brokers at Harvard treated me when I was a cold caller. I decided to wait until I lucked onto someone more like the Kid. When I got somebody like that again, I would spend time and energy in training him. Not until then. As a result, cold callers came and went. I rarely had the same two cold callers together for a month. If I didn't kick them out after a couple of weeks when it became clear that they would not or could not learn to do the job properly, they decided they hated it—and me—and quit.

I started putting my own ads in newspapers to recruit cold callers. One of my first respondents was an absolutely beautiful young woman with long dark hair. She looked like a model or an actress. I hired her just because she was a knockout. She turned out to be a lousy cold caller; she kept saying, "Um, um, um," and her voice went up at the end of every statement she made, as if she was asking a question when she wasn't. She'd say, "I'm calling on behalf of Mr. Rob Burtelsohn," and it would come out, "I'm calling on behalf of Mr. Rob Burtelsohn?"

"Look, if you aren't sure who your boss is, the prospective clients aren't going to be very interested in talking to me," I told her. "If these guys could see you, they'd buy whatever you're selling. But they can't see you. So you've got to do the selling over the phone, with just your voice." She said she understood, but she never changed. Her voice carried no confidence or authority. And her looks became a distraction, not just because I was sneaking peeks at her all day, but because all these other brokers started finding excuses to come into my office and talk to me. They never had anything to talk about, but they always positioned themselves so they could give her a couple of nice up-and-downs. A few of them tried to talk to her, and she was always happy to drop whatever she was supposed to be doing for me and talk to anybody about anything.

When I finally decided I had to get rid of her, I offered her to another broker. He hired her right away, and soon realized she wasn't any good as a cold caller. But he didn't want to pass her off, so he devised a cunning plan. He found other jobs for her to do, keeping some books or something, and told her it had to be done at his apartment. So every afternoon he'd give her his key and send her over to his apartment. It cut down on the traffic from other brokers passing through his office and let him get more work done, and it was nice to have her there at his place when he got home. As it turned out, she was happy to work for him but wasn't looking for anything else from him. She quit.

One of my cold callers was a young Russian. He had an accent, but he compensated for it with a good vocabulary and quick responses. He showed some real promise, but after a couple of weeks I was surprised that he wasn't giving me more leads. I started watching him carefully, and saw that when he had an especially long call—indicative that the person on the phone had agreed to talk to a broker—he would sometimes slip that card into a briefcase instead of into the pile of leads for me. He was stealing my leads. He was probably selling them to another broker at another firm. But I never found out for sure. I confronted him, and he just smiled at me like I was a sucker, snapped up his briefcase, and walked out.

Another of my cold callers was a very weird little guy, a ninety-pound weakling, who would come in every morning and tell me how he had stopped to visit a prostitute on the way to work. He'd go out to lunch and come back telling me he had been to a whorehouse near the office. He'd tell me he was going to two different massage parlors that evening. Either he was lying or his whores were awfully cheap, because even if he was getting it on with pros four times a day, I knew he couldn't be paying for it out of a cold caller's salary. The guy was always talking about his drinking binges, too, and about how he had blacked out and didn't know what had happened. One day he told me he had blacked out the night before, and when he woke up that morning he was lying on a patch of grass in Central Park with bruises on his face and blood all over his hands. "I wonder what happened," he said in a tone that was chilling because it seemed to carry mere innocent curiosity rather than any real concern. I was afraid of him. But he was a surprisingly good cold caller, at least for a while, so I kept him on. After a couple of months he just didn't come in anymore.

• • •

Boutique Firm's newly renovated office quickly became a shambles, and nobody seemed to care. I couldn't understand it. The Owner seemed like a good businessman, but he wasn't following through to make sure his new firm was working. It was not the atmosphere I had been looking for when I left Junior College. Far from it.

The Owner was never around, and his old mentor, the Managing Partner, did not seem to have the ability to manage his own business, much less anyone else's. The office was always a pigsty, with papers piled everywhere, including on the floor. The Managing Partner told the cleaners never to throw anything away unless it was already in a wastebasket, and he never told the brokers clean up and throw stuff away. The Managing Partner seemed to like hiring big noisy guys, most of them with Italian surnames. They hollered "Ehhhh!" a lot and called each other *paisan*. They dressed like the Managing Partner, like slobs.

When I moved in, the renovations to the office were just being completed. One of the last things to be done was the wallpaper in the reception area. It was nice wallpaper, with a kind of linen texture. One afternoon the workmen hung the first section, and then left to finish the job the next day. The next morning, however, before the workmen could return, brokers arriving in the office began grabbing little pieces of the wallpaper and walking along with it, tearing strips away. For six, eight, ten feet, there were strips where the wallpaper had been torn away, from a little tear at the start to a foot or two where the strip of paper had finally torn away completely. The work-men came in, removed the wallpaper that had the tears in it, and repapered the entire wall. It looked good. The next morning, how-ever, brokers came in and started tearing away strips again. I was disgusted. "What does it take for these guys not to tear up the new wallpaper? They work here," I complained to the Managing Partner. He shrugged.

Every morning the bathrooms were clean and tidy. By four in the afternoon they looked as if they had been used for a month by a gang of juvenile delinquents on speed. Wads of wet toilet paper had been thrown and stuck to the walls and ceiling. Paper towels and puddles of water, or worse, were all over the floor. The toilets always seemed to be jammed and overflowing. I tried to talk to the other partners, the other senior brokers who had seemed so professional when I came aboard, but they didn't seem to mind the way the office was being run.

As if the place needed to be more relaxed, one of the first officewide memos after I arrived was to declare casual Fridays. So the brokers, even the other partners, started coming in wearing jeans and sweaters. Except for me. I wore suits when I worked, Friday or not. I started closing the blinds of my office windows more and more, further setting me apart from the brokers down below in the board room. I knew the guys thought I was stuck up, and that I acted like I was better than they were. I didn't care. I *was* better than them.

When the weather got nice in the spring, they started going up to the roof of the building to smoke cigarettes and enjoy the view of New York Harbor. Pretty soon they had a white plastic picnic table and a few matching chairs up there, and they began eating their lunches up there, mostly pizza and deli sandwiches that had been delivered. I never joined them, and they never invited me.

On casual Fridays they began staying up on the roof longer and longer as the weather got warmer. Some of the guys who spent a lot of time on the roof decided they needed better furniture up there, some nice padded chairs and chaise longues. But the firm wouldn't pay for it. The guys came around asking if I would chip in, and I snarled something about how I liked to party as much as the next guy, but this was a workplace. I don't know if that was the reason, but they never got the furniture.

One day I smelled marijuana wafting down from the roof, and pretty soon a big fat guy was making regular dope deliveries to the office on Friday mornings. The brokers started looking for excuses to have parties, and before long every Friday afternoon was a bash with coolers of beer, cigars, and joints. When nobody's birthday was within a week or two past or future, they would celebrate someone's arrival or departure. One Friday they couldn't find a better reason, so they declared a going-away party for a cold caller who everybody knew was about to get fired. He was having a great time until somebody told him that his imminent departure was the reason for the party. When the brokers started having strippers in for the birthday parties, I started working at home on Fridays.

Not that there wasn't sex in the office during the rest of the week. Sex was rampant. Brokers were always leering and commenting and groping the secretaries and sales assistants, the young women who handled clerical and administrative chores for them but didn't have the office skills to be real secretaries. Groups of brokers and young women from the office often went out after work and got drunk, and affairs were frequent. A couple of times I heard that brokers and their sales assistants had standup sex in the supply closet. The receptionist was a short but buxom woman with long hair, a built-in magnet for horny brokers. They would flirt and tease, and she would give it right back to them. When one broker told her he had a sore neck, she offered to rub it for him, and pretty soon she was making the rounds giving massages to brokers at their desks, all the while rubbing her breasts, which were extraordinarily large for such a small woman, against their necks.

Before long some guys began walking right up to her and asking if they could give her a chest massage, and trying to drag her off to the supply closet. She never went, as far as I knew, but she never got mad and never told anyone to back off, either. I heard that one broker gave her a ride home, and she thanked him with a quick round of oral sex in his car in front of her building. "A great way to start the evening," the guy said. "Didn't even have to kiss her." He said he was thinking of starting a new kind of taxi service—just for the tips. Pretty soon the receptionist was getting four or five offers a day to drive her home, starting the minute she walked in the door in the morning.

Affairs between sales assistants and brokers caused all sorts of problems in the office, especially the all-too-common drunken one-night stands. The sales assistant would come in the next morning all happy, thinking she had landed a rich broker and starting to envision the cottage with the white picket fence where they would raise their kids. The broker, meanwhile, had no intention of going out with her again, and probably wasn't even sure of her last name. The sales assistant would get mad or sulky and not do her job, and pretty soon clients were calling to complain that their trades had been messed up. The whole office would be in an uproar until the sales assistant either calmed down or quit.

There were other broken promises at Boutique Firm, and other disquieting similarities to Junior College. The Owner of Boutique Firm had told me that the trading department was not a profit center. But it was. The traders at Boutique Firm did not help manipulate stock prices or create artificial spreads the way traders had at Junior College, but they were continually stealing money from us brokers: a sixteenth of a dollar here, a thirty-second there. I would write a ticket for a trade at the current market price for the stock: $5, for example. The stock trade should have been executed at $5. Instead, the confirmation would come back that the stock had been traded at $5.125. My commission was paid on the $5, and the trading department kept the other eighth of a cent as profit for Boutique Firm. My clients were paying more for stock than they should, and I was losing commissions. It wasn't a lot of money per share, but it added up. I confronted the traders, and they informed me that I wasn't their boss. They said, "Take it up with the Owner." I tried, but he resisted. On the rare occasions I got him on the phone, he said we'd talk about it over a beer sometime, but he never had time to go out for a beer.

The Owner of Boutique Firm originally impressed me as being forward-thinking and dynamic, especially for the head of a brokerage house. But he himself didn't seem to do much selling anymore, at least not in the office. Maybe he had a few mega-accounts that he handled discreetly, and I wasn't aware of them. He devoted an inordinate amount of thought to a particular obsession: a movie about himself. I don't want to say he was an egomaniac, but in an industry awash in people with inflated opinions of themselves, he stood out. He had first mentioned the movie when I was interviewing and he was describing his vision for the firm. "This will be the kind of firm that somebody is going to make a movie out of someday," he told me.

I didn't think much of the comment then, but he kept coming back to the movie every time I saw him. A broker would make a big sale, and if the Owner happened to be in the office he would say, "That'll make a great scene in our movie, won't it?" There was never any indication that anyone, a writer or producer or director or anyone else, had the slightest interest in making a movie about Boutique Firm, but that didn't matter to the Owner. He once sent around a memo to the partners with a list of the cast for the movie. The Owner would be played by Kevin Costner. The Managing Partner would be played by Paul Newman. I would be played by Nicholas Cage. I couldn't believe that the Owner, this guy who was supposed to be running a brokerage firm, had time to waste on trivial ego-tripping like this.

Besides imagining himself in a movie, the Owner loved big parties and celebrations. At Christmas, the firm had a black-tie ball in a midtown Manhattan hotel for all the employees and spouses or dates, along with some of the firm's biggest and best clients. The Owner sent a limo to pick up Melanie and me, but the gesture was wasted on us. I wasn't really friendly with anyone at the ball, and didn't want to be. Melanie and I stuck to ourselves, ate dinner, had a couple of dances, and then left early. Instead of waiting for the limo, we grabbed a cab back home. I told Melanie I figured the ball must have cost $50,000. As a 2 percent partner, I would have rather simply gotten a check for $1,000.

After only a few months at Boutique Firm, I was disgruntled. The firm had not underwritten as many stock offerings as I had been told to expect—only three, instead of five or six. I wasn't getting as much stock to sell in those deals as I had been promised, but now that appeared to be a blessing. The stocks were not doing well. The less stock I sold my clients, the less money they lost.

My book had grown, both in the number of accounts I had—about 250, with 30 to 40 of them really active—and in the amount of money I had under management, up to about $8 million. My commissions were up slightly over what I had done the year before at Junior College. But my clients were not making money off Boutique Firm's offerings. I struggled to keep them in the black, or at least even, by selling the stocks as they started to drop. This protected my clients, but didn't make me any more popular with my fellow brokers, who were still aggressively recommending the stocks to their clients as a way of propping up the price. I wasn't a team player.

There was talk of a couple of new deals coming, and the Managing Partner told me I was sure to get the $100,000 worth of new issues I had been promised. But I had been doing some checking on my own, and the two companies did not look any more solid to me than some of the microcaps that went public at Junior College. Moreover, in the previous offering handled by Boutique Firm, the Owner had farmed out a big chunk of the new shares to other brokerage houses. His idea was that they would help sell the stock, make it more liquid, and drive up the demand. His strategy backfired. The other firms sold the stock to their clients at $8, the issue price, and then as soon as it opened and went to $10, those firms sold out, mostly to Boutique Firm brokers who were buying the stock into the firm's inventory to support demand and keep the price from falling. It was a financial disaster for the firm, which was stuck with blocs of stock that had fallen below the price it had paid for them.

I told the Managing Partner I wasn't sure I wanted any of the stock in the next offerings, let alone $100,000 worth. He told me I had to take the $100,000; it was part of my contract. I told him I didn't like anyone telling me what I had to sell to my clients, especially a slob who couldn't get his brokers to tuck in their shirts or not tear wallpaper off the office walls. I'm sure he reported my insubordination directly to the Owner, who left a voice mail suggesting that we get together for a beer.

Over pints of draft Brooklyn Brown Ale at the John Street Bar, I let the Owner have it with both barrels. First, I reminded the Owner he had promised that, unlike Junior College, I would be encouraged to sell any stocks I wanted, not just the stocks in which Boutique Firm was a market maker. I complained that Boutique Firm was using its trading department as a profit center. The Owner denied that he had told me his firm would not look to make money off the trading department. He said I must have misunderstood. He said every brokerage firm uses its trading department as a profit center. That's part of the reason that brokerage firms make markets in stocks. If firms couldn't squeeze out a little profit for themselves in the spreads, they wouldn't make as many markets in different stocks, and there would be less liquidity in the market. Besides, he reminded me, I was a partner in Boutique Firm. The more money the firm made, including from trading, the more money we would all share at the end of the year. He used the same argument—that he hadn't made that promise, and that I as a partner benefited—when I complained about making it difficult for us brokers to trade stocks for which the firm was not a market maker.

Since I was unloading on him but not getting anywhere, I brought up the appearance, atmosphere, morale, and competence of the office. I told him about the drinking and drugs and sex in the office, and about how so many of the brokers in the office were incompetent. "Some of the brokers are not as professional as they should be," he acknowledged, "but one of the reasons you're here is to help train less experienced brokers in how to be more professional."

"That's not my job," I countered. "That's not why you hired me.

This is the first I've heard of training. If training people had been part of my deal, I wouldn't have come."

Surprisingly, all my bellyaching didn't seem to offend the Owner. He told me he respected me for speaking up, and said he wanted to make things better. He said he hoped I would help him.

The Owner loved to make toasts and give gifts. He liked to make any little meeting a big occasion, and that's what he tried to do then. He toasted me with his Brooklyn Brown, made a little speech about how great the firm was, how we were a great team, how maybe it would be better if Tom Cruise played me, and how he wanted to recognize me personally. Then he gave me a wrapped gift. I thanked him and took it home. It was an announcement that I had joined Boutique Firm as a partner, engraved in fancy print like a wedding invitation, in a nice silver frame. I threw away the announcement, and replaced it in the frame with a picture of my folks from their silver wedding anniversary.

26

The Last Deal

The Owner of Boutique Firm also had promised me that, unlike at
Junior College, I would be getting a lot of good, original research
about firms that I could pass along to clients. Boutique Firm had a real
live stock analyst, and he would generate real research for us brokers.

The most important stock recommendations at Boutique Firm, however, seemed to come not from the analyst but from the Owner, who
contributed his own brand of "research" that was supposed to guide us
brokers. His research was dispensed to us verbally, seemingly off the
cuff, in occasional hurriedly scheduled conference calls, usually from
his home or his boat. There were never any written reports, charts,
graphs, or background on the companies he recommended as "buys."

The Owner had a longstanding reputation on Wall Street as a good
stock picker, but that seemed like a fading reputation to me. Most of
his recommendations either went down or did nothing. The only
common link was that every recommendation was a stock in which
Boutique Firm suddenly was making a market. Before long, Boutique
Firm began changing its commission policies, tacking on extra charges
for brokers who tried to trade stocks for which the firm did not
make markets. Soon I was in the same boat as I had been at Junior

College: trying to trade stocks outside the firm's markets was not worth the effort.

I made friends with Grant, the Boutique Firm's in-house analyst. He was a clean-cut young guy who dressed reasonably well—a lot of gray flannel trousers and navy jackets rather than suits, but I didn't hold it against him too much—and seemed well educated. He always had a pithy comment, whether we were talking about the Knicks or the Dow-Jones or Saddam Hussein or oil prices. I liked the guy. More important, I thought he was smart, and that he could provide me the kind of information I needed to make money for my clients— and for myself. Grant produced a regular flow of reports and charts and graphs and statistics, and for a while I used them to help sell shares. It was always easier to sell a client on a trade if there was some research behind it—no matter how sound or unsound. Since Grant supposedly was making independent evaluations and recommendations, it didn't bother me that he, too, issued "buy" recommendations only for stocks in which Boutique Firm made a market.

One of Boutique Firm's IPOs before I arrived had been for a company that was supposed to be working on some sort of home water-recycling system. That IPO, like so many other microcap flotations, was a success at first. After coming out at $9 and rocketing up to $39, the Sink Recycling shares had settled back to the $22 to $24 range. But Grant kept assuring us brokers that the company had great prospects and the stock was just taking a breather before it made another big move. As Sink Recycling continued to slide, I occasionally pinned Grant down in private, probing whether he really believed his reports. He was convincing. He trotted out even more data, right off the top of his head, to support his recommendations.

Every now and then the Sink Recycling stock would rally a point or two, usually right after Grant came back from a meeting with the company management, or when the Sink Recycling chairman and president would come into our office and huddle with Grant. Inevitably, Grant issued new research and a new glowing "buy" recommendation for Sink Recycling, and that got us brokers pumped up to sell it some more. The Sink Recycling chairman and president sometimes came in to give us brokers personalized pep talks. They waved around Grant's latest analysis forecasting how much money they were going to make, and said the reports were wrong. That wasn't unusual. Lots of managers routinely tried to discredit analysts' reports, especially when they thought the forecasts were too optimistic and the actual results might be seen as disappointing if they fell short of the forecasts. Not these guys. They said Grant's reports were rubbish because they weren't optimistic enough. They vowed that they would do much better even than our analyst's rosy forecasts. Nobody is as susceptible to a sales pitch as a salesman, and we brokers believed what the managers and analyst told us. Fired up, we jumped on the phones and sold more stock in Sink Recycling. The stock would blip up from $18 to $19, or $14 to $15, and then fall back again in a few days and resume its painful slide.

Then Grant quit suddenly. Nobody knew why. The evening after he disappeared, I happened to be in the office late. Grant showed up. He had forgotten a few things and wanted to pick them up. The guard had let him in. Grant hadn't expected anyone to be around, but seemed glad to see me. He was awkward as he shoveled a few papers and books from his desk into a briefcase, but said something about how I was one of the few brokers who really seemed to respect his work and take him seriously. He thanked me. I asked him if he wanted to go out for a drink, and he did. Over scotch, he poured his guts out. He was only twenty-five, he told me, from a little town in Ohio, and his dream had always been to work on Wall Street. He had graduated with so-so grades from a so-so MBA program in the Midwest, and had felt like a fraud when he started applying for jobs at small, little-known securities firms. He had never heard of Boutique Firm when he applied for a job, and he hadn't even been sure what job he was applying for. When he was offered the position as Boutique Firm's analyst—his only job offer—he had accepted without really being sure what an analyst is supposed to do. But he knew it was his ticket to Wall Street.

Grant said it quickly became clear that his reports were supposed to relay the messages given to him by the Owner, the Managing Partner, and the executives of the firms whose shares were being traded by Boutique Firm. The Owner reviewed his reports and presentations before Grant was allowed to pass them along to the brokers. The few times that Grant tried to come up with something on his own, or include something that was the least bit negative about the companies, even if it was true, the Owner or Managing Partner advised him to leave that out. We brokers thought Grant was a specialist, smarter than us, specially trained as an analyst. What he said made sense to us. We accepted it, and acted on it, selling more stock to our clients even though our sales pitches were based on bad information. We were suckers.

Grant was miserable. He was working on Wall Street and making $80,000 a year. If he didn't do what his bosses at the firm told him to do, he would be fired. But he knew what he was doing wasn't right. He knew he was part of a scam. "I don't know what I'm going to do with myself now," he said. "But I knew I had to quit."

I began thinking I might have to quit, too.

About the same time, when I had been at Boutique Firm for six months, I received a call at the office from one of my former college professors. I had been friendly with the guy, at least as friendly as I was with any professor, but I hadn't heard from him since I graduated years before. He had been following my career from a distance, and had seen a notice in *Barron's* about me joining Boutique Firm. He told me he had an account with another small brokerage firm that specialized in microcap IPOs. He had opened it after a cold call. The broker had told him about an IPO, but said no stock was available. He convinced the Professor that he should buy in the aftermarket, and the Professor agreed—if the stock was doing well. The stock went public at $8, and quickly climbed to $25. That was when the Professor bought 2,000 shares—$50,000 worth of the stock, right at its top. The stock price had steadily dropped since then. It was at $9, and the Professor was wondering what to do.

The broker who had sold him the stock in the first place—and assured him it was going up—was now urging the Professor to buy another 2,000 shares and "average down." This was a common tactic among brokers trying to get more money out of their clients. It had the added benefit of making clients feel like they weren't such big losers. If the Professor bought another 2,000 shares at $9, his average price per share would have been $17, not $25, and owning it at $17 might have been a little less painful for him. In addition, if and when the stock went up, it would have to climb back only $8 for him to get even, not $16.

"I'm not sure how much confidence I should retain in this particular broker," the Professor said. He spoke in a refined, reserved, sort of old-fashioned manner. "After all, he was the financial advisor who steered me into this particular investment in the first place. I am in a quandary. I am pondering whether to invest more—average down, as the stockbroker suggests? Or perhaps I should divest, and accept my losses? Or is this perhaps one of those times when the best course of action is no action at all?"

I took a deep breath, and told him I didn't know. Ordinarily, with the usual client, I would have said the broker's strategy could make sense, the stock could go back up; if and when it did, the Professor would be better off. "I don't know," I said this time. "I just don't know, and I don't know what else to say. It's very complicated "

The Professor must have sensed that something was bothering me. He said he was going to be in New York for a conference the following week, and suggested we get together. We made a date for dinner.

Over dinner, I suddenly found myself telling the Professor, a relative stranger, things I had never told anyone, not my dad, not even

Melanie. I talked for a long time about the securities business in general and his investment in particular. I told him about the shady stuff at Junior College and the outright treachery at Prep School. I told him that brokers at firms like those didn't really care about their clients. I told him how brokers, even brokers at reputable firms such as Harvard, lied and cheated and stole from their clients. I told him brokers were experts at telling clients things they wanted to hear, as long as they persuaded clients to give the brokers more money. "I don't know if you or any other client can ever really truly believe everything a broker tells you," I said. "Certainly you shouldn't ever believe that the broker's motives for any recommendation are based solely on what's best for you and your portfolio."

I talked about how the securities business is a basic conflict of interest; the best strategy for clients is to get into good investments and keep them long-term, but brokerage houses make money by moving clients in and out of positions to generate commissions. I told the Professor about the spreads and the hidden commissions, and how stocks were manipulated. Sitting there talking to him, I felt removed from the whole business.

I told the Professor to forget about investing more to average down. I told him it was a sucker play, good money after bad. Sure, his average investment would be lowered to $17 instead of $25. But he would have more money at stake—more money to lose when the price of the stock went down to $8, then $6, then $2, and maybe lower. I told the Professor he would never get his money back. I advised him to sell immediately. If the price was still at $9, he would at least get back $18,000 of his original $50,000. The only way he could get any more back was to complain to the brokerage firm. The firm would probably ignore his complaint, and if so he would have to file a formal complaint with the NASD. He should claim that his broker had misled him and tricked him. He should allege that the broker had told him things about the company that were not true, and had promised him that the stock would go up. He should ask for all the money he had lost,

$32,000, and be happy if they offered him $5,000 or $10,000 to settle the complaint.

The Professor didn't say anything while I was telling him all this, and he didn't say anything for a couple of minutes after I finished. Finally he said quietly, "That's quite a business you're in."

"I know," I said. "I don't know how much longer I'm going to be in it."

I decided to try something on my own, something out of character for a broker at Boutique Firm or any other microcap house. I had read that one of the big European electronics companies was going to apply for a New York Stock Exchange listing. A NYSE listing would no doubt increase interest in the stock, enhance its liquidity, and probably drive up the price. There was sure to be buying interest among U.S. institutional investors, such as pension funds, that were barred from owning shares in foreign companies unless the companies were listed on U.S. exchanges.

I went to the guys in the trading department at Boutique Firm and asked them if they could buy stock in the European electronics company for me. They didn't know. No broker had ever made a request like that. They'd have to check. I asked the Managing Partner if it could be done, and he said he'd talk to the trading department about it. When I made my request, the price of the stock was at $20. By the time the trading department got back to me a couple of weeks later and said yes, they could do it, the price was at $24. I pitched it to my clients, and was able to persuade quite a few of them to buy a considerable amount—about $600,000 worth. Within a couple of weeks, amid more and more press coverage about the listing becoming imminent, the stock was up to $32. I took every one of my clients out of the position. I had made a quick 33 percent return for them, collected some nice commissions—all straight, none hidden—and boosted the value of my book by $800,000.

I had wanted to prove to my clients that I could still make money for them, and the deal worked. No one told me how much stock I had to buy or sell. The stock in the electronics company was completely liquid; I did not have to worry about other brokers giving me grief for selling out my clients at a profit. I didn't have to worry about my own trading department creating an artificial spread, or nicking profits from my clients or commissions from me. The deal felt good. I felt like this was the sort of work I was supposed to be doing as a broker. It was also my last significant deal as a broker.

Boutique Firm came up with two more lame IPOs, and I told my clients about them but didn't take up my usual aggressive account-opening campaign. Most of my existing clients weren't interested, and I was glad they weren't. The IPOs both came out at $5, went up twenty-five cents, and then tanked. Within three weeks one of them was down to $3. The other one did a little better. It took a month to get down to $3. My clients, naturally, were increasingly reluctant to buy any of the other stocks in Boutique Firm's small stable of microcaps, and I was finding it increasingly difficult to recommend that my clients buy any of them. The star IPO from the past, Sink Recycling, was down to $6, then $5. I looked for other deals like the European electronics company, but couldn't find any. My clients started to abandon me. I didn't blame them. Some called and told me to sell out their positions and send them a check for the full amount. Some simply sent in forms that transferred their holdings to other firms and other brokers. I was down into four figures in monthly commissions. And none of the other brokers at Boutique Firm were doing much better.

Melanie and I rented a ski house in Vermont for the winter with another couple, and we went up there almost every weekend, usually driving up on Friday night and coming back early on Monday. One Monday Melanie caught a ride back with the other couple, and I stayed until

Tuesday. I began staying up there until Wednesday, and finally all week. I told myself I wasn't making any commissions because I wasn't working. I'd sleep late, ski a little, hang out in the ski chalet pub, watch TV, and sleep a lot. I didn't shave all week, until Fridays when Melanie showed up. Looking back, I can see that I was depressed.

Melanie and I talked a lot that winter about my job, and being a broker. I had made a lot of money, but I was tired of the business. Even if Boutique Firm didn't work out, I wasn't sure I wanted to go to another firm, even a place like Harvard or one of the wire houses. I began to talk about what I would do if I wasn't a broker.

"Take some time off," she urged. "We've got money in the bank. No kids, no mortgage, no obligations. I'm still working and making decent money, though nowhere what you were making there for a while. We're in good shape financially. We're not in such good shape emotionally."

"I don't know if taking time off would help," I fretted. "If I don't have a job, I might go really crazy. It's a whole self-esteem thing. I've always identified myself with my job, my income. I don't know how I'll feel about myself if I don't have a job, if I'm not bringing in any money. I can feel my confidence in myself slipping away."

"Don't worry," Melanie assured me. "You need a change. Going without a job for a while might be just want you need. A chance to step back and take a career breather, to reevaluate what you want to do. You've got more confidence in yourself than anybody I've ever met. Remember when you were a cold caller? That was the worst job on earth for a person like you. But you did it. You survived it. Having no job at all is better than having a crummy job. We have plenty of money put away to live on for a while. Let's enjoy life a little, and re-group. You can handle it. I want you to try it. It will be good for you, and for us."

She told me that I had been working hard, almost nonstop, since I walked into the board room at Harvard years before. She said taking some time off would allow me to recharge my batteries and think about other ways to make a living. She suggested that I didn't even yet realize how much I had learned and what new skills I had acquired in the past five years. She assured me that I would find the right thing to do when I was ready. I was sure I could always find another good sales job, though maybe not as lucrative as being a stockbroker. But I wasn't quite ready to give it up.

Soon, however, I was ready.

When spring came I returned to the office full-time, and made zero commissions. Boutique Firm had no new deals, so I had nothing to sell and nobody to sell to. Other brokers, even the worst ones, were leaving Boutique Firm like rats off a sinking ship. I had always envisioned getting out of the securities business with a bang, making one huge score and then walking away with enough money to change my life. It didn't happen that way. One night in early May, over dinner, I looked up from my pasta, took a sip of wine, and told Melanie, "I'm tired. I'm going to quit tomorrow."

She smiled and raised her glass. "I'm glad," she said. "Here's to the start of the rest of our life."

I felt a great sense of relief, and slept better that night than I had in months.

The next day, I began calling my remaining clients to tell them I was leaving Boutique Firm and taking some time off. I could have simply sent them notes or handed their accounts over to other brokers, but I thought that perhaps I might do some more business with them in one way or another—though it seemed unlikely that I would ever be their broker again. I also wanted to say good-bye to each of them personally because I had come to like so many of them, even though they were only voices over the phone. They had trusted me, and I felt like I had done my best for them. Sure, there were times when I sold them stock that went down, but there were also times when I had sold them stock that went up. This was the microcap market, and it was wild and woolly. They knew I wasn't working for a wire house. If one of those crazy little IPOs had turned out to be the next IBM or

Microsoft, my career as a broker would have developed much differently.

Instead, I resigned and shook hands with the Owner, who seemed to genuinely wish me well even though his once-shiny little firm was dying before his eyes. I walked out of Boutique Firm, past the rows of mostly empty desks. I remember thinking that might be the last time I ever walked through a brokerage house. The Boutique Firm board room, in a failing firm riddled by defections and mismanagement, had a flat, dead feeling. I couldn't help but recall my first walk through the vast board room at Harvard, when I was electrified by the feeling of money and deals and intensity. In some ways I was different then, but in some ways I was still the same. When I stumbled into my career as a broker, I was a nervous kid who didn't know what was going to happen next but couldn't wait to find out. Now I was walking out on my career as a broker, and I wasn't nervous and I wasn't a kid. But I still didn't know what was going to happen next, and I still couldn't wait to find out.

EPILOGUE:

The Aftermarket

The life of a Wall Street broker was stressful. The mentality was to make money, as much of it as possible as fast as possible. Every day was a test. Every day I was measured according to how much money I made that day. Some days I was measured only against myself, what I had made in the past or what I thought I should be making. Most days, however, I was measured against every other Wall Street broker. The competition was intense. Everyone was driven to succeed, and the only measures of success were how much money the broker made for himself and his firm, not necessarily in that order. The harder I worked, the more extreme I was, the more success I had.

Excessive work led to success. It was an equation: Excess equals success. Excess was the common denominator in everything we did—our work, our play, our lifestyles, our spending, our personalities. Life was a Ping-Pong ball, up and down. A big sale that took minutes to complete could be followed by a devastating dry spell that lasted weeks. It wasn't the sort of life that most people could lead for very long. I knew there was such a thing as an old stockbroker. But he must have lived in Virginia or Arizona or someplace far from Wall Street, playing golf with other old guys and spending leisurely days at work in quiet little wire house branches. Most of the brokers at Harvard had been in their thirties. The Bald Shadow, pushing forty, was one of the older ones. At Junior College, and then at Boutique Firm, most of the brokers were in their twenties

For most brokers, the only sense of control in their lives came from spending some of the money they made. The rational, smart thing to do was put money away, invest it, save as much as possible so that they would be able to have a more sane, less stressful life at some hazy point in the future. Instead, the brokers I knew needed to reward themselves for their hard work. They wanted immediate satisfaction. They would go buy a Porsche, thinking about compensating themselves for the stress in their lives rather than thinking about how to reduce the stress.

After I left the business, Melanie and I finally got married. Her wedding present to me was a good mountain bike. I hadn't ridden a bicycle since high school, and I had never been much for nature or solitude. But we rented a small house in the suburbs, and I started taking the bike onto wooded trails, usually by myself. I became an accomplished off-road cyclist, and began looking for steeper hills and rougher terrain. I'd see how fast I could climb a steep path, and then how fast I could come down without crashing. I bought a bike for Melanie, and after the first time she went with me she insisted that I buy a helmet. Flying down hills, bouncing off rocks and ruts and roots, I was barely in control. It took all my concentration to keep from crashing. I taught myself that I could be exhilarated without making money.

I did little, career-wise, for nearly two years. We had twins, and they became the focus of my life. I changed diapers, pushed the double carriage around, and learned to cook dinner. We lived simply and quietly. I would have been happy to spend the rest of my life that way, but reality intervened. We wanted to buy a house. We wanted another baby, maybe two. Somebody had to pay for college. I needed to go back to work. Melanie and I began looking around for medium-sized towns with good schools and good airports, so our folks could visit us and vice versa. We found three or four towns we liked on the northern half of the Eastern seaboard, not in the New York area but within a half-day's drive, and we began looking for jobs. In the town that was on the top of our list, Melanie got a part-time teaching job, three days a week. I found a job as a broker in a suburban branch office of a wire house. The office manager who hired me seemed more impressed with the fact that I had taken off all that time to take care of the babies than with my experience as a broker. We bought a house next to a nature preserve.

In recent years, I've become a typical community stockbroker. I find clients through referrals or through coaching kids' soccer or through serving on civic committees. I play golf with my clients. They're my neighbors and friends. I never make cold calls. I don't bring home as much money as I did on Wall Street, but I'm happier. I've taught myself about investing and the markets, and I've overcome my distaste for studying enough to qualify as a certified financial planner. I'm gradually becoming what I thought could not exist—an old stockbroker.

In some ways, though, I feel a little like people must feel in the federal witness protection program. Life is safe now, but it's not nearly as exciting. Cold calling and opening new accounts for IPOs made for a high-performance, high-intensity, high-stress kind of life. I loved my life on Wall Street, even though my fellow brokers and I did a lot of things I didn't like, especially selling stock to clients primarily because it offered us the best commissions rather than because we thought it was a good investment for them. I felt like I had used my clients, though many of those clients were eager to make the kind of investments I offered, and some of them did very well off those investments.

After I left New York, I began to see that investors weren't the only ones being used. Brokers were being used, too. Managers and owners of small brokerage houses recruited as many brokers as they could, the more the better, to create bigger and better revenue streams. If the brokerage houses could get those brokers all selling the same stock to each other's clients, they could drive up demand. The firms could make a market, create spreads, collect hidden commissions, and skim off millions without the clients ever knowing it. When the pyramids collapsed and the stock prices plummeted, the owners and the managers were the only ones left standing. The clients lost their money. The brokers lost their clients, their businesses, their livelihoods. The owners and managers took their millions and retired to the beach, or else started another small firm, found a couple more IPOs, recruited some brokers, and repeated the entire exercise.

Years later, I still feel warmly about most of my IPO clients at Junior College and Boutique Firm. I am sorry for the ones who lost money because of what I sold them or didn't sell them. I am happy for the ones who did make money. I like to think that my clients knew what they were getting into with microcap IPOs. They were sophisticated, experienced investors who knew that these offerings were a high-risk, high-reward proposition. That's why I qualified them, to make sure they had enough money in the markets to be seen as experienced investors—and, of course, to make sure they had enough money to make it worthwhile to pitch stocks to them.

A year or so after I left New York, I got a call from attorneys for Boutique Firm. One of my former clients had filed a complaint against Boutique Firm and me, and wanted to go to arbitration—a common manner of adjudicating complaints that could not be settled informally but that neither side wanted to contest in a full-blown lawsuit, possibly with a trial. The firm had offered the client $3,000 to settle the suit, but he had refused. Would I help the firm defend the complaint in the arbitration? I said I would, as long as the firm agreed to indemnify me, so that I would not be personally liable for any damages. The lawyers balked until I told them I would be happy to tell an arbitrator about how Boutique Firm had used Grant, the analyst, to generate bogus research reports. The lawyer said he would get back to me. A day later he said the firm would indemnify me.

The arbitration was held in the NASD building on Whitehall Street. This was the first formal complaint ever filed against me, but I had heard about arbitrations. The arbitrator, sometimes an individual but sometimes a panel, was always from the securities industry, and arbitrators were often people who had been brokers themselves. I could never figure out why clients would submit to that, or why they thought they would get a fair shake.

In this case, there was only one arbitrator. I think he was a business professor at some small college. He took a middle position at a big oval table. The Boutique Firm lawyer and I sat on one side. The client sat on the other side by himself. The client was a guy from upstate New York, a factory owner. I knew him as a whale, a sophisticated investor. He was claiming that I had cheated him out of $12,000. He said he had agreed to buy 1,000 shares of a stock that was priced at $13, but when the order came through it was for 2,000 shares. The stock took a dive, he never sold, and now it was listed for $1. The client's position was that he had no complaint about taking the $12,000 loss on the 1,000 shares he had ordered, but he didn't want to eat the $12,000 loss on the other 1,000 shares that he thought he hadn't ordered.

When we faced each other at opposite ends of the table, I sort of gave the guy a short nod. It was the first time I had ever seen him. It was the first time I had ever met any of my clients in person, face to face, except for Naomi the New Issue Whore, who I met for drinks on one occasion *before* she became a client. He was a big guy with a ruddy complexion. He was wearing a suit, but the top button of his shirt was open and the tie was loose. I remembered that his factory made gutters or aluminum siding or both. I couldn't figure out why he was doing this. He had taken a lot of trouble to file this complaint, and then drive a couple of hours down to New York City. All for $12,000? He was a multimillionaire. He had half a million in the market. I couldn't help myself. "Walter," I said, "why are you doing this?"

He looked at me, startled and uncomfortable. "I didn't order the trade," he said.

I started to answer, but the arbitrator told us both to shut up. Then Walter told the arbitrator his story, pure and simple. He had ordered 1,000 shares, not 2,000. That was it. He had no notes or witnesses or anything else to corroborate his story. The arbitrator turned to us, and the lawyer nodded to me. I told the arbitrator that I remembered the trade, vaguely, and I didn't remember there being any doubt in my mind that I had asked Walter to buy 2,000 shares and he had said yes. I said it was possible that there had been a misunderstanding. Maybe he had talked about 1,000 instead. I didn't remember. If there was a mistake, it was an honest mistake.

I turned to Walter again. "Walter, if this trade was wrong, why did you wait two years to complain? Your next statement showed that the trade was for two thousand shares, not one thousand. You should have noticed it then. If you had complained right away, maybe I could have done something about it," I said.

Walter squirmed while the arbitrator, the lawyer, and I all waited for his answer. "I didn't notice it," he said. "That was your job to make sure the statement was right."

The arbitrator found completely in Boutique Firm's favor. Walter got zip. He should have taken the $3,000. My record as a broker remained spotless, and it still is.

Today when I pick up the phone and a cold caller from a Wall Street firm is on the line, I usually hang up. I don't feel bad about it, because I know from my own experience that cold callers themselves don't feel bad about it. Or at least they shouldn't. If they do, they're in the wrong business. Occasionally I engage cold callers and have a little fun with them. When I was working on this book, for example, I would sometimes ask cold callers if they minded me taping their pitch for research because I might want to publish it. The click of the hangup was instantaneous, the quickest way I have found to get a cold caller to hang up first.

Once in a while when I get brokers on the line pitching specific stock ideas, I'll fire back at them, asking them questions. They're often pitching a stock I know more about than they do, and they're quickly reduced to stutters and stammers. "You're not very good at your job, are you?" I'll ask them. But I try to say it gently, because in my mind it is a kindness if it gets these young guys to start reconsidering what they are doing with their lives.

And maybe that's the most important thing I have learned: Life is not like pitching stocks with the rebuttal book. I don't have all the answers.